DATE DUE			

Introduction to
LIBRARY
SCIENCE

LIBRARY SCIENCE TEXT SERIES

Introduction to Public Services for Library Technicians. By Marty Bloomberg.

Introduction to Technical Services for Library Technicians. By Marty Bloomberg and G. Edward Evans.

An Introduction to Classification and Number Building in Dewey. By Marty Bloomberg and Hans Weber. Edited by John Phillip Immroth.

A Guide to the Library of Congress Classification. By John Phillip Immroth.

Science and Engineering Literature: A Guide to Reference Sources. 2nd ed. By H. Robert Malinowsky, Richard A. Gray, and Dorothy A. Gray.

The Vertical File and Its Satellites: A Handbook of Acquisition, Processing and Organization. By Shirley Miller.

Introduction to United States Public Documents. By Joe Morehead.

The School Library Media Center. By Emanuel T. Prostano and Joyce S. Prostano.

The Humanities: A Selective Guide to Information Sources. By A. Robert Rogers.

The School Library and Educational Change. By Martin Rossoff.

Introduction to Cataloging and Classification. 5th ed. By Bohdan S. Wynar with the assistance of John Phillip Immroth.

Jesse H. Shera

Introduction to
LIBRARY
SCIENCE

Basic Elements of Library Service

1976
LIBRARIES UNLIMITED, INC.
Littleton, Colorado

020

Sh5i

100399

Mar. 1977

LIBRARIES UNLIMITED, INC.
P.O. Box 263
Littleton, Colorado 80120

Shera, Jesse Hauk, 1903—
    Introduction to library science.

    (Library science text series)
    Includes bibliographies and index.
    1. Library science. 2. Libraries. 3. Infor-
mation services. I. Title.
Z665.S4187   020   76-21332
ISBN 0-87287-173-8

TABLE OF CONTENTS

CHAPTER 7

CHAPTER 8

"One Learns Much from Books, More from his Teachers, and Most from his Students."

To my students from more than thirty years in the classroom I dedicate this book.

PROLOGUE

"Every statement I make," the distinguished physicist Niels Bohr was wont to tell his classes, "should be understood by you as a question." "How are you doing?" Scott Buchanan asked the graduates of St. John's College from time to time. "Do you believe in and trust your intellect, that innate power that never sleeps? Do you recognize the action of that power as you live and learn? . . . Have you in the course of your life before, after, and while you were at St. John's, become your own teacher? Have you yet recognized that you are and always have been your own teacher? Liberal education has as its end the free mind, and the free mind must be its own teacher. Intellectual freedom begins when one says with Socrates that he knows nothing, and then goes on to say: I know what it is that I don't know. My question then is: Do you know what it is that you don't know and therefore what you should know? If your answer is affirmative and humble, then you are your own teacher, you will make your own assignment, and you will be your own best critic."[1]

Such questions are those of a humanist, and they are particularly relevant to the librarian, for librarianship, despite its increasing utilization of the sciences and its affiliation with the social sciences, remains in its essence humanistic. It is humanistic because it is basically concerned with that elusive and subtle relationship between the human mind and the record of the great adventure. Librarianship classifies as a social science because the library, as an institution, is a creature of society, and its goal is the improvement of society by helping the individual to understand himself and the world of which he is a part. But the library is also concerned with man as a rational being. Thus, it remains primarily a humanistic enterprise. The traditional lines of demarcation among the disciplines are breaking down and in certain areas becoming almost obliterated; and librarianship, in both its technology and its services, is drawing ever closer to the social and physical sciences. But we would do well to remind ourselves of the library's humanistic origins; otherwise, in excessive enthusiasm for the technology of science and the social action of the behaviorist, we may lose sight of the individual and his needs and the humanistic values implicit in them. Shortly after the founding of the Graduate Library School of the University of Chicago, Pierce Butler set about writing his *Introduction to Library Science* in an effort to persuade his colleagues in the profession to become "more scientific" in their approach to library problems. The warning was needed in those days. But he never forgot the humanistic roots of the library, and a quarter of a century later he ended by chastising them, as he said, "for being too damn scientific." He was right on both occasions.

I would not belittle the importance of viewing the library as a social instrumentality, and I can well see what benefits science has brought to the improvement of the library, but let us not forget the humanistic values that for so many centuries shaped the library, gave it a sense of direction, and built the great collections that we know today. A library is both books *and* people, and in that sense it is a humanistic undertaking. There are many points of view represented in the pages that follow, and I would urge that you read them with the eternal *why* always in the back of your mind. You must learn to be your own teacher.

This book is an introduction, and therefore its purpose is to provide a point of entry for those for whom librarianship, as an anticipated career, is only beginning to be understood. But it is also a personal book, as it must be, for no two people view the same scene with identical predispositions and from the same point of view. I have attempted to broaden its scope by inviting assistance with some of the chapters. But these contributors, too, have brought to their task their own emphases and their own enthusiasms. Truth and objectivity, as absolutes, are not attainable, yet one must always strive for them as though they were.

This book, then, is intended to be, not a philosophy of librarianship, but a testament to the depth, richness, and comprehensiveness of librarianship as a career. No knowledge or interest is alien to the librarian. The general and special, art, humanism, and science are brought together on its shelves. Created by society to meet a basic social need, the library stands, as Archibald MacLeish has said, "against the dark," a universal affirmation that the great records of the human adventure still live and speak meaningfully to us, not just individually but, perhaps by their classified proximity, somehow all together, and that they should be freely available to all who need and can use them.

"Tell me, Pa-pa," one of Charles Dickens' children is supposed to have asked him, "Why don't you write like Mr. Thackeray?" To the query the author of *Pickwick Papers* is said to have replied, "Why, indeed, don't I?" Whether the story be true or not, I think of it every time I dip into that marvellous collection of essays on librarianship by MacLeish, *Champion of a Cause.* [2] And I do dip into it frequently, as every librarian should, so rich is it in ideas and insights expressed in such lyrically eloquent prose.

The aim of this book, then, is not to introduce, much less to formulate, a philosophy of librarianship, or even to present a "state of the art" summary, but rather to provide some insight into what librarianship is and the opportunities it offers to one who might choose it as a career. Whether or not it achieves that end must be left to what I call the Fraternity of the Lincei, those lynx-eyed critics who will review it. But if you "understand each statement as a question," if it helps you "to believe in and trust your intellect," if it promotes in you the recognition of the action of that power within you as you live and learn, then the pleasant task of writing this book will not have been in vain. "How are *you* doing?"

NOTES

[1] Scott Buchanan, *Embers of the World; Conversations with Scott Buchanan*, edited by Harris Wofford (Santa Barbara, California: Center for the Study of Democratic Institutions, 1973), pp. 1-2.

[2] Archibald MacLeish, *Champion of a Cause* (Chicago: American Library Association, 1971).

1

UP THE CENTURIES FROM SUMER

"Hell is hot. Did you ever wonder why?" With this rhetorical question J. Russell Smith began his now classic study of the geography of North America. "But," he continued, "not all Hells are hot. Among the pre-Christian Scandinavians Hell was encased in snow and eternal ice. To the Norseman blue with cold, a hot Hell sounded too pleasant to be Hell at all."[1] The distinguished geographer of Columbia University was, of course, dramatizing the relationship between the myths and legends of a culture and the physical environment in which it flourished. Social innovation, too, does not spring "full armor'd from the brow of Jove," but is rooted in and evolves from the body of practice and belief that comprise the culture of which it is a part. The library was such a social invention, brought into being when the accumulated body of experience became so voluminous that it surpassed the limits of human memory and the record of that experience could no longer be left to survival through the oral tradition.

Throughout the ensuing pages of this chapter it will be seen that over the centuries each age has formed and used its collections of graphic records to preserve and strengthen its intellectual habits and its traditional values. The cultural movements which are the warp and woof of the history of civilization have been determinative factors in shaping the library, the nature of its collections, the ways in which those collections were organized and administered, and the services the library performed. From the clay tablets of Sumer and Nineveh and the papyri of ancient Egypt, through the meager equipment of the medieval monastery and the collections of textbooks for the early schools, to the modern free public library, the library has endured a long series of transformations, each of which was conditioned by the needs of its coeval society. Every major change in the social ideal has produced an alteration in the library. Yet, despite these variants, there have been pronounced constants, too; constants that gave the library an institutional coherence that has remained essentially unaltered.

LIGHT FROM THE ANCIENT EAST

The origins of the library are shrouded in the mists of an unrecorded past, and of the first collections of graphic records we have only the fragmentary remains of clay tablets to guide us. Even these survivals give only hints of what may have been. That there were, in the early history of civilization, collections of records we can only surmise, but such an assumption is logical in the light of our knowledge of recorded history.

One may postulate that libraries began in Sumer, since it was the cradle of our civilization, and "everything" seems to have begun there. But so far as the surviving record indicates, we must look to ancient Egypt and its temples for the first known libraries. The center of all Egyptian life was the temple. Church and state were one in ancient Egypt, and the people were ruled by a theocracy. The Egyptians did have a flourishing literature and a virtual monopoly on the cultivation of papyrus, which was the generally accepted writing surface of the time. Diodorus of Sicily, in describing the monuments at Thebes, mentions a library over the portal of which was inscribed, "Medicine for the Soul." Across the Nile from Karnak were discovered the tombs of two librarians, father and son, named Miamun, who held offices under Ramses about 1200 B.C. These tombs suggest that the position of librarian, like many other public offices in ancient Egypt, may have been hereditary. Only ruins have survived to tell of the library at Karnak, which was under the protection of the god of arts and sciences as the "House of the Books." However, the library building at Edfu, which was known as the "House of Papyrus," still stands, though none of the manuscripts that it once contained has survived. On one of the walls of this structure was carved the catalog of the library's holdings. This listing was presented in two parts: the first listed the contents of twelve coffers of materials on a variety of subjects including works on the administration of the state and its functions; the second listed the contents of twenty-two coffers, all of which were devoted to works on magic, myth, and what in that day passed for medicine and science—for example: how to repulse Set, the god of darkness and discord; horoscopes; how to repulse the crocodile; how to protect against reptiles and serpents; and "the book of all the mysteries." The survival of records in ancient Egypt was favored by a warm dry climate that was hospitable to preservation, and a religious belief that encouraged the storing of materials in the tombs for the use of the deceased in the next world. But papyrus is a fragile substance under the most favorable of conditions, and, in consequence, we probably know more about libraries in Babylonia and Assyria, where they wrote on clay.

The one great library of which we have much knowledge—knowledge that has survived from the culture that once flourished in the Tigris and Euphrates river valley—dates from about 600 B.C. This was the royal library at Nineveh, inherited and greatly increased by King Assurbanipal. This great collection, which seems to have overshadowed all others, contained works on grammar, poetry, history, science, and religion. To the royal palace were brought large collections of records, many of which were copied by the scholars there and then returned to their place of origin. The collection is said to have eventually numbered in the tens of thousands. But the day of the clay tablet came to an end by the time the Assyrian Empire was no longer a power in the ancient East. With the passing of this empire, our attention must now turn to Greece.

The Greek geographer Strabo wrote that, so far as he knew, "Aristotle was the first man to collect books, and to teach the kings of Egypt how to arrange a library." But Strabo, it should be noted, wrote some 500 years after that distinguished philosopher, so his word must be taken with considerable skepticism. Nevertheless, the Greek influence in the development of Egyptian libraries did become very strong, as we shall see.

The Libraries of Ancient Greece and Rome

The world's first major libraries, like its first major body of written literature, were a product of the Greek genius, though even in Greece there was no reading public of any size before the fifth century B.C. Prior to that time, and for many years thereafter, no doubt, the mass of the people learned of their intellectual heritage from the mouths of travelling bards and story-tellers. The public scribe, who wrote and read letters for the sender and the recipient, and the messenger were the "postal" system of the time. By the close of the fifth century B.C., however, books were plentiful in Greece, though it was not until the time of Aristotle that the Greek world passed from oral instruction to the practice of reading.

There would appear to have been numerous private book collections in Athens during the "Golden Age of Pericles," in the fifth century B.C., and doubtless some of them were open to scholars of the time. The first public library in Athens was established in 330 B.C. It was erected so that the populace might have a place where they could read the authentic texts of the great Greek dramatists, Aeschylus, Sophocles, and Euripides, whose tragedies were tremendously popular but were available to the public only in very inaccurate copies. According to the historian Polybius, by the third century B.C. there were so many libraries, both public and private, in Athens that the Sicilian historian Timaeus spent fifty years engaged in research in them.

The most significant library of ancient Greece was established not in Athens but in Egypt. Alexander the Great planned to erect, at the mouth of the Nile, a great city that would rival Athens as a seat of culture, but he did not live to see his dream realized. Nevertheless, Alexandria became an important center of learning under the reigns of the Ptolemies.

In the city of Alexandria, Ptolemy I Sotor (c.367-283 B.C.), supposedly acting under the advice of the scholar, statesman, and political figure Demetrius of Phalerom, erected a magnificent building near the royal palace, in an elegant part of the city known as Bruchium. This building was to be used as a museum, a library, and an academy. To this structure were brought not only books, but also botanical and zoological specimens, artifacts, and works of art. It was Demetrius' plan to establish there a lyceum modelled after the Aristotelian ideal, and it is to Demetrius that credit has generally been given for the development of the library. However, H. J. de Vleeschauwer has argued rather convincingly that the library in its origin was as much Oriental as Greek, and that "the library itself was derived from Ptolemy and his recollection of Oriental library institutions." Thus, he holds that the library was "the work of both Ptolemy and Demetrius in their respective roles as initiator and executor."[2]

It was, however, under Ptolemy II (Ptolemy Philadelphus), that the Alexandrian library achieved its greatness. The zeal with which Ptolemy collected books has been said to have been amazing. Whenever a merchant vessel returned to the harbor, inquiry was made of any manuscripts in the cargo; when there was a manuscript, the original was kept in the library and a fair copy was returned to the owner. From Athens, Ptolemy borrowed the official state copies of the plays of the Greek dramatists, for which he paid a deposit guaranteeing their return. But he sacrificed the guarantee and returned copies to Athens, retaining the originals at Alexandria. The Alexandrian collection brought together not only Greek manuscripts but also texts in Ethiopian, Persian, Hebrew, and Hindi. Scholars, supported by royal stipend, were employed to work on the manuscripts, assure accuracy in copying, and otherwise to spare no effort in making the library, as it has been called, "The Glory of the Ancient World." The collection grew to such an extent that a second library was established in the temple of Jupiter Serapis, though the first library was by far the more important. Unfortunately, the original library was destroyed by fire in 47 B.C. as a result of the street fighting when Julius Caesar conquered the city, and the Serapum then became the main library. One version of the story has it that when Caesar's legions tried to take books from the library, the citizens of Alexandria burned the ships in the harbor to prevent their export and the burning ships set fire to the city and the library. Cleopatra, in an effort to curry favor with Augustus Caesar, is supposed to have given books from the Alexandriana for the library at Pergamum. At one time, the Egyptians were said to have placed an embargo on the shipping of papyrus to prevent the growth of any rival collection. That the Alexandriana, as it was called, was the largest library of its era there can be little doubt, and many centuries were to pass before it was equalled in size. But how many rolls it contained—estimates have been given as high as a million—no one knows. There have been various stories, too, about its destruction. One story has it that the Alexandriana was destroyed at the order of Patriarch Theophilus in 391 A.D., and another that it was burned during the Moslem invasion by Amr acting under instructions from Omar in 646 A.D. Those who have had an undergraduate introduction to the principles of logic will recall the classic example of the syllogism illustrating the fallacy of the "undistributed middle," allegedly attributed to the Arabs:

> If the Alexandrian library contained books hostile to the *Koran* it should be destroyed.
> If the Alexandrian library contained books in harmony with the teachings of the *Koran*, they were unnecessary and should be destroyed.
> The books in the Alexandrian library were either hostile to or in sympathy with the teachings of the *Koran*.
> Therefore, the Alexandrian library should be destroyed.

James Westfall Thompson, in his treatise on the history of ancient libraries, points out that the early Christians were as fanatical as the Moslems, and were equally capable of ordering the destruction of the library. Probably, over the centuries, the library was subject to a long series of thefts and depredations, until the books that remained were eventually scattered and lost. One can only speculate about the knowledge of the ancient world that perished with the library's destruction, or the riches of the Hellenic culture that we shall never be able to enjoy.

At Pergamum, in the northwest corner of Asia Minor, Eumenes II (197-158 B.C.) is said to have erected, near the temple of Athena, the second great library of the classical world, though it is known to us only through the explorations of the nineteenth-century archaeologists. The discovery of the remains of the library building has helped to identify the survivals of other library structures, but we can only conjecture as to the books it contained. The building had an open court with a two-storied portico and four adjoining rooms, which shows the antiquity of the architect's concept of a library as being built around an open area, a practice that is strongly evident even today. According to tradition, the library met its end when Anthony gave its collection to Cleopatra to enrich the Alexandriana.

Roman culture was derived from the Greek. In fact, in the early period, it was almost a carbon copy of the late Hellenic world. For the first 500 years of its history, Rome had no libraries and little recorded literature. The Romans were essentially a practical people, concerned with agriculture and trade. When the history of Rome began to be written at about the time of the Second Punic War (218-201 B.C.), it was written in Greek; only later was it translated into Latin. One should not belittle the contribution to the world's great literature of such Roman writers as Virgil, Horace, Ovid, and those others whom schoolboys in England and in this country were for generations required to read in the original Latin. Their output was voluminous. But in such library matters as the collecting and organizing of materials, the Romans can scarcely be said to have been innovative.

The flow of books into Rome may be said to have begun with the defeat of King Perseus of Macedonia by Lucius Aemilius Paullus at Pudna. Thereafter, books regularly became the spoils of the Roman conquerors as they expanded the boundaries of the empire, but probably it was the Greeks in Rome, rather than the Romans, who availed themselves of the opportunities for scholarship that these additions to Roman book collections presented. Yet, of all this booty, by far the most important was the library of Aristotle, which was taken by Sulla when he captured Athens during the First Mithradatic War, 88-85 B.C.

The story of Aristotle's library, as told by Strabo, provides an admirable example of the vicissitudes that beset the libraries of the ancient world. At Aristotle's death his collection of books was bequeathed to his favorite pupil, Theophrastus, who for thirty-five years continued the Peripatetic school of his master. At the death of Theophrastus in 287 B.C., the books went to his pupil, Nileus, who subsequently hid them in a cellar to prevent their being taken for the library at Pergamum. There the materials remained for more than 150 years, subject to dampness and vermin, until they were sold to a wealthy resident of Athens, Apellicon of Teos, in 100 B.C. The new owner directed the restoration of the books, which had suffered greatly during their long years in the cellar; but soon after Apellicon's death, Athens was seized by Sulla and the treasures were removed to the Emperor's palace in Rome. Two librarians—Tyrannio, a learned friend of Cicero, and Andronicus of Rhodes—continued the restoration of the manuscripts and organized them in a logical arrangement according to subject. That the story is authentic would seem to be indicated by the fact that Strabo was a pupil of Tyrannio.

The first "public library" in ancient Rome was founded shortly after 37 B.C. at the Atrium Libertatis by Gaius Asinius Pollio, who had abandoned politics to become a patron of the arts and letters, minor dramatist, historian, and orator. In his youth, the founder had been a friend of the poet Catullus and had studied in Athens. The nucleus of the collection was material from the libraries of Sulla and Varro, which again shows how manuscripts wandered from owner to owner and why it is difficult to write the history of a particular library. The idea of a public library, however, did not originate with Asinius Pollio but with Julius Caesar, though Caesar's plan was not realized until 33 B.C., when the Emperor Augustus established the Octavian Library, which was followed by the Bibliotheca Palatina in 28 B.C.

Rome's greatest and most famous library, and the only one that can be ranked with the Alexandriana and Pergamum, was Bibliotheca Ulpiana, founded by the Emperor Trajan (98-117 A.D.). It was composed of two structures, one for Greek and the other for Roman books. Successive Roman emperors established public libraries, but many of these, including the ones just mentioned, were destroyed by fires that swept the city from time to time. It is important to remember, also, that the term "public" library did not mean what it signifies today. These libraries were established for the use of scholars, to whom their treasures were available, but they were scarcely accessible to "the man in the street," who had little use for them, anyway. The public library as we think of it today was not to appear until nineteenth century America created it during the initial wave of enthusiasm for universal public education.

During the golden age of Latin literature, from the first century B.C. to the end of the first century A.D., there were many private libraries in Rome, maintained in their palatial estates by men of wealth and important political position. Book collecting, along with the patronage of scholars and creative artists, became a symbol of prestige and affluence. Such private libraries were available to scholars, many of whom had their own libraries as well. From one of Cicero's numerous letters to Atticus we learn that when Cicero purchased a new villa—he owned eighteen in various parts of Italy—Atticus would send his librarian to refurbish and organize the library, repair damaged manuscripts, and catalog the collection. Many of the Roman libraries contained manuscripts numbering in the thousands of rolls, and almost every villa, or estate, had its private library. So numerous were these libraries that eventually Roman law provided for their inheritance by successive generations. The Roman Empire, at the height of its power, was a vast assembly of communities that had formerly been independent city states, and many of these had maintained their "public libraries." In the early years of the fourth century, a topographic survey of Rome showed no fewer than twenty-eight libraries then in existence. But by the close of that century the decline of Roman power had begun: its weak rulers were no longer able to hold the Empire together, and the last Latin historian, Marcellinus, wrote that the libraries had been "closed like tombs."

THE MIDDLE AGES

The decline of learning in the Roman Empire had started before the invasions of the barbarians from the North. The early Christian fanatics both hated and feared classical learning because of its pagan origins. By the seventh century A.D., Greek had become practically a dead language. It was through the efforts of the non-Christian nobles that classical learning was preserved until the early fanaticism had abated sufficiently for the Church to develop such men as Cassiodorus. He and others like him honored learning and made the monasteries and cathedral schools places for its preservation. The world of learning owes a great debt to these pagan noblemen for, although paganism was dead by the fifth century, there had appeared such Christian figures as Sidonius Apollinaris and bishops like him, who were humanists at heart and sufficiently devoted to learning to defy the fanatics.

Learning Moves to the East

This transition from the ancient world to the medieval world was less abrupt and less an eclipse of classical scholarship in the Eastern Roman Empire than it was in the West. Prejudice against classical writers was less intense in the East, and the laity there did not abandon their interest in classical learning as they did in the West. When Constantinople was founded in 330 A.D., Constantine took steps to establish a library in his new capital on the Bosphorus, but it was apparently not a very large collection. He seemed to be more concerned with the formation of a fine library for his new great church than with an imperial library. Constantine's son and successive emperors evinced more interest in the imperial library than its founder had done, and in time the library became an important collection, with scholars employed to copy manuscripts and attend generally to the excellence of the collection. In 477, when the library was destroyed by fire during an uprising in Constantinople, the collection was said to have been in excess of 100,000 rolls. The Emperor Zeno, however, reconstituted the library and in a few years it was again in a flourishing state. Two other important libraries of this period should be mentioned. One was that of the Academy, which survived for several centuries; after its decline, it was followed by the library of the University of Constantinople. The University, which was founded about 850, became one of the foremost centers of learning in the Near East, and it, with its large library, played an important part in the Byzantine Renaissance of the eleventh century. The third great library of Constantinople was that of the

Patriarchs, the titular heads of the Eastern Church. There were other ecclesiastical libraries in the Empire, the pattern for which was largely established by the Abbot Theodore of the monastery at Studium, near Constantinople. In about 825, Theodore organized at Studium a library and scriptorium, for the copying of manuscripts, and a school for the education of the priesthood; this was typical of the monastic libraries of the late Middle Ages.

By the beginning of the thirteenth century, the glory that was Byzantium, which for centuries had withstood so many wars, both external and civil, slowly came to an end. It has been estimated that the Northern Crusaders brought about a greater destruction of libraries and works of art than did the Turks in their invasions two centuries later. But the significance of Constantinople in the history of Western civilization is great because it preserved so much of Greek literature and art through the Middle Ages when it was lost to the West. Even before 1200, the flow of manuscripts to the West had begun; but after the fall of the Byzantine Empire, books became a major commodity of trade with Western Europe. Thus, one might say that the foundations of the Renaissance were really Byzantine in origin.

Constantinople, however, was not the only center of culture in the Eastern Mediterranean during the Middle Ages. The Moslem era began in the early years of the seventh century, and the religion of Islam swept most of the Arabic world from Persia to Morocco. For some eight centuries, the Arabs developed a military power and a literary culture that shared with the Eastern Christians an important place in the preservation of learning. There were two influences in the spread of learning among the Arabs. The first was the development of a standardized Arabic language that was suitable for both religious and secular writing, resulting in a transition from a largely oral system of communication to a body of written literature. The second was the introduction of paper from China, brought to the Islamic world about 800. The technique of papermaking spread rapidly across the Mediterranean, reaching Spain about 950. The importance of this transition from an oral to a written system of communication, in conjunction with the development of a readily available writing material, would be difficult to exaggerate. Seldom in the history of the world have books been held in such high esteem as they then were, among the affluent classes of the population.

At Damascus, the first center of the Moslem world, the Umayyid dynasty established during the seventh century a royal library to which flowed substantial quantities of secular as well as religious writings: manuscripts dealing with law, medicine, and science which were borrowed for copying, or otherwise obtained. The collection also served as the official archives of the state, though these were later separated from the remainder of the collection. Moreover, the Arabs found in Persia a great center of Greek culture established by the Nestorian Christians when, toward the end of the fifth century, they were driven from Syria by the Emperor Zeno. These classical texts the Moslems had translated into Arabic, until, by about 750, most of the surviving Greek literature had been so treated.

The great period of Moslem learning, however, came during the time of the Abbasid rulers, or Caliphs (from 750 to 1100). The Caliphs made Baghdad the capital of the Moslem world, and there the Caliphs, and notably Harum el-Rashid of *Arabian Nights* fame, established a great university. Especially under al-Mamun the Great (813-833) the university, with its libraries and laboratories, was outstanding. Science was particularly stressed, and libraries from Spain to India were searched for relevant materials. The libraries of Baghdad were open to scholars whatever their purposes might be, and by the tenth century these libraries served as models throughout the Islamic world. A geographer, Yakut al-Hamawi, who visited the city of Madrid in 1228, wrote that some twelve libraries there were available to the public, and their lending policies were so liberal that he was permitted to have 200 volumes in his room at one time. Throughout the Moslem world, libraries were so numerous and their books so plentiful that they far outnumbered anything the Christian world of the West could present. The Moslem influence reached as far west as Spain, where libraries and centers of Moslem culture and learning were established at Cordoba, Seville, Toledo, and other cities.

The outstanding feature of the Moslem libraries, apart from their widespread distribution, was the breadth of learning that they reflected. Though they were inspired by religious zeal, it did not overshadow or limit the love of scholarship, and in this liberality they were far more hospitable to unorthodox views than were their Christian counterparts and contemporaries.

Even when judged by the library standards of today, the libraries of the Moslem era were surprisingly modern. Though religion received the greatest single emphasis, of course, the holdings ranged the entire field of recorded knowledge: poetry, fiction, medicine, law, astronomy, alchemy, magic, philosophy, mathematics, oratory, and a variety of textbooks and copybooks. The codex was the prevalent form of the book, though there were many rolls on papyrus and parchment. Arrangement of the collections seems to have been by subject, and in the largest libraries rooms were assigned to specified areas of knowledge. The books were cataloged in large ledgers, some ranging from thirty to forty volumes, and were listed by subject. The arts of fine binding, calligraphy, and illumination were practiced, and examples of the finest workmanship were found most frequently in the private libraries of the wealthy. These libraries, too, were often open to scholars.

Unfortunately, the Islamic libraries suffered the same fate as their predecessors in the Mediterranean world. Not only was there widespread destruction from war, but after the beginning of the twelfth century, there was a decline in an interest in learning, though in North Africa and Spain scholarship remained for two more centuries. But it was the Christian Crusaders from the North who, from the eleventh to the thirteenth centuries, must be blamed for the greatest damage. In Syria, Palestine, and parts of North Africa, the Christians were as destructive of libraries as had been the barbaric hordes that descended into Italy centuries before them. Nor were the libraries spared during the thirteenth century Mongol invasion under Genghis Khan. Though the Mongols did not long dominate Islam (they were driven back in 1260), they so scarred the invaded culture that it never really recovered. There was, in Baghdad, an attempted revival during the early fourteenth century, but it suffered reversals during Tamerlane's invasion in

1393. Islamic culture could have influenced Western civilization and the Renaissance far more than it did, had there not been such wholesale destruction of its resources. Nevertheless, the Moslem world, with its influence being felt largely through Spain, probably equals Constantinople in importance as a precursor of the Renaissance. And even though the Crusaders destroyed many of the Moslem libraries, they did forge a link between Western Europe and the Eastern Mediterranean.

The Medieval West

With the barbaric invasions from the North and the ultimate decline and collapse of the Roman Empire, a great darkness settled over Western Europe. The Middle Ages are a particularly difficult period for us to understand, for culturally we are more closely akin to ancient Greece and, especially, to Rome than to the Dark Ages. The medieval world has been likened to a great tunnel into which the Apostolic Church entered at one end and from which the Roman Catholic Church emerged at the other—and no one quite knows what happened in between. England, for example, was left in such turmoil and chaos by the departure of the Roman legions that it fell easy prey to the invasion of the Danes. Many battles, despite the heroic exploits of the English as recorded in the *Anglo-Saxon Chronicle*, ended, as did the battle of Ashdown, with the tragic phrase: *"þa Deniscan ahton waekstiwe gewald"* (But the Danes had won possession of the field).

No one can say precisely when the medieval library emerged from the library of the classical world, but perhaps it is sufficient to characterize the papyrus and vellum roll as symbolic of the latter and the parchment codex of the former. For centuries, however, the medieval library was a very poor thing, admittedly inferior to its Greco-Roman origins, little more than a small collection of jealously guarded manuscripts, laboriously copied by monks who were often assigned the task as a form of punishment for the infringement of monastery rules. So small were the collections that they were usually kept in chests. In the main, such books as there were, were copies of Biblical texts, writings of the church fathers, or service books used in the ritual of the church. Yet, had not these little islands of culture survived, the history of our Western cultural tradition might have been very different from what it is.

We customarily think of the medieval manuscript as a beautiful thing, ornate with miniatures and adorned with gold and a variety of colors, such as the Books of Hours, done on commission for the wealthy. But such jewels were a rarity; the typical medieval manuscript was a very dull thing indeed, carelessly transcribed by monks working under the most unpleasant physical conditions. When parchment was scarce and the monks required busy-work, old texts were scraped off and new ones written on top of them. No one can estimate the destruction of classical writings that took place during these dismal centuries in European history, but the losses must have been staggering, despite the migration of books to the East. Like the origin of the monastery itself, the origin of the Library of the Popes, the predecessor of the Vatican Library, is lost to history. In the beginning, however, it was associated with the Archives of the Papacy, though not until about 700 do we meet up with the office of librarian (*Bibliothecarius*).

So far as the history of libraries is concerned, the first important figure of the Middle Ages was Magnus Aurelius Cassiodorus, who had served as secretary to Theodoric, the Ostrogothic ruler of Rome, and who, when he retired from public life about 550, founded the monastery at Vivarium. Cassiodorus used his own extensive private library as the nucleus for the monastery's collection. But even more important than the monastery itself was his formulation of rules and principles for the administration of the monastery, its library, and its scriptorium. This *Institutiones Divinarum et Secularium Litterarum* contained a listing of books, which might be regarded as the first treatise on book selection for the development of a library appropriate to the needs of the medieval scholar. Cassiodorus is also credited with the introduction of intellectual work into the life of the monastery; along with his contemporary, Boethius, he was responsible for introducing classical learning into Western Europe.

Contemporary with Cassiodorus was the work being done by St. Benedict at Monte Cassino, founded in 529, from the doors of which went many missionaries to found monasteries and seats of learning throughout Western Europe. Even more important in this activity than Vivarium and Monte Cassino were the missionaries who came to Northern Europe from Ireland, which had been converted to Christianity by St. Patrick during the fifth century. Thus, in Ireland, where there was great veneration of the book and of the aesthetics of calligraphy, one may see the real beginning of the Renaissance. From Ireland went St. Columban (543-615) to found the monasteries at Luxeuil, St. Gall, in Switzerland, at Würzburg and Salzburg in Germany, and at Bobbio in Italy, which later received most of the library treasures of Vivarium.

In England, the monastery and its library was introduced by St. Augustine, who was sent there in 597 by Pope Gregory. He brought with him a small collection of books and the library rules drawn up by St. Benedict. With these, a small library was established in Canterbury. In the seventh century, Benedict Biscop founded a monastery and library at Wearmouth. He is reported to have made as many as six trips to Rome, bringing back books for the collections at Wearmouth and at Jarrow. Other significant centers for the growth of monastery collections were established at about this same time at Corbie in France (said to be one of the finest libraries and scriptoria in Western Europe), and at Bobbio in northern Italy. The latter reached its prominence in the seventh and eighth centuries. In Germany, during the eighth century, St. Boniface established monastic libraries at Fulda, Heidenheim, and Fritzlar. But despite the efforts of a few religious leaders, the period from the sixth to the ninth centuries was not a time of great library activity. The one possible exception to this generalization is to be found in Christian Spain, where a number of monastery libraries were established; the most important of these was perhaps the one at Seville, where Isadore, Bishop of Seville, collected a library of at least several hundred volumes, many of which were not religious writings. The collection was justly famous because of its size and the breadth of its subjects. Over each case was a poem addressed to the author, and for the whole collection there was a poem which read in part:

> Here sacred books with worthy books combine;
> If poets please you, read them, they are thine
> My meads are full of thorns, but flowers are there;
> If thorns displease, let roses be your share.
> Here both the Laws in tomes revered behold;
> Here what is new is stored, and what is old.
>
> A reader and a talker can't agree;
> Hence, idle chatter, 'tis no place for thee!

No doubt the monks, for all their piety, were addicted to "idle chatter," but the good bishop was determined to keep it out of the library.

To Tours in 782 came the scholar Alcuin, who had been educated in the cathedral school at York, England, and brought to France by the Emperor Charlemagne, who, himself, was deeply interested in scholarship and learning. At Tours, Alcuin established a school and scriptorium, and he sent to England for manuscripts to be copied. Under the influence of Alcuin as bishop of Tours, monasteries and libraries were established throughout Charlemagne's empire. The Emperor himself had two royal libraries, one at Isle-Barbe and the other at Aachen. But this revival of learning, known as the Carolingian Renaissance, did not long survive its foundation. Charlemagne's grandson, Charles the Bald, known as the first princely bibliophile of the Middle Ages, brought Duns Scotus to his palace school to supervise the scholarly work being done there. In Western Europe, the raiding Norsemen put an end to this abortive Renaissance, and feudalism again spread over the land. In England, where havoc was wrought by the invading Danes, the story was much the same. At about the same time, the Huns were invading Europe from the east and the Moslems from the south. Monastic libraries managed to survive these disruptions, but during this period there was no advance in the medieval library as an institutional form.

The cathedral schools which developed around those great churches that were the official seats of the bishops and archbishops were a kind of university for the training of the priesthood and, to a lesser degree, even the laity. The libraries of these schools developed later than their monastic counterparts and were better supported; their collections were larger and their contents less restricted to religious texts. Perhaps the most famous were those at York, Canterbury, and Durham in England, Notre Dame and Rouen in France, and Toledo and Barcelona in Spain. By the time of the late Middle Ages, however, the Church was beginning to lose its monopoly in intellectual affairs, and the nobility began to assemble libraries somewhat in the manner of the nobility during the classical age.

The antecedents of the university, like those of the library, stretch back many centuries to little bands of students clustered about a teacher, following him, as in the case of the parapetic schools, wherever he might go. At about the thirteenth century, these little groups had begun to come together, to coalesce, to form the institutions that we know today. The concept of a curriculum and degrees in recognition of academic achievement developed only slowly. The early universities, then, were federations of these student-teacher groups, not unlike the guilds of craftsmen, and the term itself comes from the Latin *universitas*: any organized body. It is quite possible that the concept of the university when it developed in France, England, and Italy, came from Moslem Spain. These early universities had no libraries. Students and teachers acquired their own books. Bookselling around the University of Paris, for example, was a profitable business and legislation was enacted by the city to regulate the traffic and insure that the students received authentic texts. The practice of students banding together in a common living arrangement slowly gave rise to the idea of the college, and many of these had small book collections for the use of the group. In 1250, Robert de Sorbon endowed the college which bears his name at the University of Paris and gave to it his own private library, along with funds for its development. From time to time other gifts augmented the collection, and in the fourteenth century other colleges at the University of Paris began to develop libraries of their own. The history of the library at Oxford University is complex, but it received a great stimulus about 1350 with a gift of books from Thomas Cobham, Bishop of Worcester. At Cambridge University, the history of the library was much the same; collections began as small concentrations of books in the colleges, which were increased by gift or bequest.

In a very real sense, the medieval university bridged the transition period from the late Middle Ages to the return to classical learning that was to become known as the Renaissance. From the universities and their libraries, modest though they were, came the learning that was to lay the foundations of that rebirth.

Any consideration of the medieval library might well end with Richard de Bury, who died in 1345 and who planned a most ambitious library development for Oxford, though it was not realized in his time. De Bury was Bishop of Durham and later Chancellor of England; though not an outstanding scholar, he was one of the most avid and influential book collectors of his day. Shortly before his death, he wrote his *Philobiblon*, a rapturous account of the joys of books and reading, which is still read today for its literary merit as well as for the insight it gives into the spirit of the medieval scholar.

THE RENAISSANCE

The Italian scholar and humanist Petrarch, who took Cicero as his model, was much more than the "morning star of the Renaissance." Together with his fellow countryman Boccaccio, he heralded a new era in library development and exerted a strong influence on Chaucer and his age. Both

Petrarch and Boccaccio formed large private libraries and encouraged the collection and use of books. Both turned their backs on the Middle Ages and fixed their attention on classical antiquity. In 1362, Petrarch gave his own library to the Basilica of St. Mark in Venice, "for the comfort of the intelligent and noble people who may happen to take delight in such things."

The influence of Petrarch, however, did not reach its height until the fifteenth century, when enthusiasm for book collecting and humanism became widespread. In Florence, Cosimo de Medici, with the aid of his "library minister" Niccoli, began the assembly of books which, under his grandson, Lorenzo de Medici, eventually became the great Laurentian library. The nobility in Italian cities besides Venice and Florence became enthusiastic book collectors, and this interest persisted through the entire fifteenth century.

The largest and most important library of the fifteenth century, however, was the Vatican, which began anew the library that had been originally assembled by the Avignon Popes but that had been lost during the period of the great schism. The real impetus for the new collection came from Pope Nicholas V (1447-1455), who had long been interested in scholarship and book collecting, and who, with the assistance of his librarian, Tortelli, scoured the book marts of Europe to make Rome and the Vatican once again an important center of the library world. Sextus IV (1471-1484) continued the work of Nicholas and opened the library to anyone who wished to use the books for scholarly work. The Vatican collection, in the breadth of subjects included, was typical of the Renaissance library; throughout the centuries it has remained one of the great research libraries of the world. We in the United States are especially fortunate in having the contents of the Vatican library on microfilm at St. Louis University.

In the Western world printing from movable type, presumably invented by Johann Gutenberg at Mainz about 1450, dramatically affected the development of libraries. It broke up the long association between the library and the scriptorium, and the library was no longer concerned with the production of books. Moreover, the ease with which books could be produced in quantity, even in those days when the printing of a book was a relatively laborious task, so increased the supply of books that they no longer had to be chained to tables or reading desks to prevent theft, as had often been necessary during the Middle Ages. Even the architecture of the library was changed. Books were shelved in a series of galleries surrounding an open court over which light was admitted through a glass skylight in the roof. The court, in addition to reading tables, provided a space for the display of artifacts and thus increased the association of the library and the museum. Most important of all, however, the invention of printing opened the world of books to a far wider audience than it had ever enjoyed. The monopoly on learning by a privileged few was broken, and the way was opened for the Reformation, the rise of scientific inquiry, and the Enlightenment.

THE REFORMATION

When Martin Luther nailed his ninety-five theses to the door of the cathedral at Wittenberg, October 31, 1517, thereby challenging the supremacy of the Pope, the Reformation may be said to have begun. This revolutionary movement, accompanied by the Peasants' War in Germany, the Huguenot struggle in France, and the Thirty Years War in England, brought the dissolution of many monasteries and their libraries. Large quantities of books, zealously collected and conscientiously preserved for centuries, were destroyed or scattered as "papist writings." But not all of the forces of the Reformation were destructive. In a letter sent by Martin Luther in 1524 to the mayors and aldermen of all the cities of Germany, he wrote in part, "Finally, this must also be taken into consideration . . . that no cost and pains should be spared to procure good libraries in suitable buildings, especially in the large cities, which are able to afford it." Luther was by no means alone in expressing such sentiments, and deeds followed words. Through such efforts, many new town libraries were established, though they were still not public in our present-day meaning of the term. Frequently, books merely passed from one institution to another. But access to these collections remained restricted to the privileged few and library growth largely depended upon fortuitous circumstance and the generosity of donors. Men of wealth also began to collect books for their private libraries, much as was done during the classical age, and in a Meissen chronicle it was written, "It is quite common for most of the nobles and burghers, even if they do not actually study, to be able at least to read and write, to bring together in their homes fine libraries with all sorts of good books of goodly writings and to attract to their hearths excellent and profitable historians, physicians, and others." Even among the artisans, book collecting, especially of scientific and technical materials, was not unknown. During the sixteenth century Germany became the center of the international book trade, and the catalogs of the famous Frankfurt Book Fair provided the most complete inventory of European literature available up to that time. In 1545, the German physician and universal scholar Konrad Gesner founded scientific bibliography with his *Bibliotheca Universalis*, a classified bibliography of world literature, of which the last two books were left unfinished because of his untimely death in the plague.

In France, the royal library prospered under the successors of Francis I, and through their love of elegance many of its holdings were bound elaborately by the French master craftsmen. The library grew by the addition of the collection assembled by Catherine de Medici, and later by that of Cardinal d'Amboise. The royal library also took an important step forward when it was moved from Fontainebleau to Paris and was placed under the direction of the librarian Grigault, who prepared a catalog of the books in 1622.

During this period, however, the royal library was greatly overshadowed by the personal library of Cardinal Mazarin, whose librarian, Gabriel Naudé, haunted the book marts of all Europe to build the most famous library of its day. This distinguished scholar believed ardently in developing a collection for his influential patron in all branches of learning. In 1627, he published the first guide or manual for organizing and building a library, his *Advis pour dresser une bibliothèque*; this was later translated into English by the famous diarist John Evelyn under the title *Advice for Forming a Library*, and it can still be read with profit and enjoyment. In this treatise, Naudé set forth his philosophy of book collecting, emphasizing the importance of modern books as well as ancient rarities, heretical works as well as those supporting the beliefs of the Church, and insisting on a classification system for arranging books according to subject in a manner that could be easily understood. When he entered Mazarin's service in 1642, Naudé found the opportunity to put his ideas into practice. Unfortunately, this great collection of some 40,000 volumes fell prey to the Fronde when Mazarin was bereft of power. When the Cardinal was returned to a position of authority, he attempted to reconstitute his collection, but by that time Naudé was dead. To understand the spirit of Naudé, one should recognize that his life coincided with the new era of Grotius, Hobbes, Galileo, Kepler, Bacon, and Descartes. It was indeed a propitious time for a librarian to be active, for books were not only being collected but also were being studied and used, and the importance of the library as the laboratory of the scholar and scientist was being fully realized. As Naudé himself confessed, he had some excellent examples to guide him.

One such example was that of Sir Thomas Bodley, a typical Elizabethan, who had studied and taught at Oxford and had become a prominent political and public figure; near the end of his life, he decided that the greatest service he could render his fellow men was to rebuild the library at Oxford University, which had fallen into neglect. In 1598, Sir Thomas proposed to the vice-chancellor of the university that he assume the responsibility for restoring the library; after he had spent five years of strenuous labor in recruiting funds from donors, building the collection, and improving the old quarters, the library was again operational. Quite properly it was named the Bodleian, in recognition of his work. He persuaded the Stationers' Company to give the library a copy of all the new books published, an early form of copyright deposit, and in his will left his property to the library. Today, the Bodleian is one of the great libraries of the world. In this same period, the Archbishop of Milan, Federico Borromeo founded the great Ambrosian Library which, among its collection of treasures, held many of the manuscripts from the monastery library at Bobbio. Also during the seventeenth century, the Vatican library made substantial gains, adding to its collections some important libraries of an earlier time.

THE ENLIGHTENMENT

The Enlightenment was that period which may be said to have stretched roughly from the last half of the seventeenth century to the end of the eighteenth. It was a time for the intense study of physical and social phenomena, under the leadership of Newton, Hobbes, Locke, and Kant—for which the way had been opened by Galileo, Kepler, Bacon, and Harvey, among others. It was a time for the organization of knowledge and its systematization, and a time for association. It was the period of the founding of the great scientific societies: the Accademia dei Lincei (the Academy of the Lynx-Eyed) was established in Rome in 1600 and survived to 1650; the Académie des Sciences was established in Paris (1666); and in London in 1660, the Royal Society owed its origin to Francis Bacon's ideas for a scientific community. During this period came not only a new drive for the development of library collections, but also substantial interest in their organization. In France, the great minister Colbert, with the aid of his librarian, the historian Beluze, followed in the footsteps of Cardinal Mazarin, and the Royal Library, which was placed under his direction in 1661, was greatly expanded and enriched. There was a growing interest, too, in the classification of the materials in the Royal Library, stimulated by the ideas of Francis Bacon on the organization of knowledge. In the middle of the eighteenth century, there was initiated the work on the great encyclopedia of Diderot and d'Alembert. Through the influence of the abbé Jean Paul Bignon, the quarters of the Royal Library were expanded and the collections were made more accessible to the scholars of the Enlightenment.

Though in France the initiative for improving the Royal Library came from the king, in England it came from Parliament. Several proposals for the formation of a great national library in London had been made during the seventeenth century, but no action had resulted. At the beginning of the eighteenth century, Richard Bentley proposed to Parliament the creation of a national library, but it was not until a generation later, through the efforts of the King's physician, Sir Hans Sloane, that action was taken. In his will, Sir Hans gave his fine private library to the nation in exchange for a sum of money to be paid to his heirs, and Parliament accepted the offer in 1753. The Sloane collection was united with the collections of Sir Robert Bruce Cotton and Robert Harley. The Cottonian collection had been given to the nation in 1700 by Sir Robert's son. Robert Harley had died in 1724 and his very valuable collection of books had already been sold, but Parliament authorized the purchase of his manuscript collection. Finally, George II gave his own private library to the growing collection and the foundations of the British Museum, which first opened its doors at Montagu House in 1759, had been laid. Today, in addition to being the national library of England, it is one of the great museums, including in its collection the Rosetta Stone, the Elgin Marbles, and other artifacts and works of art from all corners of the globe. At present, there are plans to separate the Museum from the library, adding to the latter certain other special governmental libraries, a development that would clarify the Museum's long-standing division of function.

The great leader of the German Enlightenment and, indeed, a towering figure throughout the movement generally, was Gottfried Wilhelm Leibniz, a librarian who laid down many important principles governing the duties of the librarian. An avid reader of his father's library as a youth, he became the librarian of the distinguished bibliophile, von Boyneburg of Mainz. In that role, he set forth for the first time his dream of a semi-annual catalog of books and a cumulation of these lists into "an inventory of human knowledge contained in books." It was his belief that the true advancement of knowledge was possible only when each individual scholar could quickly and conveniently survey the sum total of all previously recorded accomplishments. He visited Paris at precisely the time that Colbert was building up the Royal Library, and Beluze was numbered among his friends. At that time, also, he read Naudé's work on organizing a library. In 1676, he was appointed librarian at Hanover, and fifteen years later became director of the famous Wolfenbüttel library. Though his accomplishments in building up and organizing the collections were great, his most important contribution to librarianship was the principles he laid down in his correspondence and the proposals he wrote for the reigning princes. To be sure, many of Leibniz's ideas concerning libraries did not originate with him, he borrowed freely from his predecessors and contemporaries; but this does not diminish the importance of his work, and in the acquisition, organization, and cataloging of books his influence can be traced through many generations of librarians even to the present day.

Though scholars' concern for the new science continued, the Enlightenment as such may be said to have ended with the Romantic Movement and the French Revolution. Unlike previous revolutions, the one that shook France did not so much destroy libraries as dissipate them. It has been estimated that at this time over eight million books changed hands, two million in Paris alone. From November 1789 to the end of the Revolution, libraries were distributed among the towns and provinces to the extent that even today the scholar can find some surprisingly valuable and rare materials far from Paris, hidden in some unsuspected provincial community. The great contribution to library development of the nineteenth century, apart from continued growth and expansion, was the emergence of the public library movement; for its origins, however, one must turn to our own country.

NINETEENTH CENTURY EUROPE

As pointed out above, the excesses of the French Revolution were responsible less for the wholesale destruction of libraries than for their redistribution. Estimates of the number of volumes seized by governmental fiat in France and distributed to local and provincial libraries as well as deposited in the Bibliothèque Nationale ran into the millions. Despite this dispersion of materials, one of the major effects of the Revolution on libraries was the growth of the Bibliothèque Nationale, whose resources were greatly extended through the government's confiscatory policies. A second important result was the enunciation and implementation of the principle that books were to be accessible to the general public. To be sure, a substantial number of treasures must have been lost, not only at the time of the Revolution, but also in the decades that followed. However, the concept of the public library as an institution for all the people and not for the privileged few was becoming established and was later to be reflected in America by such figures as Franklin and Jefferson.

In nineteenth century Germany the scholarly library tradition was dominant, especially as exemplified by the libraries of such great universities as those at Göttingen and Dresden. In Germany a deepening national consciousness and changing social organization brought with it the belief that libraries should be regarded as public institutions, and along with this came a general increase in scholarly activities from which the libraries could profit. But the libraries were quite unprepared for this upsurge in scholarship. There was no class of professionally trained librarians, although Göttingen and Dresden served as useful models.

This nineteenth century German scholarship spread to American libraries as well as to American higher education. In the early decades of the nineteenth century it was not uncommon for graduates of Harvard and other Eastern colleges to continue their education through travel and study at the great German universities, bringing back a philosophy of scholarship that is still clearly discernible in our graduate schools of today. Joseph Green Cogswell, later to become famous as the librarian of the Astor Library in New York, reorganized the Harvard library according to the Göttingen scheme of classification. Both George Ticknor and Edward Everett, the two dynamic leaders of the Boston Public Library's first board of trustees, were strongly influenced by the German library tradition. Ticknor evolved his plan for a federation of Boston's libraries from his experiences at Göttingen.

In nineteenth century England the library world was dominated by two towering figures, Anthony Panizzi and Edward Edwards. The Italian Anthony Panizzi was appointed Extra Assistant in the British Museum in 1831, was promoted in 1837 to Keeper of Printed Books, and in 1856 became Principal Librarian. He touched librarianship in the United Kingdom at almost every point. "The British Museum," he is reported to have said, "is not a show, but an institution for the diffusion of culture. It is a department of the Civil Service and should be conducted in the spirit of other public departments. It should be managed with the utmost possible liberality."[3] Jared Sparks, of Boston, was so impressed by the use of the British Museum that he wrote home in 1840: "In the reading-rooms [of the British Museum] are daily congregated more than a hundred readers and transcribers, of all nations and tongues, plodding scholars, literary ladies, and grave old gentlemen with mysterious looks. When shall we see the like in the [Boston] Athenaeum?"[4]

Although Panizzi is probably best known on this side of the Atlantic for his work in laying the foundations for the Anglo-American cataloging code, from which derives our current cataloging practice, and for his scholarship in making the British Museum the great library that it is today, Edward Edwards played a leading role in promoting the *public* library movement in the United Kingdom. A man who combined theoretical insight with practical ability and untiring industry, Edwards was instrumental in promoting legislation for the encouragement of public libraries and in working with Parliament to advance such ends. Public library development in England closely paralleled that in the United States. The Manchester Public Library, directed by Edwards, opened in 1852 and in many ways was comparable in British library history to the Boston Public Library in the

United States. In 1850, Parliament had passed permissive legislation enabling communities, municipalities, and boroughs of over 10,000 population to establish, on their own initiative, public libraries. Further legislation from time to time culminated in the Public Libraries Act of 1892, which provided that every urban district and every parish in England and Wales not within an urban district should be a library district. Similar laws for Scotland and Ireland were passed at about the same time. The British Library Association was founded in 1877, the Jubilee year of Queen Victoria. A year earlier, in 1876, the establishing of the American Library Association coincided with the celebration of the United States centennial. As in this country, public library development in England owes much to the benefactions of Andrew Carnegie, and in 1913, the Carnegie United Kingdom Trust was established. Quite obviously Andrew Carnegie, the Scot, did not feel about England as Dr. Johnson did about the Scots. The most important single factor leading to nationwide coverage was the development of the National Central Library, now the National Lending Library. Established in 1916, with a Carnegie grant, as the Central Library for Students, it acts as a center of bibliographical information and as a central lending agency. With the support of the Carnegie United Kingdom Trust, it continued to expand its functions. It has had great influence in inducing library cooperation in England, as well as British cooperation with other countries.

The nineteenth century brought a period of unprecedented growth in the numbers of libraries of all kinds in Europe, especially public libraries, and in the materials it was their responsibility to collect. Increased scientific inquiry, especially during the last half of the century, brought with it a new demand for improved access to the scientific literature, particularly the rapidly proliferating journal literature. The scientist's intensified need for effective bibliographic organization was the perspective against which one must view the publication, beginning in 1851, of the Royal Society's *Catalog of Scientific Papers*, which attempted to index the scientific publications of the nineteenth century. In the closing decade of the century came the historic meeting of Paul Otlet and Henri La Fontaine, their plans for an international conference on bibliography, and the formation of the Brussels Institute of Bibliography, which eventually became the International Federation for Documentation. But further consideration of these developments must wait for Chapters IV and V.

The European influences, including those from Britain, upon the American public library were two-fold. Directly, they contributed to the promotion of the institution by the actual transfer of organizational patterns. The book clubs, the social libraries, and the circulating collections were all either derived from European models or brought to this country by enterprising merchants who sought to exploit the reading interests of the American public, just as they had capitalized on the desires of readers in their native lands. Indirectly, by the example of its own great collections and their organization, Europe suggested to the American mind the significance of the library in the integration of an emerging culture. In Peterborough, New Hampshire, and in Wayland and Boston, Massachusetts, where the initial steps were taken that resulted in the foundation of the American public library system as it is known today, the action was characteristically American, but the antecedents of that movement were largely derived from European sources.

THE LIBRARY MOVEMENT IN AMERICA

On this side of the Atlantic, the research libraries, primarily those associated with academic institutions, followed in general the pattern established in Europe, even as did higher education itself; but the idea of a public library freely available to all, and deriving its support from public funds, was a bold innovation. The American public library was rooted in the classical tradition, nourished by the Renaissance and the Enlightenment, and it came to full flower in the democratic ethic—the faith in universal popular education and the perfectability of man.

The Colonial Library

The American culture was, and to a large extent still remains, derived from England. Though it was eventually shaped and re-shaped by the new environment and by successive waves of immigrants from other lands, the English heritage is still strong, if not dominant. For a century and a half after the landing on Plymouth Rock, the colonists were surprisingly homogeneous in their national origins; they looked back constantly to the Mother Country for their beliefs, institutions, and their occupational patterns. If the Puritan ethic taught that hell is hot, the Mathers and Edwardses and the leaders of the Great Awakening did not wonder why. The idea of the library was no exception to these influences; it too came to these shores from Europe by way of England.

There is no record to indicate that when the Pilgrims landed on Plymouth Rock they brought with them any books; however, nine years later, in 1629, a band of Puritans brought to John Endicott's colony in the Massachusetts Bay area a small collection of books, which included eight unspecified titles that had been a gift from a Mr. William Backhouse, 54 "doctrinal books and pamphlets," and "two dozen and ten" catechisms. No one knows why the books were brought or how they were used, though it has been suggested that they might have been intended for use in converting the Indians to Christianity. In 1638, John Harvard died in England, leaving his property and library of four hundred volumes to the college, established two years before, at New Towne, on the banks of the Charles River. In gratitude for the gift, the new institution was named Harvard College, and the town subsequently named Cambridge. This collection, and others added to it from time to time, was made available to the faculty, advanced students, and the ministers of the area.

But the first real town library in Colonial America was the gift of a strange and rather unsavory character, Captain Robert Keayne, who died in

1656, leaving to the town of Boston money for the building of a town house which would provide rooms for a market place, an armory, and a library. To initiate the last, he left his own books, from which his immediate heirs had the right to select such as they wanted for themselves, and some manuscript writings of his own which were commentaries on the Bible. The gift was accepted by the town of Boston, the building was erected, and the library, which was augmented by other gifts from time to time and in which some of the official town records were kept, survived for almost a century. Though the original building was destroyed by fire in 1711, there was sufficient interest to stimulate the erection of a new structure, which likewise was burned in 1747 but was never replaced. A gift of books for a library was also received by the colony of New Haven in 1656, through the will of Theophilus Eaton, the collection to be held for a proposed college. By 1668, the colony had joined with the colony of Connecticut, and the collection, to which had been given other gifts, became the property of the town of New Haven. In 1689, the collection was sold to the Reverend James Pierpont, minister of the New Haven church, for "forty pounds of rye and 32 bushels of Indian corn."

On a Sunday evening in 1701, according to tradition, a group of men met at the home of Samuel Russell in Branford, Connecticut, each bearing a few books which he laid on the table, saying, "I give these books for the founding of a college in this colony." Such was the beginning of Yale. We know that James Pierpont was a member of this little group, and it has been suggested that the Eaton books mentioned above were part of this donation, but that is only conjecture. We do know, however, that when the incipient college was moved, a few years later, from Branford to New Haven, a group of irate citizens set upon the carts carrying the library and tried to seize them in an effort to prevent the loss of the college. In this melee, many of the books were destroyed, but those that have survived are now kept in the "1701 library," carefully treasured in the university library at Yale.

At Concord, Massachusetts, the town record for 1672 shows the entry: "that care be taken of the Book of Martyrs and other books that belong to the town," but that is all that we know of it. In the early years of the eighteenth century, an English minister, the Reverend Thomas Bray, became deeply concerned over the inability of the clergy in the American colonies to have access to books necessary to their stewardships, and he formed a society to purchase books to be sent to the parishes along the Atlantic coast, mostly in Maryland, Virginia, and the Carolinas, though at least one collection went to the King's Chapel in Boston and is still treasured in the Boston Athenaeum. It has been estimated that some 35,000 volumes were ultimately sent to about forty parishes through the efforts of Bray's Society for the Promotion of Christian Knowledge. With these donations came instructions for the organization and care of the collections, and Bray himself came to America to see that his work was being carried out. The books were generally kept at the parsonages of the parish ministers and eventually were scattered and lost, but for a few decades they were a kind of library network or system on the frontier of the New World. In 1719, and shortly thereafter, the town of Oxford, Massachusetts, received gifts of books for a town library; in 1731 similar gifts were made to East Sudbury, Massachusetts, and in the same year the town of Lancaster, Massachusetts, voted to purchase a copy of the Reverend Samuel Willard's *Compleat Body of Divinity*, a volume of over one thousand pages and the largest to be printed in the colonies up to that time.

The Social Library

The next development in Colonial libraries, however, came from that great statesman, scholar, inventor, and man-of-affairs, Benjamin Franklin. In the autumn of 1727, Franklin, who had recently returned from England where he had been a journeyman printer, brought together a group of young artisans like himself to form a discussion group, which met at regular intervals to consider and debate current topics of the day. It soon became apparent that the group, called the Junto, needed a library for reference and support of these deliberations. Therefore, each member was requested to bring some of his own books to the club rooms where they could be kept and made available to all the members. The plan, initiated in 1730, failed after about a year, for the obvious reason that the young men did not want to expose their possessions to loss. In 1731, Franklin founded the Philadelphia Library Company. In this voluntary association the members bought stock, and the annual assessment on this stock provided income for the purchase of books that would be for the use of all. The first books for this new venture arrived from London, March 31, 1732. This library, which in his autobiography (written some forty years later) Franklin called "the mother of all subscription libraries in North America," still exists. It has been augmented by many gifts, of which the most important was the private library of James Logan, and it is one of our most important library landmarks. We can properly assume, however, that the idea for such an association came from England, for when Franklin was there he must have encountered similar "book clubs," which were not uncommon in London and other English cities. In 1733 there was formed the Library Company of Durham, Connecticut; in 1737 the Library Company of Saybrook, Lime, and Guilford, Connecticut; and in 1739, similar undertakings were initiated in Lebanon and Pomfret in the same colony, of which the first was called the Philogrammatican Society. That any of these could have owed their origin to Franklin's venture seems unlikely; there was no magic in the name of Franklin in those early years, and it would seem much more realistic to assume that they were copied after similar associations in England. But whatever the origins of the idea, the principle of applying the technique of the voluntary association to the library needs of the community was beginning to develop. In 1747, through the generosity of Abraham Redwood, a similar library was formed at Newport, Rhode Island, and it, like the Philadelphia Library Company, still exists and is housed in the original building; membership in it is a mark of social prestige.

Slowly these little bands of people who needed books, usually the ministers, teachers, lawyers, and other professional people of the towns, spread along the Atlantic coast, formed libraries that emerged in full flower after the Revolutionary War, and moved rapidly into the interior of the country as people migrated westward. Today, the best known survivor of these so-called social libraries is the Boston Athenaeum, founded in 1807, which occupies its historic quarters on Beacon Hill, and shares of its stock are usually passed from generation to generation as an important part of the family fortune.

That those who needed books should turn to the concept of the voluntary association was natural, for many of the functions that today we regard as the proper responsibilities of the state or local government—caring for the poor, the fighting of fires, law enforcement, the provision of a water supply to individual homes—all began as voluntary associations, groups that entered into contracts with each other to secure certain benefits that no one person could provide alone. These association libraries, or social libraries, assuming various forms for specific purposes, spread throughout the country, and in a few instances still survive. Thus, there were social libraries for lawyers, ministers, young people, mechanics' apprentices, merchants' clerks, and even social libraries for women. From the end of the eighteenth century and on into the nineteenth, these libraries were very close to a public library system. There were few towns throughout the country which, at one time or another, did not have a social library, and many, over the years, had several. Often these libraries were incorporated, during the Colonial period, by act of the Colonial government and the Crown, and after the War of Independence by the state legislatures. In many states laws were passed that permitted groups to form such associations and incorporate themselves without having to appeal to the state for a special act of incorporation.

Contemporary with these social libraries, there were so-called "circulating" libraries, which today we would call rental collections; borrowers paid a specified fee, usually a daily rental charge, for the privilege of borrowing the books. These were purely business enterprises, customarily associated with a bookstore, printer, or general store, and their stocks were usually made up of current fiction and other "best sellers" of the time—the kind of reading for which there was popular demand. Such enterprises had been common in England before they were introduced into Colonial America in 1745 by James Parker, one-time partner of Benjamin Franklin, when he tried to revive the fortunes of the New York Corporation Library by renting its books to readers. In 1762, William Rind announced, in Annapolis, Maryland, a grandiose scheme for an extensive rental library which never materialized. The first really successful attempt was, however, John Mein's circulating library in Boston, initiated in 1765, which seems to have prospered. He issued a catalog of the collection the same year. But because he ran into conflict with those who wanted to break from England (he was loyal to the Crown), he fled to England a few years later and his London Book Shop and the *Boston Chronicle* that he had been publishing came to an ill-fated end. Many of these circulating libraries did prosper, at least in a modest way, and became a part of the library scene.

Because the proprietors of these libraries catered to popular taste and generally loaded their shelves with novels that were not always of the highest literary merit, they came under sharp criticism, usually from the clergy. But in England, where the libraries tended to cluster around the resort towns, the book-stocks were even worse, so much so that the Society for the Suppression of Vice advocated the regulation of circulating libraries, and parents became concerned over their children's use of them. The use of these libraries by women went so far as to raise serious doubts about the propriety of teaching the feminine sex to read. "A circulating library in a town is an ever-green tree of diabolical knowledge," complained Sheridan's Sir Anthony Absolute, "It blooms throughout the year!—And depend on it, Mrs. Malaprop, that they who are so fond of handling the leaves, will long for the fruit at last."

Beginnings of the Public Library

The faith in democracy—the belief that people were capable of making their own decisions in governing themselves—which animated the founders of the Republic was far more revolutionary than the Revolutionary War itself. The War was little more than a conventional uprising of a people who felt themselves oppressed by a tyrannical ruler. But the *Constitution* confirmed the right of the citizen to participate in the decision-making of his government, and in order for the citizen to act intelligently, he must be an educated person. Hence the need for an enlightened electorate, educated in a system of free schools, and with free access to recorded knowledge. The axiom was clear.

To the end of the eighteenth century, no library was truly public in the sense that it was freely open to all residents of its community and supported from the public treasury. Even the social libraries restricted their membership to those willing and able to pay for the privilege. The library was for the elite, the scholar, the man of learning, or the person who needed books for his work or his avocation. The idea of the true public library came with the rise in the early nineteenth century of the concept of universal public education. It was encouraged by the movement led in the 1840's by Horace Mann and Henry Barnard, who were not only promoting libraries for the school districts, to support the public educational program, but also public libraries for all the people, which would be, as Horace Mann said, "The crowning glory of our public schools." State legislation pertaining to the creation of libraries for the school districts was placed on the books somewhat earlier: in New York, in 1835, largely through the influence of Governor DeWitt Clinton; in 1837 in Massachusetts, as a result of the work of Horace Mann; and in 1839 in Connecticut, and 1840 in Rhode Island, both of which were a tribute to the educational leadership of Henry Barnard. Unfortunately, these libraries failed to achieve the promise that their promoters had hoped. The tax base was too small, the amount of revenue inadequate to keep the libraries viable, and they were often the victims of exploitation by rather unethical publishers' practices. Slowly, voluntary support for the school district library died an inglorious death. Social libraries proved to be uncertain and unreliable, since many of these association libraries survived but a short time, their promoters lost interest, moved away from their community, or died.

Nevertheless, the movement had a curious tenacity. Often, after one library disappeared, a new one was created to take its place, until it too passed into oblivion. In some places there were as many as three or four generations of these little libraries, but they were too dependent on shifts in individual fortunes to make a lasting institution, except in such rare cases as the Philadelphia Library Company, the Redwood Library of Newport, and the Boston Athenaeum. These libraries were the exception, and even they were threatened more than once with financial disaster. If libraries for the people were to be realized, a stable means of financial support had to be found.

In January 1803, Caleb Bingham, a Boston bookseller who remembered his unfulfilled need for books when he was growing up in Salisbury, Connecticut, gave to that town 150 titles appropriate to young people between the ages of 9 and 16. The collection, which became known as the Bingham Library for Youth, was to be open to all residents of the community, was to be administered by a self-perpetuating board, and was to be regarded as the property of the town. On April 9, 1810, the town meeting voted $100 from the public treasury for the support of the library, and additional grants were made from time to time for the improvement of the collection. Eventually, however, the books, which had suffered neglect, were absorbed into the present public library, the Scoville Memorial Library, which was established later in the century. Such books as have survived from the Bingham library may be seen today in the Scoville library. Salisbury, with considerable justice, claims that it inaugurated the public library movement on this side of the Atlantic, and that its library was the first of its kind anywhere in the world.

The only challenge to Salisbury's claim comes from Peterborough, New Hampshire, where the public library has a rather unusual history. In 1819, the Supreme Court of the United States handed down its decision in the Dartmouth College case, in which it held that the state of New Hampshire was bound by its contract with Dartmouth College to preserve its independence as a private institution and never to take over the institution as a state property. It was Daniel Webster, an alumnus of the college, who so ably defended his alma mater against the state intrusion. The decision was an important one in constitutional law, because it held, for the first time, that a state was as much bound by a contract as was an individual.

New Hampshire, frustrated by the decision of the Court, in 1821 imposed a tax on the capital stock of banks in the state, the revenue of which was to be used for the founding of a state university. This college, however, never materialized, and in 1828, the accumulated money was returned to the towns to be used for "the support and maintenance of common free schools, or other purposes of education." In every town except Peterborough, the money went directly into the school fund, but in this one community, the town meeting voted on April 9, 1833, that a portion of the fund, which had become known as the Literary Fund, be withheld for the purpose of establishing a town public library. One year later, the library was a reality, and the town contributed to the support of the library annually thereafter. Thus, Peterborough claims the honor of having the first truly public library because it created a library without benefit of gift and has supported it without interruption to the present day. So one can make his own choice of which town has the stronger claim. One should, perhaps, mention for the record that in 1827, the town meeting at Lexington, Massachusetts, voted $60 for the inauguration of a juvenile library, and added to this modest sum from time to time. The books were kept in the town meeting house, but support was so sporadic and inadequate that by 1839, it had gone out of existence. But one must remember, all of these towns were small and their collections were not much bigger than those of the libraries of the Middle Ages. What the public library movement most needed was action by a large and influential municipality; that opportunity came in Boston in the middle of the century.

The Boston Public Library may be said to have been born in 1841, when the citizens of Boston were addressed by a rather strange Frenchman by the name of Alexandre Vattemare. M. Vattemare, who spoke on the subject of a public library and the importance of the international exchange of official public documents as a means of promoting world peace and understanding among the nations, had been, for most of his adult life, a world-renowned ventriloquist under the name of M. Alexandre. After his retirement from the stage, he turned his attention to the hobby of exchange of documents among the nations of the world, which provided the *raison d'être* for his Boston visit. At first, the good citizens of Boston were not sure whether his ideas should be taken seriously or be disregarded as only those of a charlatan. However, through Vattemare's efforts, the city of Boston received in 1847 a gift of documents from the city of Paris. The gift was accepted and the following year the Boston city council applied for, and received from the state legislature, the authority to establish a public library. But not until 1852 did the council actually appropriate funds for the establishment of a library; at that time Mayor Seaver appointed a joint special committee, which included George Ticknor and Edward Everett, to report on plans. This report, which was almost entirely the work of Everett and Ticknor, was submitted in 1852, and the library first opened its doors for business in 1854. Thus stimulated by Boston's example, other towns began to create public libraries. In 1849, again possibly through the influence of Vattemare's second visit to the United States, New Hampshire passed the first general permissive legislation allowing towns of the state to establish public libraries, and Massachusetts enacted a similar statute in 1851.

The advent of the Civil War and the Reconstruction period materially hampered the growth of public libraries, but by the end of the century and the early years of our present era, they spread rapidly throughout the country, stimulated to a very large degree by the benefactions of Andrew Carnegie. The Carnegie libraries, so well known to many of us in our own youth, were established wherever communities agreed to continue their support. Though public libraries seemed to be well in the ascendant when Carnegie made his fortune available, one cannot but wonder how rapidly the movement would have developed had this benevolent Scotsman not made millions in the steel industry and remembered the book starvation of his youth in the highlands of his native country. The work that Andrew Carnegie had begun was carried on by the Carnegie Corporation of New York and other foundations interested in library development, such as the Rockefeller Foundation, the Ford Foundation through its Council on Library Resources, and less wealthy agencies. In the past three or four decades, the federal government has given support to libraries largely through the U.S. Office of Education, the National Science Foundation, the National Institutes of Health, and from time to time a variety of specialized commissions. The era of the large benefactions for libraries, however, would seem to be past, and at the present time grants have been directed more toward the stimulation and promotion of research, assistance to library education, and scholarships and fellowships for library study. Nevertheless, in the past under the Library Services and Construction Act, many public libraries, in particular, were able to expand materially their branch systems and other library facilities. The era of the wealthy patron—be the source an individual, a corporation, or a governmental agency—has left its mark, and such names as Morgan, Huntington, Crerar, Folger, and Pratt are writ large in the history of American librarianship.

Such, in broadest outline, has been the course of library history over the centuries; what this narrative means for libraries today and for librarianship as a career will be seen in the chapters that follow.

NOTES

[1] J. Russell Smith, *North America* (New York: Harcourt, Brace, 1925), p. 3.

[2] H. J. de Vleeschauwer and H. Curtis Wright, "Origins of the Mouseion of Alexandria," in *Toward a Theory of Librarianship: Papers in Honor of Jesse Hauk Shera*, Conrad H. Rawski, ed. (Metuchen, N.J.: Scarecrow Press, 1972), p. 90.

[3] Quoted by Alfred Hessel in *A History of Libraries* (Metuchen, N.J.: Scarecrow Press, 1950), p. 86.

[4] Quoted by Van Wyck Brooks in *The Flowering of New England* (New York: Dutton, 1937), p. 121.

SELECTED READINGS

Butler, Pierce. *An Introduction to Library Science.* Chicago: University of Chicago Press, 1933. Chapter IV, "The Historical Problem."

de Bury, Richard. *Philobiblion.* Introduction by Archer Taylor. Berkeley: University of California Press, 1948.

Ditzion, Sidney. *Arsenals of a Democratic Culture.* Chicago: American Library Association, 1947.

Harris, Michael J. *Readings in American Library History.* Washington, D.C.: NCR Microfilm Editions, 1971.

Hessel, Alfred. *A History of Libraries.* Translated by Reuben Peiss. Washington, D.C.: Scarecrow Press, 1955.

Johnson, E. D. *A History of Libraries in the Western World.* 2nd ed. Metuchen, N.J.: Scarecrow Press, 1970.

Naudé, Gabriel. *Advice on Establishing a Library.* Translated by John Evelyn, with an Introduction by Archer Taylor. Berkeley: University of California Press, 1950.

Nevins, Allan. *The Gateway to History.* Boston: D. C. Heath, 1938. Chapter IV, "One Mighty Torrent."

Shera, Jesse H. *Foundations of the Public Library.* Chicago: University of Chicago Press, 1949.

Thompson, James Westfall. *Ancient Libraries.* Berkeley: University of California Press, 1949.

_____. *The Medieval Library.* Chicago: University of Chicago Press, 1939.

Thornton, John L. *Selected Readings in the History of Librarianship.* 2nd ed. London: The Library Association, 1966.

2

THE LIBRARY AND SOCIETY

That the library was created to meet certain social necessities, and that its development is closely related not only to intellectual history but also to changes in the organizational structure and the value system of its supporting culture, should be apparent from even a cursory reading of the record. The school and academic libraries of today can trace their lineage back to the training of the priesthoods in pre-Christian eras, and they were profoundly influenced by the medieval universities. The mid-nineteenth century leaders of the movement for public libraries were well aware that they were implementing one of the greatest organizational changes in the human adventure—the attempt to qualify an entire population to participate in the control of the political and economic system in which they lived. It is axiomatic, then, that the library as a social instrumentality, is, as it has always been, conditioned and shaped by the social *milieu* within which it functions. Society is the library's trustee, and it is to society that the library must respond and be responsible. Hence, to understand what the library has been, is, and may be expected to become, one must first look at the nature of society itself and the cultural and value systems that operate within it.

SOCIETY AND CULTURE

The investigations of the anthropologists are unable to give us much insight into the life of primitive man when he lived in that dim past known as prehistory, struggling for survival. Always there seems to have been a group of some kind, a society with a rudimentary organization or structure that was recognized and accepted by the members of the group. We cannot know man, it seems, apart from association with other human beings. Even in the story of the Garden of Eden, there was Eve as well as Adam; and there was the snake, and it was not long before there were Cain and Abel, and many others whose appearances on the scene are not clearly explained. In short, there was a society, doing things in various ways, for good or ill, in accordance with, or in violation of, certain accepted standards of behavior. The concept of *society*, then, is fundamental to any understanding of human activity. A society, according to the late professor Robert Redfield of the University of Chicago, is "people doing things with, to, and for each other for the benefit of each and in ways which have been accepted by all." A society is "people with common ends getting along with each other." A society is "people doing work."[1] A society, then, is a group of cooperating individuals, be it a family, a clan, a city, state, or a nation. But always there must be organization, structure, controls, an accepted and acceptable body of belief, and a system of values. Even in primitive societies this structure has been an intricate complex of interrelated constituent parts.

But a society cannot function—indeed, it can hardly be said to exist—without some cohesive force to hold it together. That force is known to the anthropologist as *culture*. This term, which derives from the German *Kultur*, is not to be confused with the popular usage which implies the possession of certain social graces, refinement, or elegance, as one is wont to say a person is a "cultured" individual, or possesses "culture." Nor is it Matthew Arnold's culture, which he defines in *Culture and Anarchy* as "the complete and harmonious development of all the faculties that make for the beauty and the strength of human life."

The term culture, as used by the anthropologists, may be said to encompass the inventions, the arts, and the totality of ideas and beliefs that are characteristic of human behavior and that differentiate man from the other animals. Paul Sears has defined the term as "the way in which the people in any group do things, make and use tools, get along with one another and with other groups, the words they use and the way they use them to express thoughts, and the thoughts they think—all of these we call the group's culture."[2] Thus, in any one culture there may be, and in complex societies there are many, sub-cultures that may or may not be in conflict with each other or even in opposition to the generalized culture of the total society. So there are sub-cultures relating to race, ethnic background, religion, white-collar workers as opposed to blue-collar workers, and the professions of medicine, law, education, and on and on. During the present century, librarians have developed a distinctive sub-culture of their own with its body of belief, accumulated specialized knowledge, codes of behavior, and jargon. As will be seen in a subsequent chapter, the traditional library culture is now being challenged, or at least invaded, by a new sub-culture known as information science, and in this incipient conflict, both may be modified.

The nature of culture can perhaps best be understood if it is diagramed as a triangle (Fig. 1, page 44). The left-hand side represents the physical equipment, the tools and other mechanisms essential to the work being performed. Such equipment runs the entire gamut of human experience from the stone axes and spear-heads of primitive man to the most sophisticated electronic mechanisms of today's scientists and engineers. Indeed, the maturity of a culture is measured in part by the sophistication of its physical equipment. But this equipment cannot develop without the support of the other two sides of the triangle. It responds to the demands placed upon it by society, yet there is a certain reciprocity in the relationship because advances in tools also stimulate innovation in their use. Not infrequently the mere availability of a tool stimulates its use in situations where it is inappropriate. The well-engineered machine has a fascination about it that may lead to excessive or inappropriate use. Such misuse of the physical equipment exemplifies what Abraham Kaplan has called "The Law of the Instrument." Simply stated, the

Fig. 1. Culture

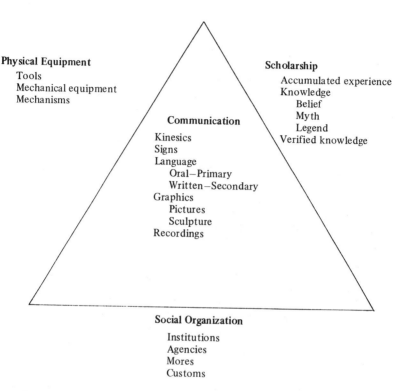

Physical Equipment
Tools
Mechanical equipment
Mechanisms

Scholarship
Accumulated experience
Knowledge
Belief
Myth
Legend
Verified knowledge

Communication
Kinesics
Signs
Language
 Oral–Primary
 Written–Secondary
Graphics
 Pictures
 Sculpture
Recordings

Social Organization
Institutions
Agencies
Mores
Customs

so-called Law holds that man tends to formulate his problems in such a way as to make it seem that the solution to his problems demands precisely what he happens to have at hand.[3] An executive who acquires a Xerox machine may suddenly come to believe that all notes and memoranda emanating from his desk must be reproduced in multiple copies, whether the need for them is real or not. In this way, not only do the means justify the end, but also they not infrequently *are* the end, and they predetermine what it is that we are going to do. The medium is the message in more ways than we would like to think. Thus, to control our excesses, we come to the second, or right-hand side, of our triangle.

This side represents what may be called the *scholarship* of the culture—the totality of all knowledge accumulated by its members, the body of verified knowledge, theory, belief, experience, myth, legends, and imaginative creations. From this scholarship derives the philosophical system, or construct, or whatever relates man to other men and to the totality of the universe in which he finds himself, and with which he must develop a satisfactory intellectual and spiritual harmony. This scholarship, codified into *mores* and operating through *institutions* and their subordinate *agencies*, or *instrumentalities*, establishes norms of conduct and social behavior. At any particular moment in time, the scholarship establishes limits for the physical equipment, and imposes boundaries upon the social organization. Tools cannot be invented unless there is the requisite knowledge for their design and fabrication, and man cannot establish a social structure, with its complex of relationships and jurisdictions, that transcends his understandings of society and human psychological behavior patterns. If he does establish such social patterns, the chances that they will achieve their aims are slim; note the failures of such utopian societies as those of New Harmony, Indiana, or Oneida, New York, which failed to achieve their goals because, according to the popular view, they were "contrary to human nature."

The base of the triangle represents *social organization*, the institutions and their agencies that "drive," or give reality to the culture. A culture must have organization, system, to qualify as a culture. Today, in our Western civilization, the organization is complex and highly specialized, though even in primitive societies specialized roles may be present. The variety and character of these roles determine, in large measure, the degree of sophistication of the culture, and, of course, a single individual may play a number of roles: as parent, as teacher, as wage earner, as a participant in community activity, to name but a few possibilities. The older term "division of labor" is, of course, an expression of the role.

If a culture is to survive, these three aspects (physical equipment, scholarship, and social organization) must be kept in reasonable harmony. If any one lags too far behind the others or advances too rapidly, the culture becomes warped. Today, in the United States, we see some of the consequences of a social organization that has failed to balance technology and scholarship. Many believe that our technology has seriously exceeded our intellectual resources to control it. Similar maladjustments may have been responsible for the decay and eventual demise of earlier cultures.

The organization of a culture is a vast tissue of reciprocal activities, differentiated into interwoven systems and sub-systems, the pattern of which is determined by social *institutions*. These social institutions are a cluster of social phenomena, conventions, or formalized structures whereby a society fixes the limits of, exercises control over, and imposes form upon the activities of the members of the society. Institutions are the instruments by which a society imposes its will upon the populace, shapes the behavior of the individual in accordance with the goals and values that the culture seeks to achieve, by granting sanctions, imposing *tabus*, establishing *mores*, and in general lording it over all aspects of human life. An institution may be rigid or flexible, and it may discharge its functions through agencies, associations (voluntary or compulsory), or other appropriate groups. So close is this relationship between institution and agency that it is not always easy to distinguish the one from the other, but always it is the institution that establishes the norms of conduct from which the individual departs only at his peril. Such institutions as the family, law, religion, and education give rise to their respective subordinate agencies or instrumentalities as the household, the courts, the church, and the school. The library, then, along with the school, the college, the news media, and other manifestations of the "knowledge industry," is one of the agencies through which the institution of education exerts its influence. That the library is such an instrumentality may help to explain why, over the centuries, it has tended to follow in the wake of social innovation, to reflect the goals society seeks, rather than to initiate change. One must also remember that such social instrumentalities are creatures of their society, and when, for any reason, they fail to fulfill their established roles, their missions, society can, and will, reject them. The great enemy of the social instrumentality, such as the library, is ossification, the failure to keep pace with needs. Today, our institutions, some of which have stood for many centuries, seem themselves to be undergoing change; this change confuses the social structure and makes it more difficult for the instrumentalities to which the institutions have given rise to perform adequately their assigned functions. If the library finds itself confused, it may be because the goals that our society seeks have changed and are unclear. The library (particularly the public library) and other agencies of its kind must be alert to the desirability of re-examining priorities and services to make certain that they are aligned with the needs of society and are continuing to fulfill those needs.

COMMUNICATION

In the center of our triangle should be placed *communication*, for culture is impossible without some medium for the transmission of thought. Human thought is social as well as personal, and communication binds the culture into a cohesive whole and makes possible the control which it exerts within society. Just as culture, through the communication system, shapes us as a species, so too it shapes us as individuals. Indeed, the very word *communication* means *share*, and when two or more people are communicating, they are a sharing unity. Culture, then, can be regarded as people in communication sharing customs, behavior, and belief. Because of the importance of communication to the structure, organization, and activities of society as well as to the character of the individual, it is central to the study of librarianship. The library, then, is not only a social and cultural phenomenon, or instrumentality, it is an important segment of the communication network, and an understanding of that network is essential to the librarian.

In the beginning was perhaps not the word, for verbalized communication, language, presupposes a relatively high degree of cultural sophistication. In the beginning was probably the gesture (kinesics), along with the grunt, or the exclamation connoting some basic emotion—fear, apprehension, fright, joy, or pain. Such signals, whether intended as such or not, are common in our communication repertoire and are not unusual even among the higher animals. Indeed, we probably make more use of kinesics in our social contacts than we realize. But language is, of course, the basis of our communication system and carries the burden of information transfer; yet because language is so basic, we tend to take it for granted and forget what a mysterious phenomenon it is. The ability to communicate by means of language may be what separates man from the animals—man was not man until he spoke.

"Language," wrote Susanne Langer, "is, without a doubt, the most momentous and at the same time the most mysterious product of the human mind. Between the clearest animal call of love or warning or anger, and a man's least, trivial *word*, there lies a whole day of Creation—or in modern phrase, a whole chapter of evolution . . ."[4] Conventionally, one thinks of language as *speech*, but there are other languages as well. From the grottoes of Combarelles and Altamira to the galleries of the Louvre, the walls bear mute testimony to man's need to express his thoughts and communicate them to others in graphic representation. Music and the dance "speak" in their own conventional languages, which are sometimes regarded as "universal." But all forms of communication are closely related to the culture, so the Westerner may not understand, and probably does not even appreciate, much less comprehend, the true meaning of Oriental art forms or those of the American Indian or the Eskimo. But language as speech so dominates our daily lives that the two have come to be almost synonymous. The philologist and linguistic purist, of course, would be quick to point out that *language* means *tongue*, hence *speech*, and all other uses represent aberrant forms; yet all are aspects of communication, hence, all are relevant to the library as part of the communication system.

Because language implies the ability to attach meaning and values to a wide variety of symbolic systems, it is not easy to define. Charles Morris has given us what is probably the most scholarly definition, though to appreciate it one must strip away a certain amount of technical jargon that in itself demonstrates the problem of language comprehension. Language, Morris says, is a plurality of signs that can be produced by human beings. The significance of these signs must be sufficiently standardized to be known and understood by a number of individuals. These significances must remain constant, or at least relatively so, within differing situations, and they must be set in patterns that are sanctioned by the community in which they are used. There will, of course, be some variation in individual interpretation—no communication is perfect, there is always some loss—but such variation will be due largely to the fact that human beings are rarely able to do more than suggest what they desire to express; thus, it may often be left to the recipient of the message to fill in the gaps.[5] We must also remind ourselves that language can set limitations to communication: we cannot communicate that which we cannot say. In certain cultures there are phenomena that cannot be expressed because there are no words in the language to express them. Indeed, there is no agreement about whether even thought is possible without some kind of language, some kind of medium to express it. Can we think what we cannot say? remains a debatable question. Science, of course, is constantly inventing new words to express new concepts, and jargon may be used to conceal truth or mask ignorance rather than to communicate. Some cynical linguists have expressed the belief that "language was made for lying."

Though one thinks of communication generally as being a social phenomenon involving two or more individuals, there is also a communication system within the human body, but that will be considered in the chapter that follows. Whether the communication is internal (neura) or external, it is always composed of four elements: a transmitter, a receptor, a message, and a medium of transmission. In speech, the medium consists of alternate crests and troughs—vibrations—in the air. Communication may also be direct or indirect depending upon whether there is an intermediary agent imposed between the transmitter and receptor. Such an intermediary may be a document, a phonograph recording, or any other device that may in one way or another shape the message. The first may be considered as primary or direct communication, and the second as secondary or indirect. This dichotomy, however, is not always easily distinguishable, for there may be a blending of forms which evince the characteristics of both—the smoke signal, the telegraphic message, the image on the television screen, even the conversation over the telephone. Such fine distinctions as these are, however, probably not important. Our primary concern here is with those forms of secondary communication that result in a graphic record—the book, for example, which can span space and time, and can enable the receptor to receive messages from someone miles distant from him, or someone who lived in a past that existed centuries before his birth. "Time-binders," the general semanticists have called these graphic records, and it is with these that the library is primarily concerned, and it was for their preservation that the library was originally conceived.

One other distinction is important here, for its oversight has caused some confusion in thinking about the social function of the library. Personal communication is an individualistic matter; it enables the recipient to "talk back," and to some degree, at least, he can, by the process of selectivity in what he chooses to read, exercise some control over the message. Much of such communication is sought out by the recipient. He must come to the library and must seek out for himself those messages to which he wishes to be exposed; those messages must be selected from the total store of the library. Mass communication, by contrast, is under the complete control of the transmitter. He determines what messages will be broadcast to a mass audience, and the receptor has no alternative but to turn off the television set or cast the newspaper aside. A library is not an agency of mass communication simply because people come to its doors in large numbers. They do not all receive the same message, as they do on television or radio; instead, each seeks out individually those messages that are relevant to his needs. Moreover, the messages are there for him to return to again and again if need be; they are not flickering shadows on a fluorescent screen or the transitory vibrations of a cone-shaped diaphragm. Perhaps it would not be excessive to say that the mass media are basically authoritarian, the library essentially democratic.

This implicit commitment to the democratic ethic by the library, particularly the public and academic library, raises problems that ramify through all its policies and procedures. Such a commitment represents a break with the tradition that stretches back to the origins of the library. From its beginnings the library had been designed and operated for the elite, those individuals with scholarly competencies or interests. Thus its patronage was relatively small and reasonably well defined, with rather homogeneous informational needs. But the advent of democracy brought to the library a "general public," whose needs were not well-defined or understood. All of this represented a sharp break with tradition. How best the library could, and should, respond to this new clientele became a serious problem. What is the role of the library in a democracy? What, precisely, are its responsibilities during a period of social change? Can it reverse the trend of its history and lead rather than follow social change, and if it can, should it? As a public institution, should the public library give its constituency what it wants? What should be its response to charges of censorship? What are its obligations with respect to the disadvantaged? What relationships does the role of the library bear to the roles of other service agencies in the community? Admitting that the program of the library should be "dynamic," just how dynamic should it be, and what does this dynamism mean?

THE ROLE OF THE LIBRARY
IN ITS CULTURAL SETTING

Like the individual members who comprise the society, social instrumentalities, including the library, have roles to play, the boundaries of which are established by the culture and the institutions of which it is composed. The traditional role of the library as a part of the communication system is the preservation and transmission of the cultural heritage. The library can, of course, communicate the values of other cultural systems, and indeed, it properly should; but if it departs too far from the attitudes and value system of its own culture, it is certain to be in trouble. The library, then, reflects a particular "world view," a "paradigm," to use Thomas Kuhn's term, or an "image," to borrow from Kenneth Boulding. Such paradigms, or images, may change through time in response to changes in the culture, and the library that is unable to adjust to such alterations may discover that it no longer has a social purpose and the culture has cut it adrift. Up to this point in our argument, the social imperative, or precept, of the library is a relatively simple admonition; the tough questions come when one must decide how best to exercise this responsibility—when one must decide between what is and what should be.

The proper study of the librarian is man—collectively as well as individually. A generation ago Douglas Waples, of the Graduate Library School of the University of Chicago, devoted many years to the consideration of the social effects of reading, but he was never able to do more than to ask the fundamental questions, to lay the foundations of a new discipline that I have subsequently called *social epistemology*. By this term, I have proposed a new study, or science, that will not be a reworking of the old area of mass communication, but will be a body of knowledge about knowledge itself. How knowledge has been developed and augmented has long been a subject of study, particularly by the philosophers; but how knowledge has been coordinated, integrated, and put to work, still remains an almost unrecognized field of inquiry. We have, from the most ancient times, our systems of logic and our formalizations of scientific method, and we know with some exactness how scientific knowledge is accumulated and transmitted from one generation to another. In this area of inquiry, the historians of science have been of great assistance. Philosophers have long speculated about the nature of knowledge, its sources, its methods, and the limits of its validity. But the study of epistemology has always revolved about the intellectual processes of the *individual.* Psychologists carried the philosophers' speculations into the laboratory and have made some progress in examining the growth of knowledge and its effect on behavior, but again with reference only to the individual. But neither the epistemologists nor the psychologists have developed an orderly and comprehensive body of knowledge concerning intellectual differentiation and the integration of knowledge within a complex society. The sociologists and the cultural anthropologists, though they have directed their attention to the behavior of men in groups, have paid scant heed to the *intellectual* forces shaping social structures.

Social epistemology, as I envisage it, is fundamental to the librarian because it should provide an effective philosophical frame of reference within which can be viewed and understood the complexities of the intellectual processes of society—an understanding of how society as a whole seeks to achieve a perception of its *total* intellectual and social environment. The focus of this discipline should be upon the production, flow, integration, and consumption of all forms of communication operating throughout the entire social pattern. From such a discipline should emerge a new body of knowledge about, and a new synthesis of, the interaction between knowledge and social activity. We know that society knows both more and less than the individual—this is fundamental to the work of the librarian. Society "knows" the contents of all the encyclopedias that have ever been written, but it cannot "know" the beauty of a sunset or the emotional impact of a great poem. How does society know what it knows, and how does that knowledge influence the total social environment? That question lies at the very heart of the role that the librarian plays in society and the role of the library as a social instrumentality. Only armed with such knowledge can we make valid decisions about what the library should become. The answers to such questions as have been raised above are the great issues that confront librarianship today, and are likely to persist into the foreseeable future.

Lacking such precise evidence as social epistemology might provide, the librarian has no choice but to proceed in the faith that reading maketh a full society as well as a full man, to paraphrase Francis Bacon, and there are scraps of evidence to support this view. The most notable, perhaps, has been the effect of the acculturation of the immigrants who sought our shores during the last decades of the nineteenth century and the early years of the twentieth. The biographical literature of those immigrants and their children is replete with references to the public library and the services that its store of books performed in helping them to adjust to the new world and to become, as so many of them devoutly wished, "true Americans." One should not forget, however, that this zeal for learning, for "making a go of it" in a strange new world, was fostered by a family environment in which learning was honored. The library provided the opportunity for fulfillment more than it stimulated a basic desire. To what extent today's "outreach" programs can compensate for an environment at least indifferent to, if not actually hostile to, learning remains to be proved.

THE INTEGRITY OF THE BOOK COLLECTION

Years ago, the slogan of the American Library Association was "The Best Books for the Most People at the Least Cost." Without quibbling over the mathematical impossibility of maximizing three variables simultaneously, the motto at least focused attention on the basic fact that the librarian is, first of all, a bookman, and his primary responsibility is to place on his library's shelves only those books that contribute most to the intellectual growth of his clientele. Perhaps a somewhat more appropriate slogan is that of the Special Libraries Association—"Putting Knowledge to Work." Knowledge, specifically recorded knowledge, is the librarian's business and must be his first concern. Such a declaration does not imply that the library may not have other functions than the pursuit of accurate information. The development of taste, the pleasures of recreational reading, the excitement of vicarious adventure, the robust joy of good humor, and the thrill of the detective or mystery story all have their places in the enrichment of human life and should be represented in the library stacks, but knowledge remains the supreme good, and its dissemination places a heavy responsibility upon the librarian.

In the school library, in the college or university library, and in the so-called special library serving business and industry, the librarian is in a favorable position when he reviews the development of his book collections. All are favored by a well-defined clientele and a relatively precise definition of purpose. In the school and the academic library, the primary objective is to support the parent instructional program and, in the academic library, the research needs of the faculty and advanced students. In the special library, the definition of function is perhaps even more clear. Moreover, in all of these situations, the librarian is favored by a faculty or research staff whose personalities, interests, and needs are well known to him. These people may also be an important reservoir of bibliographic knowledge on which the librarian can call in choosing the most important materials to be provided. Nevertheless, in all of these there is a growing tendency for the librarian to assume ever-increasing responsibility for the selection of the materials, and the librarian must prepare himself to meet that responsibility.

It is in the public library that the problem of book selection becomes the most difficult. Its objectives are much less well defined than are those of the other library types, and it frequently lacks the reservoir of expertise that the academic and research communities can provide. As a consequence, two schools of thought have developed concerning book selection policies for the public library. The first, which has been called the *demand theory*, holds that, because the public library is a public institution supported from the municipal treasury, it should respond to the demands of the public it is supposed to serve; that is, it should give the public what it wants. Of the fallacy inherent in the demand theory, Kathleen Molz told the faculty and students of the Library School of Case Western Reserve University:

Society, with its shorter view that the public should get what it pays for, has so chipped away at the concept of the public library that, in all too many communities, it has become little more than an information hodge-podge furnishing its staff and resources as a solver of riddles for the community's contestants, a reference arm for the burden of community homework, and a supplier of cheap best sellers for the titillation of the middle class.[6]

As a consequence, she says that the public library "stands dead center in the midst of muddle." These may seem to be harsh words, but they were enunciated by Bernard Berelson in his study of *The Library's Public* long before she wrote, and the situation has changed little since his investigation was made. Certainly, in the matter of book selection policy, the public librarian must be more self-sufficient than any of his colleagues in other library fields.

The counter theory to that of *demand* is the *value* theory, which holds that it is the librarian's responsibility to stock only the "best" books. But this philosophy raises the vexing question of what books are "best," for what purposes, and for whom? In the end, the librarian must rely on an understanding of his community and its needs superimposed upon a philosophy of what the library should be and supplemented by his own good judgment, sense of values, and literary taste. The librarian can, and should, augment his own scholarship by including on his staff professional people with a variety of competencies in the fields of knowledge that are appropriate to the library and, beyond this, by enlisting a stable of experts drawn from the community; but he should not take such steps until he has formulated in his own mind a philosophical framework for what he proposes to do.

In 1938, Douglas Waples concluded an address to the participants in a conference at the University of Chicago with:

Over many American lunch counters hangs the sign "the banks have agreed to sell no sandwiches and we have agreed to cash no checks." How about a sign in front of the loan desk, "Mike Flanagan's drug store, for obvious reasons of self-interest, has agreed to stock no books of importance to the serious reader, and we, for the same reasons, have agreed to stock nothing else."[7]

Even after almost half a century, Waples' half-facetious advice is still sound. Even though the effective implementation of a book selection policy is no easy task, the ideals of value and excellence should ever be before us.

Milton, in the "Areopagitica," likened Truth to the god Osiris, who came into the world "a perfect shape most glorious to look upon," but whose lovely form was hewn "into a thousand pieces," and scattered to the "four winds" by the Egyptian Typhon and his conspirators. "From this time ever since, the sad friends of Truth, such as durst appear, imitating the careful search that Isis made for the mangl'd body of Osiris, went up and down gathering up limb by limb still as they could find them." The myth has particular relevance for the librarian, who, like the devoted Isis, must relentlessly search for Truth fragmented "into a thousand pieces" by that "great blooming buzzing confusion" that is human experience. What motivates the good librarian is not, as has been so frequently said, the love of books, but love of Truth—Truth, wherever and in whatever form it may be found. For the end of knowledge is wisdom, and wisdom is the power to perceive truth in all its relationships—therein lies the unity of librarianship in all its forms and practices, and for all its patrons, however diverse they may be.

This unity that is librarianship, Ralph A. Beals has symbolized as the highest expression of the anthologist's art.[8] Historically, an anthology is a collection of choice flowers skillfully woven into a garland to be used for whatever purpose a garland may be expected to serve. Thus Meleager, the unknown author of *The Circle*, and, most of all, the pages of the great *Greek*, or *Planudean Anthology*, wove into anthological patterns the unity of Hellenic life, thought, and feeling. With the coming of the sixteenth century, the anthology became more highly specialized, and there began to appear collections of charters, treaties, state papers, laws, legal precedents, and a variety of contemporary and historical materials. In time there appeared anthologies of such subjects as religion, morality, politics, and economics, and at a still later date there were brought together lay interpretations of physics, chemistry, geology, and medicine, as well as writings on the practical and domestic arts.

Libraries, like anthologies, must rest on unity with respect to their underlying principles of selection, arrangement, and interpretation. But the librarian, unlike the anthologist, is threatened by the ever-present danger of regarding books as only physical objects when his main concern is with them as metaphysical entities, capable of influencing in a variety of ways the thoughts and actions of those who read them. "What is a book in a collection?—a book in a library?—to a librarian?" asked Archibald MacLeish. "Is it merely the unit of collection, a more or less fungible (as the lawyers put it) object made of paper, print, and protective covering that fulfills its bibliographical destiny by being classified as to subject and cataloged by author and title and properly shelved? Or is it something very different? Is it still a book? Is it, indeed, something more now than a book, being a book selected to compose with other books a library? If so, what has it become?"[9] The distinguished poet and former Librarian of Congress replies that the library stands as a silent affirmation that the books that man has written speak—"not alone but somehow all together."[10]

MacLeish's thesis that books derive much of their meaning from association with other books provides the key to the librarian's art. A garland is not a garland until it is woven in such a way that each flower both contributes to the beauty of the whole and enhances its own particular charm through association with its fellows. The value of a library lies in the unifying purpose with which its books have been brought together. A miscellaneous agglomeration of books is not a library, it is only an assembly of books. The true librarian is an anthologist, a weaver of garlands, a descendant of Isis.

Greek thought was unified by the search for first principles. Plato's dialectic was a method of study of those principles, and Aristotle unified them in a science of metaphysics. Medieval scholarship was logically ordered by a theology in which were set forth, with due proportion and emphasis, the truths relating God to man, and man to man, and man to nature. The Enlightenment was distinguished by a search for a rational explanation of the universe, and all human behavior was measured against the cold clear light of reason. Today, a world characterized by specialization and threatened with conflict and fragmentation seeks a new unity that will give purpose and direction to human life. The age of relativity has weakened the old norms, attitudes, and values by which man's relation to all the forces in the universe and his relation to his fellow men were once, rightly or wrongly, judged. Man abhors chaos and uncertainty as much as nature is supposed to abhor a vacuum. Science, we have discovered, is not the savior of mankind, nor the standard by which all conduct is to be measured. Science is not enough. There would seem to be an increasing tendency even to reject science in a new kind of anti-intellectualism. Our society needs, as never before, the ordered accumulated knowledge and wisdom of the ages.

"For those to whom truth is an invariant," writes Norman Hackerman, president of Rice University, "that is, something engraved in stone, it must be unsettling to be told that even long-standing natural 'laws' are subject to alteration in light of fuller understanding. This must be especially unsettling when the same proposition is applied to human 'truths.' "[1]

"When I was a young man at the University of Cambridge," Alfred North Whitehead once told a group of his students, "I was taught science and mathematics by brilliant men . . . Since the turn of the century I have lived to see every one of the basic assumptions of both set aside . . . and all this in one life-span—the most fundamental assumptions of supposedly exact sciences set aside."[2]

There would seem to be in the human being an innate hunger for unity, a sense of order that relates all things and establishes eternal verities and principles. To this need for order the library can well respond, with its long experience in systematizing human knowledge. But the unity which it is the power of the librarian to give lies not alone within the ordering of the books on the shelves or their representation as entries in a bibliographic tool, useful though they may be in the display of the library's contents. As metaphysics ordered Hellenic thought, and theology that of the Middle Ages, librarianship can become the great unifying agent that gives order to the intellectual life of our times and relates man to his total environment. It is this creation of synthesis of man's knowledge to the end of promoting wisdom that is one of the most important contributions the librarian can make to man's intellectual life; his is the gift of order and relationship. It is this relationship that makes "a book now something more than a book, being a book selected to compose with other books a library."

The unlettered child poring over a picture-book and a theoretical physicist searching the literature for a better insight into the problem before him, are one and the same. Each in his own way seeks a better understanding of the world in which he finds himself; each seeks to put together into a system those verities that will give meaning to his life. Each has a special claim upon the librarian in his search for Truth, and neither must be denied.

SOCIETY'S RIGHT TO KNOW

No one librarian can, of course, obtain every book; no library can meet every need. Libraries cannot keep on growing forever. There must be an optimum size for every library, though it doubtless varies from situation to situation, even though we do not know what that optimum may be. Selection there must always be, even for the largest libraries. Not all books have permanent value, and far too many books have little value at all. Only the greatest books are "immortal." Books, like people, have a "right" to die. A library is "a growing organism," observed S. R. Ranganathan, the great Indian librarian and scholar, by which he meant that a library grows by replacement as a living organism grows by the renewal of cells. Selection can no more exist apart from rejection, than there can be sunlight without shadow. Unfortunately, rejection raises in the mind of many the spectre of censorship, which has long been anathema to librarians.

The American Library Association, first through its Intellectual Freedom Committee and later with the resources of its Intellectual Freedom Foundation, established to provide assistance to librarians unjustly accused by those who would stifle freedom of thought and expression, has fought courageously and often successfully in behalf of those freedoms guaranteed by the *Constitution of the United States* and enunciated by the "Library Bill of Rights," which says:

> The Council of the American Library Association reaffirms its belief in the following basic policies which should govern the services of all libraries.
>
> 1. As a responsibility of library service, books and other library materials selected should be chosen for values of interest, information and enlightenment of all the people of the community. In no case should library materials be excluded because of the race or nationality or the social, political, or religious views of the authors.
>
> 2. Libraries should provide books and other materials presenting all points of view concerning the problems and issues of our times; no library materials should be proscribed or removed from libraries because of partisan or doctrinal disapproval.
>
> 3. Censorship should be challenged by libraries in the maintenance of their responsibility to provide public information and enlightenment.
>
> 4. Libraries should cooperate with all persons and groups concerned with resisting abridgment of free expression and free access to ideas.
>
> 5. The rights of an individual to the use of a library should not be denied or abridged because of his age, race, religion, national origins or social or political views.

6. As an institution of education for democratic living, the library should welcome the use of its meeting rooms for socially useful and cultural activities and discussion of current public questions. Such meeting places should be available on equal terms to all groups in the community regardless of the beliefs and affiliations of their members, provided that the meetings be open to the public.

No one can rightly quarrel with such statements of high purpose, but, unfortunately, fear of accusations of censorship has not infrequently led to a weakening of standards of excellence in the library's book acquisition policy. Academic freedom is the right of the teacher to teach the truth as he sees it without interference, and the librarian should be given the same protection without fear of allegation that he is a censor. The library should be at least as free as the classroom, and the librarian as educator should be protected in his right to exclude those books that he considers unworthy.

Because we do not know, with any precision, "what reading does to people," or how it affects social behavior, the profession can be magnanimous in admitting to library shelves books that present "all sides of a subject." Did we but know with certainty the ways in which reading influences conduct, we might be much less tolerant than we now purport to be of those writings that conflict with our own notions of truth. We cannot run with the hare and hunt with the hounds in the belief that "bad" books will do the reader no harm, while "good" books will bring him untold benefits. The position of the librarian would be greatly strengthened if he would say that "good" books can confer benefits, and "bad," or at least unworthy, books can be ruinous to the public's sense of taste. No librarian worthy of the profession would permit a patron the privilege of a book if it were known that anti-social consequences would result. Magnanimity may be no more than the mask that conceals ignorance.

Excessive concern with pornography, which is not very important to the welfare of society, has all too often led the opponents of censorship to neglect the larger issue of keeping from the public that information to which it has a right. All too little attention has been paid to increasing restrictions on the release of essential information concerning the operations of government at national, state, and local levels; the destruction of the environment, and other aspects of conservation; the critical dangers of over-population; the machinations of big business and big industry; and all the other forms of knowledge control that threaten even the very existence of our civilization. These, and many like them, are dangerous topics and librarians, awed by fears of recrimination from boards of trustees and other foci of social power, have walked softly where courage was most needed, and where censorship was most to be feared.

THE LIBRARY AND THE CHILD

One cannot, of course, in a survey such as this treat every aspect of librarianship—administration, cataloging, reference work, and all the various library specializations; but there is one segment of library work that, because of its importance, merits some consideration, and that is library service to the young. When Frances Henne once addressed the students at the Graduate Library School of the University of Chicago, she began her lecture on work with children and young adults by saying, "I am going to talk to you about the most important of all phases of librarianship." Subsequently, one of my friends in the student body reported to me, "At first I thought she was only being facetious, but I'll be damned if she really didn't mean it." I replied, "I am sure she did mean it, and I agree with her." I think my friend was a bit surprised that I should take this position, since my own specializations have been directed more to the scholarly services of the library, but I was quite sincere.

Library service to the young *is* vital, not only to the future of the library but also to the welfare of society. "The salvation of our culture rests in the education of the young," Clarence Darrow told a Yale audience in the 1920s, and Darrow, having been the tough-minded criminal lawyer that he was, the defender of Leopold and Loeb, should know whereof he speaks. The child of today will be the voter of tomorrow, and how can he support libraries if he is ignorant of the benefits they can, and should, confer? Votes are made by the remembrance of things past, and "the thoughts of youth are long long thoughts." The shapes of things to come are molded in the children's room, and the librarian's service to children requires as much scholarship as any other part of the library profession.

I have long taken the position that the good children's librarian comes very close to representing the ideal in library service, first because she knows her materials, and second because she knows her clientele. But to be a good children's librarian requires a very special kind of skill—a skill which, unfortunately, all too few people possess. Basic is the ability to communicate with the child, to understand his needs, interests, and desires. But beyond this rare capacity is a sense of literary values which will enable the librarian to winnow the good materials from the inferior, and there is much of both in today's book production. We are concerned here with the formative years, and failure will negate the need for automation, information science, and all the social responsibilities in which librarians are wont to take such pride. Moreover, the public library has the autonomy to attempt that which the school library, tied mainly to the curriculum, finds it difficult to do.

One can admire, and rightly, the physical resources that architects have incorporated into some of our modern central library buildings, but the focus of children's services should be the neighborhood, in order to increase the library's resources to the maximum. This dispersion is as desirable for libraries of the wealthy suburbs as for those of the ghetto. Collections should not be static but should be rotated from branch to branch, keeping in mind always their appropriateness for the community served. Children more than any other audience, except perhaps the aging, need library service brought as closely to their homes as conditions permit.

This area of the library's service is one in which volunteer and part-time assistance can be effectively used. We are wasting a rich resource of talent in not utilizing more fully than we are the unemployed housewife or the retired person who has a natural facility for working with the child. Such assistance should, of course, be chosen with the utmost care, for a well-intentioned but inadequate worker can seriously injure any program. Supervision is, therefore, essential, but the rewards can be great. Ideally, of course, such volunteers should receive a proper economic reward, if for no other reason than that it promotes supervision of the work being done and the ability to demand standards of excellence in performance. In every large metropolitan area, as well as in smaller communities, there must be substantial numbers of housewives and others who would find their greatest reward in the work itself; but their generosity should not be imposed upon in the name of economic stringency.

The aim of children's services is, of course, the expansion of the child's intellectual horizon and his understanding of his environment, and books and the library personnel are the major resources for achieving this. But such services do not have to be, and indeed should not be, restricted to the printed page—recordings, story-telling, group activities, and a host of other forms of constructive activity are appropriate to the library's offerings. In suggesting such programs, one thinks immediately of the Children's Library in Sao Paulo, Brazil, and the rich and varied fare that it sets before the child. The library should not become a day-care center where parents can dispose of a child during necessary periods of absence from home. But if some attributes of the day-care center creep into the program while the library's resources are brought to children who would otherwise never experience them, the line of demarcation should not be drawn too sharply. Above all, the child should not mature with the impression that a library is a refuge to which one flees from the rigors of reality. The library is not a "children's home," for daytime "orphans"; it must be presented as a place one seeks out happily in enthusiastic anticipation of intellectual stimulation and excitement.

Frances Henne was right. We must not let our justifiable pride in and concern with our very substantial accomplishments in developing sophisticated library techniques obscure the virtues in conventional library service to youth. Despite the Biblical injunction, we must *not* "put away childish things."

ONE MIGHTY TORRENT

Ours is a paper culture, a civilization built on paper bearing symbolic marks. We talk glibly of the "knowledge explosion," but it is not an explosion at all. An explosion is spherical, it exerts pressure in all directions; but the growth of our accumulated knowledge is not spherical, it is amorphous. Some areas of knowledge grow much faster and extend much farther into the unknown than do others; some may be said to grow scarcely at all. Moreover, our knowledge has not expanded as rapidly as we might like to think, but we are threatened by a paper flood.

One could argue that it is our *ignorance*, or at least our awareness of our ignorance, that is "exploding," rather than our knowledge. Hackerman suggests that "maybe ignorance should be treated as a constant of nature. Or maybe it appears to be constant and continuous up to some critical point beyond which everything starts over. In any event, ignorance seems to be the driving force impelling us to refine truth constantly."[13] De Solla Price sees in the growing proliferation of scientific literature the possible future demise of science through suffocation in its own record. Among the "diseases" of science, he hypothesizes that at some future date science will be unable to progress because it can no longer master the literature it has produced.[14] There are few tasks more challenging or more appropriate to the professional responsibility of the librarian than that of bringing recorded knowledge under manageable control.

If we are effectively to utilize the accumulated knowledge of society, some way must be found to control the inundating flood of print. Librarians are the managers, so to speak, of recorded knowledge; it is their responsibility to acquire, organize, and service the transcript, in whatever form it may appear—the product of the human intellect. Thus, it follows that bibliography in its broadest sense is central to the practice of librarianship; it is what librarianship is all about. In that venerable slogan of the ALA: it is the "best books" and the "most people" that define the librarian's goals. But even the "best books" do not a library make unless they are brought together into a unity, the unity that is knowledge itself—a collection that has direction and purpose, a garland, if you will, in which there should be no weeds and in which every blossom makes its own contribution to the beauty of the whole. Thus, it is the task of the librarian, as it was the task of the descendants of Isis, diligently to seek out and bring together from wherever they may be found, the scattered fragments of Truth.

NOTES

[1] Robert Redfield, *Human Nature and the Study of Society* (Chicago: University of Chicago Press, 1962), p. 418.

[2] Paul B. Sears, *Who Are These Americans?* (New York: Macmillan, 1940), pp. 78-79.

[3] Abraham Kaplan, "The Age of the Symbol," *Library Quarterly* 34 (October 1964): 303.

[4] Susanne K. Langer, *Philosophy in a New Key* (Cambridge: Harvard University Press, 1942), p. 83.

[5] Charles Morris, *Signs, Language, and Behavior* (New York: Prentice-Hall, 1946), pp. 35-36.

[6] Kathleen Molz, "The Public Custody of the High Pornography," *American Scholar* 36 (Winter 1966-1967):103.

[7] Douglas Waples, "People and Libraries," in Carleton B. Joeckel, ed., *Current Issues in Library Administration* (Chicago: University of Chicago Press, 1939), p. 370.

[8] Ralph A. Beals, "The Librarian as Anthologist," *D.C. Libraries* 12 (January 1941): 19-21.

[9] Archibald MacLeish, "The Premise of Meaning," *The American Scholar* 41 (Summer 1972): 357.

[10] Ibid., p. 362.

[11] Norman Hackerman, "Ignorance Is the Driving Force," *Science* 183 (March 8, 1974): 907.

[12] Alfred North Whitehead, *Dialogues of Alfred North Whitehead, as Recorded by Lucien Price* (Boston: Little, Brown, 1954), p. 131.

[13] Hackerman, "Ignorance Is the Driving Force," p. 907.

[14] Derek J. de Solla Price, *Science Since Babylon* (New Haven: Yale University Press, 1961), Chapter V.

SELECTED READINGS

Berelson, Bernard R. *The Library's Public.* New York: Columbia University Press, 1949.

Boulding, Kenneth. *The Image; Knowledge in Life and Society.* Ann Arbor: University of Michigan Press, 1956.

Childe, V. G. *Society and Knowledge.* New York: Harper, 1956.

Conant, Ralph W., ed. *The Public Library and the City.* Cambridge, Mass.: MIT Press, 1965.

Conant, Ralph W., and Kathleen Molz, eds. *The Metropolitan Library.* Cambridge, Mass.: MIT Press, 1972.

Egan, Margaret E. "The Library and Social Structure," *Library Quarterly* 25 (January 1955): 15-22.

Ennis, Philip H. "The Library Consumer; Patterns and Trends," *Library Quarterly* 34 (April 1964): 163-178.

Garceau, Oliver. *The Public Library in the Political Process.* New York: Columbia University Press, 1949.

International Encyclopedia of the Social Sciences. New York: Macmillan, 1968. See: Anthropology, Culture, Society, Language, and related topics.

Linton, Ralph. *The Tree of Culture.* New York: Knopf, 1957.

Machlup, Fritz. *The Production and Distribution of Knowledge in the United States.* Princeton, N.J.: Princeton University Press, 1962.

Maquel, Jacques J. *The Sociology of Knowledge.* Boston: Beacon Press, 1951.

Martin, Lowell A. "The American Public Library as a Social Institution," *Library Quarterly* 7 (October 1937): 546-561.

Shera, Jesse H. *The Foundations of Education for Librarianship.* New York: Wiley, 1972. Chapter II, "Society and Culture"; Chapter III, "Communication, Culture, and the Library."

3

KNOWING MEN AND BOOKS

"This is no book," a reviewer once wrote of Walt Whitman's *Leaves of Grass*; "who touches this touches a man." Whitman himself wrote of the same book in his preface to *November Boughs* that the poems were "the out-cropping of my own emotional and other personal nature—an attempt, from first to last, to put *a Person*, human being (myself, in the latter half of the Nineteenth Century, in America) freely, fully, and truly on record."[1] Nikos Kazantzakis, in his introduction to *Report to Greco*, denies that the work is an autobiography. "The sole value I acknowledge in it," he writes, "was its effort to mount from one step to the next and reach the highest point to which its strength and doggedness could bring it; the summit I arbitrarily named the Cretan Glance." Therefore, he says, "I call upon my memory to remember, I assemble my life from the air, place myself soldier-like before the ground, and make my Report to Greco." To make his report, he says, "I collect my tools: sight, smell, touch, taste, hearing, intellect."[2] Every product of the human intellect, in whatever form it may be expressed, is a part of the creator's life; and the stuff of which libraries are made is autobiographical. As the products of the intellect are threads in the warp and woof of the creator's life, so they become a part of the life of those who are exposed to them. The act of reading is a very intimate act, a dialogue between author and reader, and in this intimacy the librarian, if he is to be a mediator rather than an interloper, must share. He can mediate effectively only when he knows the materials in his care and the clientele who use, or will use, them. Yet, of all aspects of the librarian's profession the implications of this act of mediation are, perhaps, the most neglected.

THE GREAT UNKNOWN

"Reading maketh a full man," wrote Francis Bacon, but the distinguished Baron Verulam did not specify that with which the man might be made full. Douglas Waples and his associates once wrote a book called *What Reading Does to People*, without discovering what the effects are. Many cultures have existed and even prospered without widespread literacy. Nevertheless, our Western civilization depends heavily upon the written word, and that dependence grows as our culture increases in complexity. The ability to read has long been the hallmark of scholarship and learning, and today illiteracy, even functional illiteracy, is a serious handicap and a source of embarrassment. The educational system of the West has always been book-centered, despite the growing use of non-book materials and other media. The very existence of the modern public library is predicated on Bacon's dictum and the belief that reading "is good for people." The early advocates of the public library based the major portion of their argument on the virtues of reading as essential to future economic success and social advancement. Moreover, reading would be a bastion against the corruption of youth, keeping the reader away from the grog shops or other places of iniquity.

Yet, despite these hopes for the efficacy of reading, Americans have long held a curious ambivalence about the act. The learned professions— education, medicine, the ministry, and the law—have received the highest community esteem, while at the same time there exists along with this distinction a certain distrust of "book larnin'." The man who has not had any "practical experience," who has "never met a payroll," is apt to be condemned as "a visionary and idealist" whose judgment is not entirely to be trusted, and the boy who prefers reading to football is at least "a bit queer."

The ability to determine with precision the effects of reading is impeded by the obvious fact that the written word is only one way in which one assimilates information and knowledge. Indeed, in many situations reading may account for only a relatively small part of the total intake of information. Man communicates through and receives communication from all his senses, kinesics, all the arts, and all forms of social contact. Studies that have been made of the information-gathering habits of scientists, for example, suggest that such people derive a large portion of their accumulated knowledge from conversation with their peers and their superiors, through attendance at professional meetings, and through other means for the promotion of professional contacts. The general public, unfortunately, derives much of its "knowledge" from hearsay, gossip, and a host of other sources of unreliable information. Such phenomena do not detract from the importance of the library. Our civilization could hardly have achieved its present state of sophistication without repositories for the preservation and utilization of the transcript of the culture; but it is important for the librarian to see in proper cultural perspective the institution over which he presides, and to recognize his position in the total cycle of information gathering and dissemination. The library, important as it is, is not the *sine qua non* of man's recourse to information and vicarious experience.

Because the library exists to serve everyone who needs it, librarians become dismayed when not all those who need the library actually use its services. Because we who are librarians tend to be compulsive readers, we come to assume that reading is indigenous in all men and that it is essential to existence. You and I are compulsive readers, we read everything that comes within our range of view. We read what is printed on the cereal box as we eat our breakfast, not because we want to know what is said (we knew it already, we read it yesterday morning and the morning before that); we read because we cannot help ourselves. We find it almost impossible to think of life without reading, and we count that day lost when some serious reading has not been done. But not all people are such as we; for many, reading occupies a relatively small portion of their waking hours. Reading, especially serious reading, is hard work, and for many the transfer of thought from printed page to eye to brain, and thence to overt behavior is almost an impossibility.

To be sure, many people flock to the doors of the library, but this does not imply that the library is an agency of mass communication. Use of the library is individually motivated; unlike the radio and television, the library does not "spray" the audience with the message. Mass communication has many outlets but only one message; the library is a single outlet, which collectively includes its branches, but it disseminates many messages. In the mass media the sponsor dictates the message according to his own interests, but in the library the patron must seek out for himself the message that most nearly meets his needs. Moreover, the level of tolerance, or acceptance, is much lower in the mass media than it is for even light reading. No serious reader would spend his time reading a "soap opera," but he will watch, if he watches at all, such productions on television that do violence to his standards of taste. The mass media may direct their appeals to the lowest intellectual level, the library should aim at the highest. A picture, according to an old adage, may be "worth a thousand words," but only if they are written in "basic English." A picture presents only surface impressions; and though these impressions may be vivid, they are seldom capable of transmitting reflective thought.

Librarians, especially public librarians, are wont to speak of the "general reader," as though he were some kind of biological and psychological specimen that could be identified, characterized, and motivated in a particular way. But this general reader no more exists than does the "economic man." Every reader is "special" in his own eyes and should be so treated by the librarian. The first three of S. R. Ranganathan's five precepts of librarianship (he called them "laws") are: Books Are for Use; Every Book Its Reader; and Every Reader His Book. For generations librarians have preached the doctrine of service to the reader; yet even today there are many people who still hold to the image of the librarian as a kind of Fafner guarding the Niebelungen gold and demanding nothing less than a Siegfried to release the treasure.

Not all the shortcomings of librarians are of their own making. No doubt every librarian, at one time or another, has heard the story told of Langdon Sibley, librarian of Harvard College from 1856 to 1879, who, according to the tale, was crossing the Harvard Yard on a bright June morning, when he encountered President Charles W. Eliot. "How are things at the library?" inquired the President. "Oh, very well," replied the librarian, "All the books are in except two; Agassiz had those and I'm going over to get them now." The episode, if indeed it ever took place, is supposed to prove that librarians are more concerned with the care and custody of the books in their collections than they are with use. What the narrative does not reveal is that, according to the statutes of Harvard College in those years, the overseers required the librarian to have all the books in the library and accounted for once a year on the day of the annual meeting of the board. Sibley was not guilty of indifference to the needs of Harvard scholarship, he was only being a good librarian fulfilling his responsibilities and obligations as set forth in the statutes of the college.

The good librarian must, of course, be concerned with the preservation of the books in his collection, but preservation must be seen in terms of the needs of future generations. Except for a few museum pieces, such as the *Gutenberg Bible*, books are for use, as Ranganathan has said; but they cannot be used if they are not preserved. Today, when books proliferate at an exponential rate and seemingly by parthenogenesis, preservation is, perhaps, somewhat less important than it was in an earlier day, when all books could be called "rare." Nevertheless, important books still go out of print, and no library can be constantly invading its book budget for replacement of titles that have permanently strayed from the shelves.

Perhaps only the harassed doctoral candidate, working against time and within the limitations of financial resources, and feeling the whiplash of his dissertation professor, can truly appreciate the sting of despair when the librarian, for whatever reason, good or bad, answers his request with a positive "no." Librarians are not paid to say "no," and, John Milton to the contrary, they do not serve "who only stand and wait." Service speaks with an active, not a passive, voice.

Knowing books and men—knowledge of the materials and their sources, and empathy with the patron and his needs—these are the twin pillars upon which library service rests. Yet, what are the proper dimensions of that service, and how can it best be translated into effective action? These are the basic questions of librarianship. We know that just as the book is only one part of the total educational experience, education is only one part of the total function of the book. Moreover, education is only one part of the total responsibility of the librarian, just as use of the book is only one part of the total arsenal of the teacher. The librarian may, and often does, act in the role of the educator, but in any formal sense he is not an educator—he is a librarian. Neither is the librarian a social worker, a doctor, a lawyer, or a psychiatrist. The librarian's concept of service, then, demands an understanding of his limitations as well as an understanding of the proper areas for the exercise of his professional competencies.

It is the librarian's responsibility to bring the best of the world of books to the user in ways that will most nearly meet his needs, assuming, of course, that those needs are legitimate and not inimical to the best interests and welfare of society. The domain of the librarian might be represented as a triangle, as in Fig. 2:

Fig. 2

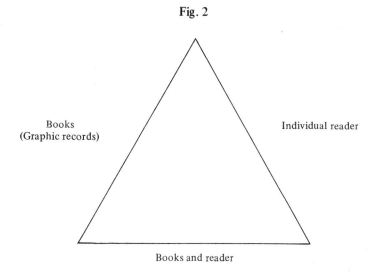

It is at the base line of the triangle that the world of the librarian exists. The librarian operates in three spheres (see Fig. 3).

Fig. 3

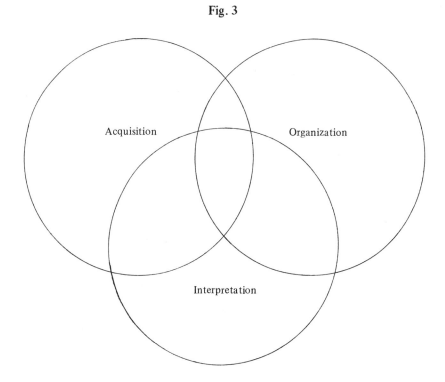

Acquisition means knowing what to acquire, in terms of the user's, or assumed user's, legitimate needs, and where and how to acquire it. The task of acquisition requires a sound knowledge of the substantive subject field, or fields, involved; the bibliography of that area; and the relevant book trade.

Organization relates to the arrangement of materials in the library so that their contents will be accessible; the bibliographic resources of the field, including the fabrication of bibliographic instruments for the library's own holdings; and the technology for gaining access to other sources of relevant information.

Interpretation is the act of bringing the reader and the book together. It is the *raison d'être* for the library, but it cannot exist in the absence of the other two spheres.

The body of knowledge and understandings that define the role of the library might be presented a second way, as shown in Fig. 4.

Fig. 4

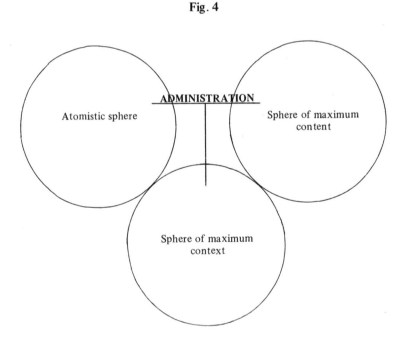

The **atomistic sphere** encompasses all the minutiae, mechanisms, procedures, and processes that comprise the technology of librarianship. The **sphere of maximum content** represents the intellectual content of the library in whatever form that content may appear—books, films, recordings, tapes. The **sphere of maximum context** symbolizes the environment, both social and cultural, in which the library operates. In the realm of the public library, the context is the public sector; in the academic library, the students, faculty, and staff of the educational institution; in the school library, the students and teaching staff of the school; and in the special library, the staff of the parent organization. All three spheres are coordinated, synthesized, and unified into an effective operation by the administration. The duties of the administration are, to use the phrase of Robert Maynard Hutchins, "to align means to ends."

<h2 style="text-align:center">WHAT IS A BOOK
THAT A MAN MAY KNOW IT . . .</h2>

What, then, is a book? We all know it as a physical object, customarily as a codex, a sequence of leaves (bearing symbols, either phonetic or non-phonetic such as pictographs, which represent the author's thoughts filtered through his powers of expression), these leaves being held together at the spine and the whole covered with an appropriate binding. But we are not here concerned with the physical form of the book: it can present many shapes and come in many sizes. The graphic record can be a tape, a record, a film and still qualify as a graphic record, the physical embodiment of what its creator thought he put there. Our attention is directed here to the book as an intellectual production, for that is the primary concern of the librarian.

Many people have attempted to define a book, usually in descriptive terms or by analogy; the latter definition tends to take rather elaborate, not to say somewhat sentimental, forms. A book, for example, has been likened to a window—it can exist to get a view of the outside world, it can be a source of illumination, and it can ventilate the mind; it can exist for none other than aesthetic purposes, like the great rose window at Chartres. But of all the analogies, perhaps the most nearly accurate is that attributed to the eighteenth century German physicist, Georg Christoph Lichtenberg, who said that a book is a mirror, *"Ein Buch ist ein Spiegel."* A book is a mirror because if a jackass looks into it he will not see St. Paul looking back.[3] The analogy is not only amusing, it is quite true, for what a book is to any given reader depends on what it "says" to him. Like beauty, the message of the book is in the mind of the beholder.

Intellectually, a book is an unstable commodity, being, as it is, a product of the human mind. Any one book can mean many different things to many people, and even different things to the same person at varying times in his life. A book is a reflection of the reader. We conventionally say, "A book says . . ." but a book says nothing until it is given life by the intellect of the reader.

In my own experience, *King Lear* is not the same play that it was when I first read it as a young man in his sophomore year of college. Then I saw it as the tragedy of an old misunderstood man and the filial devotion of his youngest daughter. Today, I read it as the tragedy of human pettiness, selfishness, and greed brought to a focus in the mental aberrations of a senile old man who wanted "to eat his cake and have it, too." I do not mean to imply that I now regard the play as a lesser work of dramatic art than I once thought it was; quite the contrary, to me it has become Shakespeare's greatest work, not excepting *Hamlet*. Probably many people, some of them distinguished Shakespearean scholars, may disagree with me, but that is their affair. *Shakespeare* is what *Shakespeare* means to them. No one knows what Shakespeare himself thought, or how he conceived the "message" of *Lear*. His characters, as he himself admitted, "are such stuff as dreams are made on." The librarian's "vines" do, indeed, have tender grapes, and their juices are intoxicating.

For the very reason that books do stimulate us in a variety of ways, we attribute to the book certain anthropomorphic traits and characteristics. A book, the intellectual contents of which are, for whatever reason, incomprehensible to the potential reader, "says" no more to him than does a mirror to a blind person. The reader must wring the message from the book, and many books do not give up their messages easily.

As we saw in the preceding chapter, Archibald MacLeish raised the question of whether a book changes its character by being associated with other books in a library collection, and thus he has broadened the scope of our inquiry into the nature of a book. He was not, of course, suggesting that the book itself underwent some mystical metamorphosis respecting its physical form or intellectual content. Rather, he believed that a book in concert with related books could evoke in the mind of the library patron concepts, relationships, and avenues of reflective thought that a book alone could not induce. Thus, a true library is not merely an agglomeration of books brought together by a series of fortuitous circumstances, but a meaningful creation designed to stimulate in the user purposeful cerebration. Two books, like two heads, may be better than one. The addition of a book to a collection, or the withdrawal of one from it, alters the character of the whole, and the importance of the book determines the magnitude of the change. Thus the building of a library collection is itself an act of scholarly creation, and if the librarian is to be the architect of his "house of intellect," he must know both books and men, and the uses to which the former is put by the latter.

... AND A MAN
THAT HE MAY KNOW A BOOK?

What, then, is a man as a rational being? Obviously he is far more complex than a book and, unlike the book, he is subject to change. The problem of man as man has baffled the philosophers, the medical doctors, and the psychologists, not to mention the poets and other creative artists, from the beginning of recorded time. To Guildenstern's protestations that he lacked the skill to play the recorder, despite Hamlet's insistence that it was "as easy as lying," Hamlet replied:

Why, look you now, how unworthy a thing you make of me! You would play upon me, you would seem to know my stops, you would pluck out the heart of my mystery, you would sound me from my lowest note to the top of my compass; there is much music, excellent voice, in this organ, yet cannot you make it speak. 'Sblood, do you think that I am easier to be play'd on than a pipe? Call me what instrument you will though you can fret me, you cannot play upon me.[4]

"Cogito ergo sum"—I think; therefore I am—wrote Descartes in his *Discourse on Method*, to which Ambrose Bierce, in the *Devil's Dictionary*, replied, "I think I think; therefore, I think I am." But, cynical or otherwise, both men were acknowledging that what marks man as man is the power of rational thought; the ability to generalize from specifics, the capacity to reason. Yet, though brain research has made impressive progress during the past half-century, there are still vast areas of the human brain that have baffled all attempts at scientific exploration, and that leave behavior patterns still unexplained. We cannot even agree on definitions of consciousness, cognition, or knowledge, much less comprehend them. So far as our understanding of learning is concerned, we have progressed little further than the conditioned reflexes of Pavlov's dogs. We observe the behavior patterns of mice in "learning" to negotiate a maze, or which door conceals the cheese and which an electric shock, and then make the leap from mouse to man without any assurance that it is a valid inference, or that what we are observing is really "learning."

What, then, is the brain? Superficially, and somewhat disrespectfully, it is a "blob" of electro-chemical substance, weighing approximately 1,500 grams, that can be held in the palms of the two hands, and is the apex of the central nervous system. In part, at least, it is a vast and intricate network of neurons numbering ten to the tenth power, through which flow minute electrical currents. But attempts to explain its operation by analogy to a computer, merely because a current flows or does not flow—the binary or "all or nothing" nature of the nerve signals—is a misleading, or gross, over-simplification. Actually, the synapses themselves may be viewed as minute computers. Moreover, the locus of the response in the brain is not a constant but may shift slightly to any given signal or stimulus.

We do know that the brain operates by association, by relationship, by patterning. Sir Charles Sherrington, the distinguished British neuro-physiologist, called the brain "the magic loom," because it weaves patterns of thought. We cannot "think" chaos. Nor can the brain continue to function rationally under conditions of sensory deprivation. It must constantly receive external stimuli or it will begin to turn upon itself, so to speak, with hallucinations; it will become, in the argot of the criminal, "stir crazy."

"Order is heaven's first law," not only in the world and in the universe, but in our minds as well. That a library and the tools of the librarian must be organized is not the consequence of some crotchety librarian's whim.

Classification is essential to the operation of the library, and the closer that organization approaches the organization in the mind of the library user, the more successful will be his search. Use of the library involves the matching of two patterns, the pattern of the organization of the library and the pattern of the patron's approach to it, and it is the degree to which these two patterns coincide that determines retrieval effectiveness and hence patron satisfaction.

If we but knew with precision what takes place in the human mind when it is confronted by a library file, we could greatly improve our tools of bibliographic organization. Classification, the arrangement of the books as they stand on the shelves, has long been thought to be the key to subject access to the library's store, and the catalog was conceived as a supplement to it. Long before Melvil Dewey and his distinguished successors, Charles Ammi Cutter, Charles Martel and J. C. M. Hanson, S. R. Ranganathan, and Henry E. Bliss, to name but a few, men were devising schemes for the arrangement of books. The early schemes were little more than large groupings of books in the major subject fields, but as libraries grew in size these groupings became as inadequate for the modern library as the Greek classification of the elements into fire, water, earth, and air would be for modern science.

So the classification theorists of the late nineteenth and early twentieth centuries set themselves to the task of designing classification schedules that would serve the growing needs of the library. But scholarly as these men were, and their contributions should not be minimized, they conceived of library classification in terms of the organization of *knowledge*, rather than the organization of knowledge *in books*, and there is a vast difference. Furthermore, they attempted to devise a "universal" classification that would be all things to all men. But there can be no "universal" approach to a library; everyone approaches an array of books in a different way and with a different purpose. Similarly, books are not a single unit of knowledge; each encompasses bits of knowledge, units of thought, that approach infinity. A book as a physical object in a library classification, as it stands on the shelf, has *position*—that is, propinquity to the book to the right of it and the book to the left—but it has a single dimension. Intellectually, however, books are multi-dimensional, and the only way we have been able as yet to introduce additional dimensions into the book stock is through the use of entries in a card catalog or bibliography which can be multiplied as dictated by the intellectual dimensions of the book. These "surrogates" for books are, at best, a crude device, but until a new form of bibliographic organization is devised, perhaps through the use of the computer, which will separate the intellectual content of the book from the book as a physical entity, they are the best that we have. Thus, brain research is particularly important to the librarian for, in the future, it may point the way to the improvement of bibliographic instruments and procedures.

Throughout all the library's operations and procedures the librarian must be concerned with patterns of human thought, with relationships as they are understood by the users of books. This awareness may be seen in the work of the cataloger as differentiated from that of the bibliographer. The cataloger starts with a particular book, analyzes its contents and its subject matter, and decides where it should be classified so that it will be most likely to be found by those who need it. He also selects from a standard list those subject headings that in his opinion seem most succinctly to describe the substantive content of the book. In short, the cataloger begins with the book and moves to the presumed subject, or subjects, of the patron's interest. That the work of the cataloger and the interest of the patron meet as often as they do may be attributed to the skill of library pioneers who designed our systems of classification and our subject heading lists, for the library user starts at the other end of the tunnel and proceeds from subject interest to book. The two approaches to the library store may be roughly diagrammed thus:

Cataloger — Book — Subject — Patron

Patron — Subject — Book

But the subject bibliographer, like the patron, begins with the subject about which he is compiling a bibliography and proceeds from subject to book. The compiler of a bibliography is, in effect, a patron, or at least a representative on the library staff of the patron:

Bibliographer — Subject — Book
(Patron)

The more successful the librarian is in achieving an understanding of the patron's frame of reference—his needs, desires, and limitations—the better will be the service to the clientele. The proper study of the librarian, as for mankind, is man. Yet, how complex even relatively simple relationships are, how many ways to go astray in the library's operations may be seen from the diagram of the reference process (Fig. 5 on page 72).

Thus, the interrogation of a library collection may be seen as a series of screens, or filters, involving the total act of communication between human being and graphic record, and between human being and human being. For the understanding of a relationship as complex as these, though it is one that the reference librarian experiences every day, Pavlov's salivating dogs are of little help.

Years ago, Enrico Fermi, in an address to the graduates of the University of Chicago Laboratory School, observed that, no matter how deeply the physicists penetrated into the inner nature of the atom, Nature always seemed to keep a jump or two ahead of them—"there was always someplace to go." So it is with man's relation to the book, and that mysterious reaction between eye and brain, and brain and cognitive thought. Of the science of psychology, Sigmund Koch, professor at Boston University, wrote:

Fig. 5

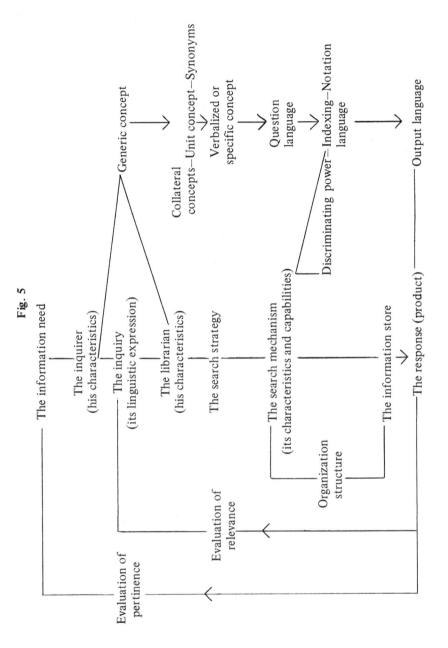

Many social critics have been concerned about the tendency of modern man—especially American man—to prize images, pictures, more than the realities for which they stand. . . . Scientific psychology was stimulated into life in the late nineteenth century. That intensely optimistic age, understandably dazzled by the apparent cognitive and technological fruit of the natural sciences, decided to try out a hopeful new strategy: that of extending the methods of natural science to all human and social problems. At the very beginning, there was some degree of realism about the magnitude and difficulties of such a task. But the *image* had been created, and in almost no time at all the ever-autistic character of man under challenge asserted itself. The hypothesis was soon prejudged! The *hope* of a psychological science became indistinguishable from the *fact* of psychological science. The entire subsequent history of psychology can be seen as a ritualistic endeavor to emulate the forms of science in order to sustain the delusion that it already *is* a science.

. . . .
Strange things happen when image is seen as fact! . . . What is perhaps worse than any single symptom of psychological science, is the demeaning image of man himself at the basis of its presumably tough-minded conceptualizations, an image that mankind cannot but accept and strive to emulate because of its association with the iconology of science. In its austere form, it depicts man as a stimulus-response mechanism or, worse, a mere mathematical point of intersection between stimulus and response processes, and steered by socially "manipulated" rewards and punishments. According to this form of the image, the laws of human and social "behavior" can be derived from rigorous study of the variables controlling the rate at which a hungry rat in a small, dark box presses a lever to obtain tiny pellets of food. The more sophisticated and recent form of the image holds man to be an information-processing entity operating on the principles of a binary digital computer programmed to conform to payoff criteria similar to the rewards of the previous case.[5]

Professor Koch's verdict on scientific psychology could well be brought, and in almost the same terms, against librarianship, for it, too, was caught up in the onrush of science that followed the close of World War II. This impact of science upon the work of the librarian, its accomplishments, failures, and possible future, will be dealt with in the remainder of this chapter and in the succeeding chapter.

THE UNFULFILLED PROPHECY

In 1938, Frederick J. Keppel, then president of the Carnegie Corporation of New York, wrote in an anthology on the future of the library:

> As to cataloging cards ... I blush to think how many years we watched the so-called business machines juggle with payrolls and bank books before it occurred to us that they might be adapted to deal with library cards with equal dexterity. Indexing has become an entirely new art. The modern index is no longer bound up in the volume, but remains on cards, and the modern version of the old Hollerith machine will sort out and photograph anything that the dial tells it. ... We librarians must keep up with all these applications of science, and I admit it takes a fair share of our time to do so.[6]

Keppel, who envisaged himself as a modern Rip Van Winkle, hypothesized his innovations as taking place in 1958, twenty years after he wrote. His words passed almost unnoticed by librarians, though during World War II a small group of us in the Central Information Division of the U.S. Office of Strategic Services, in Washington, began to experiment with some primitive techniques in the use of IBM sorting equipment for the indexing of postal intercepts from abroad delivered to us daily in large bundles by the U.S. Office of Censorship.

But it was that distinguished scientist, Vannevar Bush, of the Massachusetts Institute of Technology and the Carnegie Institution of Washington, who first fired the imagination of librarians and others over the potential of the computer for the subject analysis of library materials and the automated retrieval of information. In an essay entitled, "As We May Think," published in the *Atlantic Monthly* in 1945, this "Father of the Modern Computer" envisaged "Memex," a personal information retrieval mechanism that utilized computer technology for the recording and analysis of scientific literature.[7] The concept represented a long-standing concern of Bush's over the inadequate availability of recorded scientific information due to the absence of effective bibliographic control. This interest was prompted in part by the authenticated story that for thirty years Gregor Mendel's basic work on the principles of heredity remained unknown to those scientists who could use it because it was lost through "the crudity with which information is transferred between men." Unlike Mendel's writing, Bush's words did not lie fallow and unnoticed for thirty years. Partly because of the distinguished reputation and influence of the author and partly because of the wide circulation of the journal in which the essay appeared, Bush's vision fired the imagination of librarians and others. By 1950, serious work had been initiated in places like the library of the U.S. Department of Agriculture, under the leadership of Ralph R. Shaw, directed toward just such "push-button libraries" as Keppel and Bush had hypothesized. Stimulated by support from fund-granting agencies (the National Science Foundation, the Office of Research and Development of the U.S. Air Force, the National Library of Medicine, to name but a few), there emerged a variety of mechanisms and systems using a wide variety of technologies for the subject analysis of research literature and data processing for the research scientist. In addition to the push-button library, scientists even more than librarians began to talk of mechanical indexing, machine translation, and "artificial intelligence," this last term being loosely used to cover a wide variety of activities involving "non-biological" intelligence—character or pattern recognition, automated generation of abstracts, machine translation, and the like.

The decades of the fifties and sixties were exciting years, filled with high hope, confidence in ultimate success, faith in a new kind of librarianship, with debate and argument, claims and counter-claims, controversy and polemics because we believed implicitly in what we were doing. But the goal of a true information system still eludes us. What emerged from these years of exploration and invention, unsupported by basic research, were systems for *document*, rather than *information*, retrieval. We found ourselves with ingeniously designed but quite inadequately selective electronic card catalogs that flooded the user with quantities of bibliographical references rather than the precise information for which the search was initiated. These machines, and their soft-ware, the programs used with them, still lack adequate discriminating power. Moreover, the machines, unlike the human brain, cannot automatically adjust to changes in the intellectual environment of the search, they cannot alter a course of action for which they have not been programmed. Shifts and refinements in an inquiry resulting from what has, or has not, been found are impossible. Yet every searcher, every reference librarian, constantly makes such alterations in his search strategy. Serendipity is quite beyond the powers of the machine. Modern computer technology can simulate "thought" to a rather striking degree. Impressive progress has been made in character and pattern recognition. It is now possible to analyze speech by computer and then "reassemble as it were" the parts of the analysis so that the machine reproduces speech to a degree of intelligibility that makes possible the identification of the linguistic background, the national origin, of the original speaker. Computers can, and do, disgorge vast quantities of bibliographic citations from their "memories," but the user must winnow the output for himself. The ability to search at fantastic speeds and to manipulate complex programs with many inter-related variables, however, does not compensate for the absence of selectivity. We have not yet achieved mechanized cognition. So we find ourselves with "mechanical stack-boys"; diligent, conscientious, and tireless in the performance of their tasks, but not very bright, always needing instruction when a decision must be made, and certainly a poor substitute for the intelligence, experience, and imagination of a competent reference librarian or literature searcher.

By 1965, Vannevar Bush wrote that, though he had not lost faith in Memex, it would be a long time in coming and that we would first have large networks, computer-centered with on-line connections providing information services in specialized fields or disciplines.[8] Indeed, as we shall see in the chapter that follows, such services are now in the making in medicine, chemistry, and related disciplines.

We must not lose sight of the fact that the book has not been, and doubtless will not be for the foreseeable future, replaced as the most effective container of ideas that man has yet devised. It is portable; it provides random access; it can be read with no instrumentation more elaborate than a pair of glasses. In the 1960s, Robert Maynard Hutchins hailed the computer as the greatest invention since Gutenberg gave us printing with movable type, and there is no doubt that the modern computer is a powerful tool. But a tool it is, and a tool it must remain. There is a growing fear that Emerson may be right: things *are* in the saddle and ride mankind. We cannot turn a deaf ear to Lewis Mumford's warning of a world dominated by mechanization. Thus he has written in "Reflections—Prologue to Our Times:"

> I still look forward to, as a valid possibility, the slowing down of the pace of automation and depersonalization great enough to permit us to safeguard the immense treasuries of knowledge and technical facility now at our command.[9]

Mumford readily acknowledges that automation has an important contribution to make to our lives so long as it is kept under human control, but he continues,

> Even at their best, all these improvements, however helpful, remain peripheral: they fail to do justice to man's central concern, his own humanization. In letting depersonalized organizations and automatic contraptions take charge of our lives, we have been forfeiting the only qualities that could justify our existence: Sensitiveness, consciousness, responsiveness, expressive intelligence, human-heartedness, and . . . creativity.[10]

The very values that Mumford most seeks to preserve are those that are nourished by the library, and the librarian, of all professionals, should be alert to the dangers inherent in the capacity of automation to depersonalize its services.

It is not the intention here to imply that all the effort to develop automated information retrieval systems and the push-button library envisaged by Keppel and Bush was a waste—far from it. We learned a great deal from all the *Sturm und Drang* of the past twenty-five or more years. We achieved a new insight into the uses to which recorded knowledge is put, and into the complexities of the reference and search process. We have learned to view the library from a new perspective and have gained a better understanding than ever before of its role in the human adventure. The machine has brought with it a new respect for the reference librarian and the demands he or she must face. We can now appreciate the magnitude of the problems that must be solved before we can interrogate the machine and get the answers we want.

There is no guarantee that scientific innovation will go on indefinitely. Research, like all other forms of human activity, moves in cycles, and it is not impossible that we may be reaching a plateau; the futurists of the 1960s may have been premature in their prognostications of the potential for man-machine relationships. Artificial intelligence is still human stupidity. Computers can, indeed, perform feats of computation, and even retrieval, that seem to be beyond normal human mental powers. But even the largest, most advanced, computer cannot be made to understand sentences which a four-year-old child can comprehend without hesitation.

Perhaps the greatest lesson of all that we have learned from our exploration of automata is not that computers are any less wonderful than we have imagined, but that human intellectual abilities, and the brain itself, are far more wonderful than we had even dreamed. When we set ourselves to the task of programing computers to understand simple sentences, we were forced into the realization of the tremendous number of logical steps, the brilliant inferences, and the vast body of knowledge necessary to a process that we previously had merely taken for granted. The Age of the Computer may turn out to be golden after all, if only because it reveals to us the miracle in what we consider most ordinary in our lives.[11]

But so far as the computer and the library are concerned, we are laying the foundation for a new technology to assist the profession, and a new science of information processing—information science—and all that it implies of future understanding of how recorded knowledge is manifested in society.

We still may not know what a book is or a man that he may know it, but at least we are recognizing the problem and its importance to the future welfare of mankind.

NOTES

[1] Walt Whitman, "A Backward Glance O'er Travell'd Roads," Preface to his *November Boughs* (1888); from *Walt Whitman: Two Prefaces*, ed. Christopher Morley (Garden City, New York: Doubleday, Page, 1926), pp. 65-66.

[2] Nikos Kazantzakis, *Report to Greco* (New York: Simon and Schuster, 1965).

[3] The original German is, "*Ein Buch ist ein Spiegel; wenn ein Affe hineinsieht, so kann kein Apostel herausgucken.*" Georg Christoph Lichtenberg, *Aphorismen, Briefe, Satiren* (Düsseldorf/Köln: Eugen Diederichs, 1962), p. 48. I have taken the liberty of changing the monkey to a jackass, and identifying the apostle as St. Paul.

[4] *Hamlet*, III, ii.

[5] Sigmund Koch, "The Image of Man in Encounter Groups," *American Scholar* 42 (Autumn 1973): 636-637.

[6] Frederick J. Keppel, "Looking Forward—a Fantasy," in *The Library of Tomorrow*, ed. Emily Miller Danton (Chicago: American Library Association, 1939), p. 5.

[7] Vannevar Bush, "As We May Think," *Atlantic Monthly* 176 (July 1945): 101-108.

[8] Vannevar Bush, "Memex Revisited," in *Science Is Not Enough* (New York: William Morrow, 1965), pp. 75-101.

[9] Lewis Mumford, "Reflections—Prologue to Our Time," *New Yorker* 51 (March 10, 1975): 50.

[10] Ibid.

[11] See George Leonard, "In God's Image," *Saturday Review* 2 (February 22, 1975): 12-13.

SELECTED READINGS

Adler, Mortimer. *How to Read a Book.* New York: Simon and Schuster, 1939.

Berelson, Bernard R. *The Library's Public.* New York: Columbia University Press, 1949.

Cherry, Colin. *On Human Communication.* Cambridge, Mass.: MIT Press, 1967.

_____. *World Communication: Threat or Promise?* New York: John Wiley, 1971.

Greene, Marjorie. *The Knower and the Known.* London: Farber and Farber, 1966.

Mumford, Lewis. *The Myth of the Machine: Technics and Human Development.* New York: Harcourt, Brace, and World, 1966.

Ong, Walter J. *In the Human Grain.* New York: Macmillan, 1967.

_____. *The Presence of the Word.* New Haven: Yale University Press, 1967.

Ottinger, Anthony G. *Run, Computer, Run: The Mythology of Educational Innovation.* Cambridge, Mass.: Harvard University Press, 1969.

Piaget, Jean. *Rhetoric, Romance, and Technology.* Ithaca, N.Y.: Cornell University Press, 1971.

_____. *Scientific Education and the Psychology of the Child.* New York: Orion Press, 1970.

Shera, Jesse H. *Foundations of Education for Librarianship.* New York: John Wiley, 1972. Chapter I, "Communication and the Individual."

_____. *Libraries and the Organization of Knowledge.* London: Crosby Lockwood, 1965.

_____. "What Is a Book That a Man May Know It?" In *Knowing Books and Men; Knowing Computers, Too.* Littleton, Colo.: Libraries Unlimited, 1973, pp. 65-74.

Sherrington, Sir Charles. *Man on His Nature.* Cambridge, England: Cambridge University Press, 1963.

von Neumann, John. *The Computer and the Brain.* New Haven: Yale University Press, 1958.

Waples, Douglas, Bernard R. Berelson, and Franklyn R. Bradshaw. *What Reading Does to People.* Chicago: University of Chicago Press, 1940.

Wooldridge, Dean R. *The Machinery of the Brain.* New York: McGraw-Hill, 1963.

_____. *Mechanical Man: The Physiological Basis of Intellectual Life.* New York: McGraw-Hill, 1969.

Young, J. Z. *Doubt and Certainty in Science.* New York: Oxford University Press, 1960.

4

DEUS EX MACHINA

by LaVahn Overmyer
Associate Professor of Library Science
Case Western Reserve University

"Thinking," observed Ralph R. Shaw in one of his most facetious moods, "is what we expect machines to compensate for our lack of." This distinguished librarian, teacher, and pioneer in library automation, despite the fact that he was the inventor of the Photo-Clerk and the Rapid Selector, always maintained a wholesome suspicion of the machine as a potential substitute for the human intellect. He was a scientist by training and a humanist at heart, and the two qualities were always mixed in him as they are in many librarians today.

In the preceding chapter attention was called to some of the yet unfulfilled promises of the machine; the intent of this chapter is to set forth some of the benefits that automation is already bringing to librarianship. If some ambivalence remains in the mind of the reader, this is an almost inevitable consequence of the rapid and dramatic development of computer technology and its application to library practice. Machines have come a long way since Shaw wrote "From Fright to Frankenstein."[1]

Electronic computers are a phenomenon of the last half of the twentieth century, but our modern idea of manipulating data by machine has been in a continuous process of research and development since late in the nineteenth century.

The Industrial Revolution of the eighteenth and nineteenth centuries was directed toward expanding man's physical capabilities. Machines were designed to dig, lift, push, pull, transport, cut, and punch in order to relieve man of hard physical labor. Many recent technological developments have concentrated on extending man's mental capabilities.

Computers and associated data storage and transmission equipment are today's major tools for recording, manipulating, and transmitting information to assist man in his intellectual work. These machines provide him with the means to interact, cooperate, and communicate over great distances more easily than was ever possible in the past. It is this type of technology, rather than the factory machines of the Industrial Revolution, that assists in the operation of libraries.

BRINGING RECORDED INFORMATION
AND USERS TOGETHER

As our world changes and our civilization becomes more complex, it becomes increasingly necessary for recorded information to be available in a wider variety of forms for a wider audience than ever before. Today's information needs are met by two types of institutions—the old and established library and the newer information agency.

For centuries libraries have been the traditional institutions in charge of acquiring and storing recorded information for those who wish to use it. In the past they served mainly the scholarly and educated and had no great problems in delivering satisfactory service; but this century has witnessed major sociological changes and greater advances in education, research, science, and technology than in any previous period in history.

Today's libraries reach people of all ages from all economic levels in many different environments. In this country this heterogeneous group is served by a huge complex of library systems—public, academic, and school as well as many different kinds of special libraries.

The output of recorded information has never been greater. By World War II it became apparent that libraries could no longer carry the entire burden and that the country needed additional ways to process and disseminate information. A few non-library information services had existed, and with generous support from the government these were expanded and new ones were established. Their purpose was to complement rather than replace libraries by providing a range of new services that most libraries had been unable to offer.

These agencies have no single identity, for they package and disseminate information in a variety of ways in many subject areas and disciplines. Some abstract and/or index the world's literature in one or more subject areas, such as Chemical Abstracts and Science Citation Index. Others serve as information centers, referral centers, distribution centers, or clearinghouses; and the actual work is done in government agencies, professional societies, commercial organizations, and universities. At first most were concerned with the literature of the physical sciences and technology, but now the social sciences and, to a lesser extent, the humanities are also represented.

Almost without exception these non-library agencies are concerned with the detailed analysis and dissemination of contents of documents rather than with documents per se—with individual articles of journals rather than the entire issue, and with chapters of books rather than the entire book. The limited catalog information provided by libraries for the whole book or journal is inadequate for research and scholarly requirements. A multitude of publications and computer services emanate from these adjunct information facilities for extensive use by librarians, researchers, scholars, and the general public.

Computers and associated technologies are becoming increasingly important to both types of institutions. In libraries the use of these technologies is labeled *library automation*; in non-library agencies, *information retrieval*. Neither term is precise or discrete, but the distinction is made to provide a convenient division of responsibilities for the discussion that follows.

LIBRARY AUTOMATION

Library automation is a generic term often used in discussing the use of computers and related equipment to help libraries handle and manage the physical materials that comprise library collections. For philosophical and semantic reasons some prefer to use "library mechanization" or "data processing in libraries"; all these terms refer essentially to the same activities. Since no universal definition of library automation seems to exist, a functional explanation appropriate to this chapter is: "the use of electronic data processing equipment and supporting technology to assist in acquiring, processing, storing and maintaining the collection; and in making the collection available to users by circulation, reference services, interlibrary loan, and telecommunications. Technological assistance has been most effective in creating and maintaining the many records, including the bibliographic apparatus (catalogs), necessary for proper control of the collection and for providing service to library users."

Although books are still the mainstay, the "collection" represents a wide variety of recorded information, print and non-print, available in today's libraries.

Print materials include not only books but also serials (periodicals and the like), government documents, technical reports, manuscripts, maps, pictures, drawings, sheet music, and microrecords (miniaturized records such as microfilm, microfiche, and microcards).

Non-print materials found in a library often include audio and visual items such as films, slides, and recordings. A much newer form that is now available to all types of libraries, though it is not yet common in library collections, is machine-readable data (information recorded on a medium such as magnetic tape that can be processed by computer).

These different materials do not, of course, have equal importance in any one library. Libraries specializing in the physical sciences and technology often consider journals, technical reports, certain government documents, and perhaps internally generated data more important than books because their contents are more current and detailed. Libraries dealing with maps, manuscripts, archival-type materials, art works, and music are primarily interested in non-book materials, both print and non-print. School and academic libraries are frequently responsible for non-print materials used for instructional purposes. Regardless of the forms that exist in a library's collection, however, all must be processed in some way before they can be used.

Library automation is concerned with using existing electronic data processing equipment to assist in handling and controlling these print and non-print materials ("documents") as physical entities. Although electronic computers represent our most advanced data processing equipment, the possibility always exists that some day they may be replaced by a different technology.

A library's ability to meet user needs and the extent to which a collection is used are measures of success and satisfaction. To meet these needs each library develops its own set of routines for getting the work done; but unless every routine, process, and service is directed toward serving its users, there is little reason for a library to exist. Although the specifics vary from one library to another, the responsibilities can be grouped into three broad categories:

Selection and acquisition of materials.

Preparation, storage, and maintenance of each item (individual document); and bibliographic control (classifying, cataloging, and recording) of each item.

Use of materials by dissemination and service (circulation of items in a local collection, user assistance through various levels of reference service, and use of materials from other libraries and information agencies via interlibrary loan and telecommunication).

These categories of operations and services are both typical of and unique to the library; essentially they describe what is common to all libraries, but not found in other institutions.

Management/administration serves as the umbrella to control and coordinate the three categories and to provide general services such as personnel, accounting, legal, and public relations. Although management is vital to any organization, much of library management work is not unique to the library, and administrative practices vary widely. This aspect of library operations, therefore, is not discussed in this chapter.

INFORMATION RETRIEVAL

Information retrieval is also a generic term that covers a broad range of activities more concerned with the analysis and dissemination of the contents of parts (e.g., articles in journals) than with the whole document (e.g., journal issue). It involves use of the computer in abstracting, indexing, extracting, content analysis, SDI (selective dissemination of information), current awareness and retrospective searching, and related activities that help to make the information available to users.

Here again, terminology is not completely clear; "information processing," "information handling," and "machine literature searching" have been used to describe aspects of these activities.

Library automation and information retrieval involve some tasks that are similar and overlapping, but at present their operational procedures have not been integrated. Most agencies involved directly in the production of "information retrieval" products are not attached to libraries. A notable exception is the National Library of Medicine, which produces *Index Medicus*, MEDLARS (**Med**ical **L**iterature **A**nalysis and **R**etrieval **S**ystem), and MEDLINE (**MEDLARS** on-**line**).

The services provided by these non-library facilities fill a great need in meeting today's information requirements. Their greatest use is probably in reference departments of libraries. Many abstracting and indexing services are available in both printed and machine-readable form, and other information centers are providing machine-searching services of one or more data bases. An increasing number of reference departments are taking advantage of these newer sources of reference information.

Since this book is about libraries and librarianship, the use of these products rather than their actual production is of interest in this chapter.

TECHNOLOGICAL DEVELOPMENTS

Neither library automation nor information retrieval as defined here would be possible without equipment that can accept alphanumeric characters (letters, digits, and symbols), convert them for processing and manipulation, and restore them to alphanumeric form. Furthermore, neither would be practical unless results could be accomplished more rapidly, more accurately, and more consistently over extended periods of time at reasonable cost than would be possible by manual methods.

Specifically, what can be accomplished at any given time with machines is, of course, dependent on what the available machines are capable of doing. Computer technology of the 1970s bears little resemblance of the first computers of the 1940s and even less to data processing equipment developed late in the last century, but a brief review of yesterday can provide a better understanding of today.

Man is forever looking for better and faster ways to do things. History records the use of punched cards and punched paper tape in the seventeenth and eighteenth centuries and credits the work of Charles Babbage in the early nineteenth century with furnishing some basic ideas for the development of today's computers. Although these events are interesting as history, ancestors of present equipment were developed more recently.

Punched cards and punched card equipment (often called Unit Record or Tabulating Equipment) as we know them today are a direct result of the work of Dr. Herman Hollerith, a statistician in the U.S. Census Bureau, in the late 1880s. He and his colleagues had just spent seven years manually sorting and tabulating great masses of census data for fifty million people. They estimated that it would take ten years to complete the 1890 census, using the same manual methods.

A friend, Dr. John Shaw Billings, Librarian of the Army Surgeon General's Library and later the first Director of the New York Public Library, suggested the use of mechanical means to perform the tedious, time-consuming counts and tabulations.

With the encouragement and assistance of colleagues, Dr. Hollerith began developing a machine-processing system. He designed a code to represent alphanumeric characters (A-Z, 0-9, and a few symbols). Each character was identified by a unique pattern of holes punched in cards or paper strips to be "read" by a magnetic principle. The very familiar 80-column punched cards of today, often called "Hollerith cards," still use the original "Hollerith code."

Dr. Hollerith then invented machines to "read" the punched patterns of holes and process the data in various ways. Although slow and crude by today's standards, the machines helped to complete the 1890 census of sixty-two million people in just over two years instead of the predicted ten years.

Others were encouraged by this success, and for the next fifty years punched card equipment was the principal means for processing data rapidly, accurately, and inexpensively.

Punched card equipment, even the modernized version, consists of a group of unconnected machines. Each machine can perform only one, two, or three specific tasks; but by using the machines as a group, cards can be punched, verified, printed, sorted, matched, merged, selected, and duplicated; paper printouts can be produced, and simple calculations performed. Individually the machines are known as printing keypunch, verifier, interpreter, sorter, collator, reproducer, and printing accounting machine.

It would be a mistake to underestimate their value, for they have been indispensable in certain types of jobs. The trend in recent years, however, has been to use them as supporting equipment in computer centers rather than as independent systems, since they have definite limitations and lack versatility. They can process only punched cards—one card at a time (a *unit* record); each machine is specialized; most are controlled by pre-wired boards; and an operator must move the cards from one machine to another to complete all processing steps.

These limitations were recognized by scientists and engineers, as well as users, as early as the 1930s. The idea of a single multipurpose machine to perform and coordinate many separate tasks had considerable appeal, and in the 1940s several one-of-a-kind experimental computers were assembled in research laboratories in the United States and England, most of them under government sponsorship for government use. Although never marketed, they provided much basic technology for all electronic computers that followed.

The first production computers, "first generation," reached the commercial market in 1953 and were used for the remainder of the decade by government agencies and a few large corporations. Truly "monsters" or "giants," as they were frequently called, they operated with vacuum tubes and electrical relays and were gigantic in size with enormous requirements for electrical power, humidity control, and heat control. They were slow, costly, and unreliable; but they did introduce new concepts in machine design and were able to perform mathematical calculations and data manipulations that were impossible to accomplish with previous equipment. Thus their successes were sufficient to attract the attention and appreciation of business and industrial leaders and to assure continuing research and development.

With the development of transistors, diodes, and magnetic recording in the late 1950s, manufacturers were able to produce the popular "second-generation" computers, which were much faster, more versatile, and more reliable. They were less expensive, smaller in size, and more economical to operate. This generation of computers awakened the public to their value as powerful tools in education and information processing (in libraries and information centers) as well as in business, industry, and government. There was a sharp upturn in usage, and computer technology became increasingly influential in American life.

From the beginning, changes and improvements in the technology have been rapid and continuous, supported by intensive and extensive programs in research and development. "Third-generation" computers were introduced about 1965 with integrated circuits for better performance. Capacity and operating speed were increased, and costs and energy consumption were reduced. Compatibility among different makes and models became possible, and programming (the writing of instructions for the computer) techniques were improved.

Experts do not seem to agree about the generation of computers available in the mid 1970s—fourth, third-and-a-half, or still in the third? Whatever the label, of more importance to librarians is the fact that many improvements of the past ten years have been of direct benefit to libraries.

Modern computer systems—the computer and associated input, output, storage, and communication components—are very complex in structure and performance. Systems are available in a wide range of models, sizes, capabilities, and costs, from small micro- and minicomputers of less than $5,000 to huge multi-million-dollar inter-connected systems. They can be independent or joined together. Users at remote locations can be directly connected to some systems via telephone lines or other telecommunication apparatus, and many systems can simultaneously handle the work of hundreds of users. The smallest computer of today, occupying a few square feet of space, is faster, more powerful, and more versatile than those of the first and second generations. Even the slowest model measures its internal processing speed in microseconds (millionths of a second), and some measure in nanoseconds (billionths of a second)—one thousand to one million times faster than the millisecond (thousandths of a second) speed of the first generation. One minute of computer computation equals at least fifty years of manual work, and the achievement of one million additions in less than one second is not uncommon.

Many large volumes would be required for a detailed explanation of computer technology, and the information would be incomplete because of new developments. Hundreds of books are available on all aspects of computer systems. Nevertheless, for those readers with little or no knowledge of the technology, a simplified introduction to basic structure and terminology seems appropriate.

At first, computers were clearly divided between *analog* and *digital*, and digital was further divided between *scientific* (mathematical) and *general purpose* (business, data processing). Some present computers are combinations of all. The capabilities of interest to libraries are found in *digital, general-purpose computers.*

There is no typical computer, not even a typical digital general-purpose computer. In spite of differences, however, all electronic computers do share common characteristics that distinguish them from other machines and technologies.

All have internal main storage, often called "memory," and the ability to accept operating instructions from internally stored programs.

Even the simplest systems consist of *hardware* and *software*. Hardware is the battery of machines or actual physical equipment. Equipment is required to get the data into the system (*input units*), to process the data (the *computer*), and to provide results (*output units*). All hardware is worthless unless *programs* (detailed sets of instructions) are provided to tell each component what to do. Every system requires many kinds of programs because computers do many kinds of jobs, and *software* is the collective term to identify the programs just as hardware identifies the physical equipment.

Thus, any operating computer system must have *both* hardware and software and the absolute minimum steps of:

INPUT   **PROCESSING**   **OUTPUT**
              (computer)

In actual practice this is much too simple for the types of processing done by computers, but it is adequate to explain some basic points.

Computer

The computer is where work is actually done. It accepts input, performs innumerable processing steps according to instructions in the programs, and produces desired output.

A computer has no moving parts but performs all internal work electronically, which accounts for its tremendous speed and the fact that there is nothing to see. By using combinations of the presence or absence of electrical impulses or magnetic cores magnetized in one direction or the other to represent 0's or 1's (zeroes or ones), it is able to make a unique combination of "bits" (impulses or cores) to represent each alphanumeric character in the prescribed character set. The combination of 0's and 1's used in all computer processing is based on the *binary* system of numbers and is known as "machine language"—the language of the computer, which is unreadable by humans.

All computers not only use machine language and have no moving parts, but they also consist of three basic components: the *main storage unit* (memory), the *control unit*, and the *arithmetic/logic unit.* Some authors group the three into the *Central Processing Unit* (CPU) or main frame; others consider only the control and arithmetic/logic units as the CPU; and still others group control and arithmetic/logic as a combined unit. Of importance here is the fact that each component has definite work to do.

The *main storage unit* is a "passive" unit that has been likened to an electronic filing cabinet. All instructions (programs) and data to be processed (e.g., a purchase order) enter the main storage area from an input unit for "storage." Instructions then move to the control unit, one at a time, and data to the arithmetic/logic unit for processing. Processed data are then returned to storage before output. Data in memory are "transient," so storage needs only enough capacity to store the program(s) required, plus the largest element of data to be processed (one purchase order). The size of main storage in a computer system is one of the most important factors in determining a system's capacity and therefore its over-all capabilities.

The *control unit*, often likened to a telephone exchange or the central nervous system, serves as the manager. It receives the instructions and contains complicated circuitry to direct all operations for input, output, and processing; but it does no processing of actual data.

The *arithmetic/logic unit* is where the actual internal processing of data is done. Very complicated data processing and mathematical problems can be solved by reducing each problem to a series of very elementary steps and using the capabilities of adding, subtracting, multiplying, dividing, moving, shifting, comparing, and testing.

Early computer systems could serve many users but only one user at a time; others had to wait their turn. A user accumulated individual transactions (e.g., purchase orders) into a job or batch and took the batch to the center for processing; this procedure is known as *batch processing.* If the computer was busy, he could wait hours or days for the results. For many types of work batch processing is very satisfactory and it is still the most economical; but in the early days it was the only mode of operation available.

By the mid-1960s techniques were developing to permit many users to use the same computer simultaneously (*time-sharing*) and to have direct interactive communication (*on-line* or *in-line access*) from remote locations. These advances were possible because of improved speed and capacity of large systems, improved input-output units, and improved data transmission systems.

Dramatic advances in microelectronics have resulted in the miniaturization of logic, control, and memory circuitry, where over 20,000 circuitry components can be stored on a tiny silicon "chip." The reduction in size of processing units has not only further reduced costs in medium-sized and large computers, but has also contributed greatly to the success of a group called "minicomputers," so named because of their small physical size rather than their performance. In fact, some can outperform those that are much larger, and they are far superior to all of earlier generations.

By the early 1970s further miniaturization resulted in the "micro-computer," where all circuitry is contained on a silicon chip less than a quarter of an inch square. One manufacturer has produced a complete microcomputer on a single plastic card measuring 9¾ by 5¾ inches; it has limitations, of course, but it is available for less than one thousand dollars.

Very small computers have many practical uses. Some are used in independent systems, but many serve as satellites or auxiliary computers to large complex systems. While they lack the versatility and processing power of today's large systems, they can perform many kinds of standard operations just as well and at much less cost than the large ones.

Because computer hardware is inoperable and useless without adequate programs, much more attention is now given to improving software and assisting users than was done in earlier years. As mentioned, both programs and data are processed in machine language; this means that the computer must convert all input from punched cards, paper tape, etc., to machine language and all output back to the language or codes of the output units.

The very earliest programs were written in this tedious machine language, a series of 0's and 1's. This was soon replaced by symbolic language (mnemonic codes), a bit easier but still very demanding. Improvements continued, but until procedure-oriented, higher languages were developed, all programs were "machine-dependent," meaning that each program had to be written for a particular make and model of computer.

The higher level languages, such as FORTRAN, COBOL, ALGOL, BASIC, PL/1, and many others, are not machine-dependent. A user can write his application program in one of the languages without needing to know very much about the computer he is using. The computer then needs a suitable compiler to convert the statements to the machine language of that particular make and model.

Modern computer systems require many different kinds of programs operating together. Some authors divide these programs into software and user programs. When this distinction is made, software consists of generalized programs, subroutines, compilers, assemblers, executive routines for control, programs for operating the system, and many others related to the computer. These types of programs are often provided by the manufacturers or commercial companies specializing in software. User programs, on the other hand, are prepared for a user's specific application; and some progress has been achieved to make it easier for users to prepare their programs.

Input, Output, Secondary Storage Units

Though the computer itself is the heart of a system, its operations are not observable; users have very little control over the operation, which becomes remote and impersonal. By contrast, the equipment used to get data in and out (I/O) and to store machine-readable data can be seen. Known as *peripheral equipment*, these auxiliary devices are directly attached to and are under the control of the central processor (CPU). The computer and all peripheral equipment thus comprise a computer system.

Both *input* and *output* are generic terms and can refer to *contents*, *medium*, or *device*.

In the input process, *contents* refers to both instructions and information to be processed (e.g., information to appear on a purchase order) that are to be "read" into the computer. All contents must first be converted to machine-readable form—i.e., some code that the computer can accept, such as holes in a punched card.

The *medium* is the physical means for holding the contents—punched card, paper tape, magnetic tape, magnetic disk, etc.

The *device* is the peripheral machine used to "read" the contents of the medium into the computer, such as a card reader, paper tape reader, magnetic tape drive, or magnetic disk drive.

In the output process *contents* refers to the actual information "written" from the computer, such as the contents of a purchase order form. The *medium* again refers to the physical form of the contents—a printed page (e.g., purchase order form), punched card, paper tape, magnetic tape, etc. The *device* is the machine that holds and controls the medium, such as a printer, card punch, paper tape punch, or magnetic tape drive.

Although a user may have very little influence in the initial selection of peripherals, it is the user's responsibility to decide content and form of output, preparation of input, and the media and devices to select from among those available.

Decisions were not difficult to make in the early years, because choices were limited to punched cards, paper tapes, and printed paper. Now the media and devices available to get information in and out and store for later use are many and increasing; fortunately, most are useful to libraries.

Development of magnetic recording (magnetic tape and magnetic disk) for second-generation computers proved to be a major improvement in input, output, and permanent storage. Although punched cards still have a place, especially for programming, they are too slow and lack the versatility that libraries require.

Magnetic tapes provide much faster input-output and inexpensive, compact storage. Data are recorded as magnetic bits and the number of characters (density) stored on one inch of tape has increased from 200 characters per inch to 1600 as a standard; tests have been made on tapes of 3600 density. One inch of magnetic tape at 1600 density can store the equivalent of twenty 80-column punched cards.

Magnetic disks and drums provide even faster input-output and offer additional advantages of random storage and direct access, both essential for interactive communication. Whereas the use of magnetic tapes requires that data be recorded in some predetermined order, disks and drums can accept data in any order. Furthermore, since tapes are on reels, searching for a record must be done sequentially, that is, each previous record must be passed before reaching the desired record. Disks and drums permit "direct access"—going directly to the desired record without passing all previous ones.

Magnetic recording has promoted the development of input devices other than keypunches and paper-tape typewriters, but most systems still require the laborious task, by human operator, of "keying" the information letter by letter on a keyboard. Data recorders are available to key directly to magnetic tapes or magnetic disks. The IBM MTST (magnetic tape selectric typewriter) records data on a tape cassette that is converted by a special device to magnetic tape. The IBM Selectric typewriter with OCR (optical character recognition) font records data on hard copy (paper or card). OCR fonts contain characters of special design that can be "read" by an optical scanning device and transferred to a machine-readable medium such as a card, tape, or disk for further processing.

Further development of OCR is of special interest to libraries since many are converting current bibliographic data for their catalogs into machine-readable form and are interested in doing the same for older catalog information. Using an operator to key each record is much too expensive. From time to time the Library of Congress tests OCR equipment designed to read the many fonts in which printing appears. Although not yet perfected, progress is encouraging. When an OCR scanner can identify many types of printing accurately, the possibilities of providing materials in machine-readable form are virtually unlimited.

In addition to the development of OCR, within recent years the economic feasibility of interactive devices has been most attractive to libraries. At the present time the types most used are terminal typewriters and video terminals such as cathode-ray tubes, called CRT's, with small TV screens and keyboards. Both enable human operators to have two-way communication directly with computer-stored data from remote locations. This type of equipment enables a user in New York to "access" a computer in California or Europe, for example. Telephone lines and special cable systems are the most common means for transmitting data to and from remote locations. Typewriters are relatively slow but provide a hard copy of the "dialog"—the query of the user and the response of the computer. CRT's are much faster but provide no hard copy unless an auxiliary printer is attached.

Improvements in printers have also been beneficial to libraries. From the beginning, most computer printers have had a very limited character set of 26 upper-case letters, 10 digits, plus a few symbols, such as many keypunches have. Although adequate for business uses and a few library applications, such as orders and book cards, the incomplete character set is totally inadequate and unsuited for maintaining permanent bibliographic records. Producing catalog cards or book catalogs in an unattractive format without adequate punctuation does not interest most libraries. Fortunately many late-model printers have a character set of upper- and lower-case letters, a full complement of punctuation marks and other symbols, and in some cases diacritical marks and non-roman characters, as well as the limited set of upper-case only. Since a larger character set slows the printer and is thus more expensive, users must decide which is preferable at any given time.

For those desiring publications that look like regular printing, the more complex and sophisticated technique of photocomposition is available. Copy is prepared and coded in machine-readable form and stored on magnetic tape; it is then projected on a CRT screen and photographed on film. The final product is produced by offset printing. Photocomposition provides a very large character set that can include both roman and non-roman alphabets, a large variety of type fonts (e.g., block, roman, italics), and fonts with different size characters. Although photocomposition is expensive, the gap between costly photocomposition and regular computer printing is narrowing.

An increasing number of large libraries and information services that process many foreign language materials in a number of alphabets are using photocomposition for their publications. *Index Medicus* from the National Library of Medicine has been photocomposed since 1964, one of the first publications to use photocomposition. The book catalogs of the New York Public Research Libraries are a more recent example.

COM (Computer Output Microfilm) is yet another medium for storing computer-generated output. Machine-readable data, often stored on magnetic tape, are projected on a CRT screen, photographed, and stored on microfilm or microfiche. COM also is being used in libraries as another method of output production and compact auxiliary storage.

CIM (Computer Input Microfilm) is not yet as well developed or widely used as COM. Microfilm images are converted to machine-readable form, using the principle of optical character recognition.

COM, CIM, and inexpensive compact microfilm storage appear to have considerable potential in libraries of the future for catalogs and other records.

Research is continuing on appropriate media for storing large data bases created from machine-readable data. Storage is a major economic consideration in operating computer systems since an important reason for converting anything to machine-readable form is to use it many times in many different ways. Magnetic tapes and magnetic disks are now the most common media for storing permanent or semi-permanent records for re-use in computer processing, but the need for less expensive, reliable "bulk" storage appears to be increasing. Contents of the catalogs of large libraries or the data bases of large networks can total billions of characters, so the need for an efficient means to store these masses of information is of practical concern.

Input, output, and storage components have improved significantly in the last ten years, and more are on the drawing boards. Perfection of OCR equipment capable of reading any kind of print rather than stylized characters only will perhaps make it practical for libraries to convert their retrospective catalog data into machine-readable form. Very high-speed laser printers are now on the market for faster and less expensive printing. Laser recording, magnetized film strips, and further developments in microphotography are additional possibilities for bulk storage. What is impossible or impractical today may become both possible and practical in a few short years. What was once much too expensive is now economically feasible because as computer power and reliability have increased, the trend in computer costs has been steadily downward.

Changes occur rapidly and usually for the better, so one responsibility of practitioners is to keep informed and up to date on technological developments that are relevant to the current needs of his institution.

DEVELOPMENT OF AUTOMATION IN LIBRARIES

Libraries are by nature conservative, but they are not static. As social institutions, they do reflect societal changes, eventually if not always immediately, for major changes tend to be gradual rather than sudden—evolutionary rather than revolutionary. In the use of technologies, libraries have most often adopted and adapted what others have invented and developed; this has been especially evident in the use of computers and other data processing equipment.

Punched card equipment, computers, telecommunications, micro-records, and all other devices designed to handle information have been developed to assist mathematicians, chemists, physicists, engineers, records managers, accountants, and a host of others in business, industry, and government. Manufacturers, in the beginning, were not thinking of libraries; only within the last ten to fifteen years have they begun to recognize the information industry as an important customer group. In spite of this unconcern on the part of manufacturers, libraries began to use data processing equipment forty years ago.

The University of Texas installed a punched card circulation system in 1936. Through the 1940s and 1950s about twenty other libraries used punched card equipment and/or paper-tape typewriters for circulation control, ordering, book cards, accession lists, serials holdings lists, book catalogs, account control, and statistics.

These libraries were looking for labor-saving devices to eliminate or reduce some of the monotonous, repetitive, time-consuming manual processing that existed in so many day-to-day operations. By today's standards these machine efforts were very elementary, but libraries had begun to accept the technology of the time.

In the early 1960s universities, government agencies, and commercial organizations acquired second-generation computers. Associated libraries were encouraged to use them—to take advantage of this "new and powerful technology"—and an increasing number of them did. Some earlier users of unit record equipment simply transferred their work to the new computers, while others converted manual records and routines to machine-readable form for computer processing.

Most of the early work represented independent efforts by individual libraries to "automate" at most two or three applications, and by 1963 fifty to seventy-five libraries were attempting to do something. Much was done by "trial and error," and there was frequent "re-invention of the wheel"—each library tended to start from the beginning without benefitting from the experiences (successes and failures) of other libraries. Often there was little coordination of work within a library, and cooperation among libraries was minimal.

As one would expect in any new and untried venture such as library automation, some work was successful and some failed. Mistakes and frustrations were plentiful, and critics were many. Failures were due to many reasons, including the fact that second-generation computers were not capable of meeting some basic library needs effectively and economically.

Libraries as a group undoubtedly process the greatest quantity and the widest variety of variable-length alphanumeric data of any group of institutions in the world. Materials are acquired in many forms, print and non-print, unpredictable in length and structure. The bibliographic content of library catalogs, which describes, analyzes, and classifies this mass of material, represents some of the most complex data a computer can be expected to process.

Computer components of the second generation fell somewhat short of meeting these complex needs. Punched cards and paper tapes were clumsy and slow, and the upper-case-only printer was considered unsuitable for production of most catalog records. Magnetic tapes and magnetic disks improved the storage and searching requirements, but on-line interactive devices, adequate character sets for the printer, and sophisticated software to meet library needs were not yet readily available. Though no one was proceeding on very firm ground in expanding beyond housekeeping routines and circulation control, there was an intuitive awareness that much more was possible with computers than with punched-card and paper-tape equipment.

The computer concept of capturing source information once, updating (changing, adding, or deleting) and manipulating it as required, and generating a variety of outputs for use in many places for many different purposes was beginning to be understood. The idea of a "system" which would coordinate numerous tasks of different types was emerging; and a number of public, academic, and special libraries were making feasibility studies and surveys with the development of a system in mind.

Information retrieval was also undergoing significant changes. The greatest growth in research, development, and implementation in different kinds of information centers began in the early 1960s. Indexing and abstracting in a wide range of disciplines as well as a number of associated services were begun or expanded, and the majority of these services were using computers to assist in processing. Today many centers are providing computer-generated products in both printed and machine-readable form. While most of this work continues to be performed outside a library environment by non-library agencies, the products of their work have become indispensable tools for library reference departments.

What transpired during this period provided valuable and often enduring lessons. Librarians learned that the introduction of computer technology into libraries, even at the simplest level, is a complex, difficult, time-consuming, and expensive undertaking. It is much more than a simple transfer of manual operations to a machine. It requires a type of planning and a team approach that most librarians had not been expected to use in the past. Computers have no magic properties and cannot solve all problems; but they can lend powerful support to meeting library needs when librarians accept their responsibilities for planning the work. Librarians also learned that each advance in computer technology was offering capabilities that were increasingly attractive to libraries.

As library automation has progressed, librarians have realized that no library, not even the Library of Congress, can operate independently. Increases in the quantity of publications, sharp increases in cost of materials, personnel, and general operations, plus demands for more services from a better educated public have led to the development of networks, sharing of resources, and other cooperative projects.

Two important events occurred in the mid-1960s that strengthened the faith all "believers" had in library automation—first, the introduction of third-generation computers, and second, activities at the Library of Congress.

Fortunately for all computer users, third-generation computers were introduced about 1965. Significant improvements in both hardware and software offered more versatility, more power, and greater reliability at less cost than those of the second generation. Fortunately also for libraries, the Library of Congress was becoming actively involved in automation.

As far back as 1958 the Library of Congress had an automation committee, but very little was done until 1963, when an outside team made a detailed survey and feasibility study. The team concluded that automation of the major operations within the Library of Congress was both desirable and feasible and that immediate action should be taken to establish an extensive program. Of even more importance to other libraries was the conclusion that the immediate objective of automation should be to solve the pressing problems facing large research libraries, especially those problems of *bibliographic organization and control*—i.e., cataloging. When the team's conclusions and recommendations were published in *Automation and the Library of Congress*[2] in 1964, libraries that had been quite indifferent to automation became actively interested.

The report recommended goals and targets that were new and different. It suggested that automation efforts be directed toward cataloging rather than acquisitions and circulation. This suggestion was of interest to librarians because they could visualize a possible expansion of services to their libraries from the Library of Congress. Ever since the Library began selling printed cards in 1901, most libraries of this country have depended on the cards for a significant portion of their descriptive and subject cataloging.

The fact that LC did begin work in bibliographic organization and control, as was recommended, provided a much-needed sense of organization and discipline and has proved to be a vital force for the promotion of library automation in the libraries of this country and throughout the world. From this time forward the combination of improved technology and Library of Congress involvement pointed library automation in a different and more productive direction.

Within a matter of months after publication of the report, a separate unit was established within the Library to handle all automation activities, and MARC (**M**achine-**R**eadable **C**ataloging) became the first major project. Since the beginning LC has recognized its dual responsibility—to itself for its own internal operations and to other libraries, especially those of this country. As a result, communication with librarians from all types of libraries has been frequent and informative through meetings, conferences, workshops, seminars, and publications.

MARC is an operational system for converting current bibliographic (catalog) information to machine-readable form and storing it on magnetic tapes; tapes are sold to subscribers for processing on their computers. MARC has had a long, exciting, and very productive history; only a few highlights are mentioned here, however, since its progress and accomplishments have been well documented in available library literature.

As with most major endeavors, MARC began in a limited way. The bibliographic records of monographs (books) were selected as the first to be processed. The decision was made as to what should be included in the machine-readable record—contents, order of contents, and identifiers (content designators) for fields and parts of fields (data elements). For example, the imprint field is divided into separate data elements of place, publisher, and date. The result was the MARC I format for monographs.

After sixteen selected libraries had tested and experimented with the MARC I format for more than a year as part of the MARC Pilot Project, and after further consultations with catalogers and other librarians, the format was greatly revised and expanded. It became the MARC II format, the basic format in use today. A MARC record includes everything that appears on a printed catalog card, plus appropriate identification for each field and data element and additional information for control and retrieval purposes.

The format was accepted by the library community, and in March 1969 the MARC Distribution Service began. For an annual fee the subscriber receives each week a magnetic tape containing cataloging done at the Library the previous week. In the beginning MARC records were limited to English language books cataloged at LC, the file for which goes back to the beginning of 1968. Later the current cataloging of books in French, German, Spanish, and Portuguese was added. Shortly all other roman-alphabet languages will be included, and languages in non-roman alphabets will follow. MARC formats and separate distribution services are also available for serials, maps, and films; and formats have been completed for manuscripts and music. The development and distribution of formats for these different materials are having influence throughout the world and are discussed later in the chapter.

While the MARC project has had the greatest visible effect on other libraries, the Library of Congress has many other automation projects. These projects are in varying stages of development and operation, and all are also well documented. Some have been developed independently; others are direct results or by-products of MARC. Long-range plans call for integrating as much of the work as possible. For example, a record entered in the Order Division will make its way through all the processing steps with appropriate updating until it becomes a complete bibliographic record in machine-readable form available for MARC distribution, card production, book catalog production, search and retrieval, and the data base for other publications.

Name and subject authority files and the National Union Catalog are among the numerous files and publications in machine-readable form; other files are scheduled for conversion.

The Library uses the latest technology when it proves to be appropriate. Interactive terminals are used throughout the Library for different purposes ranging from the input of original data to search and retrieval. OCR (optional character recognition), COM (computer output microfilm), and photocomposition are actually in use or under study.

Computer software and application programs are constantly being revised and updated. Some, such as those used in the format recognition process, are available for purchase. *Format recognition* is a technique for computer analysis (editing) of bibliographic records. When a record is prepared manually for input into the MARC system, an editor assigns content designators and other identifying data before giving it to the typist for keying. Format recognition eliminates the prior editing; the typist keys the record without editing and the format recognition programs do the analysis. The editor's role is that of proofreader who handles exceptions and corrects errors. The technique has been highly successful in speeding up production and improving accuracy.

The Library of Congress, as one of three national libraries, has resources not available to the usual library. Its resources in manpower, technology, funding, materials, and organizational know-how enable it to do much more than other libraries can do. It tests and evaluates new equipment as it comes on the market; it conducts pilot projects and makes useful statistical studies; and it is able to solicit the advice and cooperation of libraries throughout the world.

LC has been working with the National Library of Medicine and the National Agricultural Library to make the records of the three national libraries more compatible. It has also been working with Unesco and IFLA (International Federation of Library Associations) to develop international programs, including the exchange of bibliographic information between nations.

An early step toward standardization has been the *MARC Communications Format*—i.e., MARC II, the one used by the Distribution Service to distribute MARC records on magnetic tape. This format has been accepted by national and international organizations for the *exchange* of bibliographic information among libraries. The order and identification of the contents of each record follow a prescribed pattern so that recipients know exactly what to expect. It has provided a level of standardization that some thought would be impossible to attain. The communications format does not prevent a library from making changes during internal processing, but it guarantees that records sent from one library to another in this format will be standard.

As one might expect, standardization of a machine-readable format has progressed further in the United States than elsewhere. Libraries in this country are accustomed to using LC's printed catalog cards, which are also prepared according to prescribed patterns and have served as a standard for the last seventy-five years.

Great Britain and Canada, both English-speaking countries, also find it possible to make their bibliographic records compatible with the MARC format and have developed BNB (British National Bibliography) MARC and Canadian MARC. In fact the British National Bibliography and the National Library of Canada are exchanging MARC tapes with the Library of Congress on a regular schedule for the imprints of each country. LC no longer has to do original cataloging for British or Canadian materials, and the other libraries accept LC's cataloging for U.S. imprints. Each country can make modifications according to its internal practices and incorporate the changes for its own distribution services.

The hope is that this practice can eventually be extended to non-English speaking countries although it will be much more difficult and may take years to attain because of language differences. A high percentage of LC's collection is in languages other than English. The Library processes materials in hundreds of languages and dialects, grouped into about seventy major languages and written in more than thirty different alphabets. The Library has been doing original cataloging for most of these acquisitions.

If some agreement can be reached for the national library in each country to assume responsibility for cataloging the imprints of its country according to a mutually acceptable format, redundancy and duplication of cataloging effort in the world should be reduced appreciably, and an easier and more rapid exchange of the world's recorded information should result.

What this would mean, for example, is that the French national library, Bibliothèque Nationale, would be responsible for the cataloging of all works published in France for the international exchange of bibliographic records. If that library uses the accepted international format, libraries in other countries, such as the Library of Congress, would accept the cataloging without appreciable modification. The number of national libraries participating would determine the amount of original cataloging other libraries would have to do.

No one is suggesting that a venture of this magnitude will be easy to accomplish; in fact, there are those who doubt that international cooperation to this extent is possible. Those who are more optimistic, however, are working to overcome the barriers, and some steps have already been taken.

Several years ago a number of committees of IFLA developed an International Standard Bibliographic Description for both monographs and serials; they are known as ISBD(M) and ISBD(S). ISBD, as the name implies, provides an international standard for describing a bibliographic record. The standards for monographs and serials are different but similar; both use standard marks of punctuation to separate fields of information and data elements within fields. This scheme enables a person unfamiliar with a language and/or an alphabet to identify different parts of the record. Although ISBD has no direct connection with the development of an international machine-readable format, ISBD punctuation began to appear in the records on MARC tapes in 1975 and also on the printed cards generated from the tapes.

Work also continues on the MARC International Format, another project of IFLA. It is expected that whatever international format is adopted will be used between national agencies of countries but perhaps not within countries.

Serials, while not receiving the early attention accorded monographs, are also involved in a growing number of national and international activities in addition to ISBD(S) and the MARC format.

CONSER (Conversion of Serial Records), representing American and Canadian libraries, is a project to build an on-line national serials data base. Its primary objective "is to establish a relatively comprehensive bibliographic data base of serial titles quickly enough to avoid continuing redundant and expensive conversion efforts on the local, regional, and national levels."[3] By centralizing responsibility and channeling the work into one place, expensive and wasteful practices of several groups doing the same thing can be avoided.

The CONSER group is working with NSDP (National Serials Data Program), which is based at the Library of Congress. NSDP is the U.S. representative in ISDS (International Serials Data System), which is established within the framework of the UNESCO/UNISIST programme, a program to develop an international information system. The ISDS " . . . is an international network of national and regional centers responsible for the creation and maintenance of computer-based data banks which contain essential information for the identification of serials."[4] These centers are also responsible for the registration of International Standard Serial Numbers (ISSN) for serials published within their countries. The purpose of ISSN is to provide a unique identification number for each serial published in the world.

ISSN for serials has a counterpart for books, ISBN (International Standard Book Number). Agencies responsible for the registration of ISBN are located in various countries in an effort to provide a unique identification number for each book published in the world.

It appears that almost every major project in library automation is now directed toward cooperation of some type—exchange of bibliographic data, sharing of library resources, national and international union lists, and networks, as well as a multitude of smaller projects of great importance to the libraries involved.

Within individual library systems, which may or may not be involved in cooperative efforts, there is a broad range of activities that are ever changing and too numerous to describe in detail. What is certain is the fact that there is no "typical" project in library automation. Some libraries limit their work to ordering, circulation, and other less difficult tasks, just as they have been doing for a number of years. Others have integrated many processes including bibliographic control of materials and serials processing with automated check-in of issues.

The impact of MARC is difficult to measure precisely, but each year more and more libraries of many countries are affected by the MARC project, either directly or indirectly. Although the number of subscribers to MARC tapes has consistently remained under one hundred, the libraries receiving services from the tapes now number in the thousands in this country alone. There are numerous examples of libraries joining together to use MARC tapes and other computer-produced data.

One of the oldest, most ambitious, and most successful of these networks is the Ohio College Library Center, known as OCLC. It is based in Columbus, Ohio, and began with a membership of about fifty academic libraries in Ohio. It now serves more than four hundred libraries from coast to coast, and the number is growing. Membership includes public and academic libraries of all sizes—small, medium, and large—federal libraries, and libraries in other established networks. This is an example of how one subscriber to MARC tapes serves hundreds of libraries throughout the nation, and it explains why the MARC subscription service is not larger.

OCLC is an evolving system with plans to include acquisitions, perhaps circulation, and direct communication between libraries via on-line terminals. At the present time the system is centered around shared cataloging where members input original cataloging, accept cataloging done by others, and order computer-printed catalog cards. What actually takes place is best illustrated by a simplified example.

Each member has at least one CRT (cathode ray tube) interactive terminal in the library connected to the computer in Columbus; most have more than one. Each also has an identifying symbol used in all transactions. A library receives a book ready to be cataloged. A staff member first queries the data base stored in the computer in Columbus by keying in at the CRT terminal one of several search keys. If the record appears on the screen and is accepted, the operator depresses the "Produce" key. This sends the order for catalog cards and adds the identifying library symbol to the holdings field appearing at the bottom of the record.

If the record is not in the system, a manual search is made for LC catalog copy. If it is found in the National Union Catalog, a printed catalog card, or some other source, it becomes the source document for input. The operator calls up a "work form" and keys in all information including the necessary content designators. This record is then transmitted to the computer and becomes a record in the data base for others to use. Catalog cards are ordered and the library symbol appears in the holdings field.

If no LC catalog copy is found, the library may input original cataloging according to the steps given in the previous paragraph. A MARC record appearing at a later date will replace a library's original cataloging and become the official record.

The machine-stored data base of OCLC thus includes records taken from MARC tapes and also other LC records and original cataloging input by members. Since each record includes symbols identifying the libraries that hold the book, a large union catalog is being created at the same time.

Orders for cards are transmitted via the terminal. Actual production of cards is done by batch process according to "profiles" prepared for each library. Profiles give the specifications for printing the cards and the number of sets of cards to be prepared. Large academic library systems with many separate libraries may have more than fifty different profile requirements. This capability gives the cards a "custom-tailored" feature not common in computer-produced cards. The character set includes a full set of diacritical marks for roman alphabet languages, and the print is easy to read. After printing, the cards are sorted ready for filing and are delivered within a few days.

Recently serials were included in the data base, and in 1975 OCLC became the interim host for the CONSER data base. As the data base increases in size, it becomes more and more useful as a union catalog and as a tool for ordering, interlibrary loans, and general reference. When libraries can communicate directly with each other via the terminal, OCLC will become even more valuable for reference and interlibrary loan.

OCLC began its shared cataloging operation in 1971, so its data base now represents only partial holdings of each library. For the time being, most members expect to maintain their card catalogs as they have done in the past. There are some libraries, however, that have already closed their card catalogs or expect to do so in the next few years, including the Library of Congress.

By 1979 or 1980 the Library of Congress expects to have all current cataloging in machine-readable form and available for distribution. This is no small undertaking; but if plans for international cooperation materialize even partially, chances for success are greatly enhanced. Ultimately, the Main Card Catalog of the Library will probably be closed and the contents made available in book form. Whether these retrospective catalog records will ever be machine coded remains a question. Complete cataloging data of current materials will be computer stored and available to the Library staff via on-line terminals. Book catalogs containing abbreviated records will be prepared for less sophisticated uses by the public. If the need arises, card catalog supplements may also be prepared.

The New York Public Research Libraries closed the public card catalogs in 1972 and are producing photocomposed book catalogs each month for current materials. They report a substantial reduction in the cost of catalog management.

Other large libraries report similar plans, because the time has come when machine-readable bibliographic information is less expensive to produce and maintain than an old, large, unwieldy card catalog.

The machine-readable data bases of abstracts and indexes, mentioned earlier in this chapter, are produced by different kinds of organizations. The National Library of Medicine (national library), Chemical Abstracts (professional society), the New York Times (newspaper), and the Institute of Scientific Information (an "information business") are examples of the types of organizations and institutions involved in the handling and processing of information. More and more these data bases are becoming available to libraries through various means, including on-line access for searching. It is thought that most libraries will not buy or lease the machine-readable records for "in-house" processing but will use the on-line search capabilities available. On-line direct access searching services are available from some producers, but the trend seems to be toward commercial enterprises that acquire the machine-readable data bases from many producers and combine them into a large system. Specialized services of this type are increasing; and access to these data banks as another reference service is becoming possible and economically feasible for even the small libraries.

Networks are in varying stages of development throughout the country, encouraged by the National Commission on Libraries and Information Science, which was created in 1970 as a mechanism for coordination at the national level.

An increasing number of libraries are using COM (computer output microfilm) for the storage and production of catalogs, union lists, shelf lists, holdings, and internal records.

New developments in laser recording for the inexpensive storage of data in massive quantities and the high-capacity transmission of data over distances may enable a greater number of libraries to have their complete catalogs in machine-readable form and may enable them to transmit complete documents rapidly and at reasonable cost. Much of the developing technology bodes well for libraries.

RESPONSIBILITIES OF LIBRARIANS

Professional responsibilities of librarians expressed in broad terms change very little over the years; they are committed to establishing and maintaining policies and objectives that will provide satisfactory levels of service to meet the needs of those who use libraries. But time does not stand still; just as needs change, so the means to attain desired results never remain exactly the same.

In some periods of history progress has been slow and gradual; at times, almost dormant; at other times, more rapid and dramatic. There are always economic, political, sociological, humanistic, and technological factors that determine what is attainable at any given time. At this time we seem to be in a period when changes tend to the rapid and dramatic. Of concern here is the extent to which technology is affecting the profession of librarianship and some specific professional responsibilities.

Advanced computer technology, telecommunications and micro-recording, and the non-print audiovisual materials give libraries a much wider choice of ways to serve their users, to communicate with each other, and to perform their daily work. Several challenges facing present and future librarians cluster around these technologies—how best to use the technologies and how best to establish useful functioning networks.

When more choices are possible, more decisions are required, and this fact in itself puts an additional burden on those responsible for deciding what seems best for any given task or service at any given time. Furthermore, new ventures inevitably create problems that never existed before.

It is vitally important that librarians meet the challenges, accept the responsibilities, and make the decisions that affect the future of the profession and the future direction of libraries. What has often been overlooked in a discussion of computers and associated technologies is the importance of individuals—the human resources that continue to be the foundation of any successful system regardless of the number and sophistication of machines.

Computers, in spite of their power and speed, cannot think, create, or reason. The programs and circuitry that enable a computer to display its power are products of the minds of men. "Garbage in; garbage out" is a short way of saying that computers process fast and accurately whatever is put in, right or wrong.

Librarians should be responsible for output, the products and results that computers can give—their design, their form, and their contents. It is for them to decide the details of what they want. They should also be responsible for supervising the design and preparation of input—the information processed to create desired output.

Computers are changing the personnel structure and job requirements in libraries, just as they have done elsewhere. Both professional and non-professional positions are undergoing revisions. Admittedly, the introduction of computers is a traumatic experience for some, and it must be handled with understanding and patience. Everyone must be made aware of what is happening and of his part in the total program. In-house training and opportunities to attend outside training programs are means used to keep employees informed.

Library patrons may also require additional attention. Interactive terminals such as CRT's are becoming more common in all types of libraries. In some they are available in public service areas for public use. If the general public is to use these devices to any extent, the system must be simple to operate and the training aids short and easy to understand. Just as librarians have been giving assistance in the use of the card catalog, they will be expected to assist in the operation of electronic devices.

Some professionals have already become "data processing" or "automation" librarians, positions created to design, develop, and supervise an automated system; they have been successful in bridging the gap between library and computer. These are important new positions that represent the library point of view.

In general, however, most librarians will not become computer experts, though many are already involved in automated systems. Their need to have free and informed communication with computer people is essential to the success of any such system. Most failures and near failures in computer systems everywhere can be attributed directly to human rather than technological inadequacies.

It is each librarian's responsibility to understand the technology, with all of its implications, to the degree necessary for satisfactory performance of his position. This means keeping up on advances in technology and their potential for use in libraries. It means embarking on a program of continuing education that will extend through one's entire professional career.

Continuing education can take several forms: self study, membership in professional associations and attendance at their meetings, formal credit classes in universities, short courses such as non-credit classes, and so on. Continuing education has been a matter of interest to the library community for many years, but much has been unguided and uncoordinated. Some sections of this country have had a wealth of programs, and others have had none.

In an effort to provide guidance, organization, and coordination, a report to the National Commission on Libraries and Information Science contains recommendations and a proposed model for the creation of a nationwide network for continuing education in library and information science.[5] A companion publication relates the experiences of other professions in conducting continuing education programs.[6] Automation is given high priority as a field of study.

Library schools have a responsibility to update their curricula to meet the professional needs of present and future librarians. They too must participate in continuing education as well as maintain strong curricula of formal credit courses.

The introduction of technology into libraries, if interpreted correctly, never promised to reduce the responsibilities of librarians; at most it implied that computers, for example, can offer assistance with many tedious, time-consuming tasks.

The professional associations of this country and other countries have taken active leadership roles in recognizing the importance of both library automation and information retrieval. The American Library Association (ALA), through its Information Science and Automation Division (ISAD), and the American Society for Information Science (ASIS), through a number of its special interest groups such as Library Automation and Networks (SIG/LAN), have been especially active. The Special Libraries Association (SLA), the Association of Research Libraries (ARL), and the Medical Library Association (MLA) have also participated, though to a lesser extent.

Professional associations in other countries, such as ASLIB in Great Britain, the Canadian Library Association, and, at the international level, Unesco, IFLA, and FID (International Federation for Documentation) are devoting much time and effort to promoting the use of advanced technologies in libraries and information centers. There is abundant literature to assist both student and practitioner in becoming knowledgeable and keeping informed.

What is presented here does little more than expose the tip of the iceberg. Library automation and information retrieval offer exciting and challenging opportunities for imagination, research, and innovation. Much more investigation and exploration need to be done, and the library profession should bear that responsibility.

NOTES

[1] Ralph R. Shaw, "From Fright to Frankenstein," *D.C. Libraries* 24 (January 1953): 6-10. Cf. Jesse H. Shera, "Automation without Fear," in *Documentation and the Organization of Knowledge* (London: Crosby Lockwood, 1966), pp. 85-96.

[2] Gilbert W. King, *et al., Automation and the Library of Congress* (Washington, D.C., Library of Congress, 1963).

[3] *Library of Congress Information Bulletin* 33 (November 29, 1974): A246.

[4] The quotation, with ellipsis, was taken from *Library of Congress Information Bulletin* 34 (June 20, 1975): A105.

[5] Elizabeth W. Stone, Ruth J. Patrick, and Barbara Conroy, *Continuing Library and Information Science Education* (Washington, D.C., American Society for Information Science, 1974).

[6] Elizabeth W. Stone, *Continuing Library Education as Viewed in Relation to Continuing Professional Education Movements* (Washington, D.C., American Society for Information Science, 1974).

SELECTED READINGS

In addition to the works listed here, the reader should consult many of the periodicals and annual reviews listed in Chapter 6, especially the *Annual Review of Information Science and Technology.*

Austin, Derek, and Peter Butcher. *Precis—A Rotated Subject Index System.* London: British National Bibliography, 1974.

Chapman, Edward A., and Paul L. St. Pierre. *Library Systems Analysis Guidelines*. New York: Wiley-Interscience, 1970.

Dougherty, Richard M., and Fred J. Heinritz. *Scientific Management of Library Operations.* Metuchen, N.J.: Scarecrow Press, 1966.

Hayes, Robert M., and Joseph Becker. *Handbook of Data Processing for Libraries.* 2nd ed. New York: Wiley-Interscience, 1974.

Heileger, Edward, and Paul B. Henderson, Jr. *Library Automation: Experience, Methodology, and Technology of the Library as an Information System.* New York: McGraw-Hill, 1971.

Illinois. University. Graduate School of Library Science. *Proceedings of the Clinic on Library Applications of Data Processing.* Urbana, Ill.: Graduate School of Library Science, University of Illinois, for the years 1964-1970 and 1972-1973.

Lancaster, F. W., and Emily Gallup. *Information Retrieval On-Line.* New York: Wiley-Interscience, 1973.

Lickleider, J. C. *Libraries of the Future.* Cambridge, Mass.: MIT Press, 1965.

Marcuson, Barbara, *et al. Guidelines for Library Automation: A Handbook for Federal and Other Libraries.* Santa Monica, Calif.: Systems Development Corporation, 1972.

Meadow, Charles T. *The Analysis of Information Systems.* 2nd ed. Los Angeles: Melville Publishing Co., 1973.

Morse, Philip M. *Library Effectiveness: A Systems Approach.* Cambridge, Mass.: MIT Press, 1968.

Overhage, Carl F., and Joyce Harmon, eds. *Intrex.* Cambridge, Mass.: MIT Press, 1966.
    Report of the famous conference on Information Transfer Experiments held at Woods Hole, Massachusetts, in 1965. Supplementary bulletins on the progress of the experiments at MIT have been issued from time to time.

Overmyer, LaVahn. *Library Automation: A Critical Review.* ERIC Report. ED 034. 107. 1969.

Palmer, Richard P. *Case Studies in Library Computer Systems.* New York: R. R. Bowker, 1973.

Swihart, Stanley J., and B. Hefley. *Computer Systems in the Library.* Los Angeles: Melville Publishing Co., 1973.

5

LIBRARIANSHIP IN A NEW KEY

Librarianship is primarily a service enterprise, and it has been so ever since its inception. Its aim, as has been said in the earlier chapters, is to make the accumulated record of man's intellectual activity as readily available as possible to the user, or the potential user. To achieve this end it developed over the years, decades, and even centuries a substantial body of procedures and techniques as a result of certain assumptions about man's use of recorded knowledge. This *ad hoc* technology was refined by trial and error and tested over years of experience. The approach was essentially pragmatic—if a procedure worked, or seemed to work, it was adopted. Actually, the system worked rather well as long as the problems of organizing recorded knowledge remained relatively simple.

Knowledge may be thought of as being organized in a structure of subjects recorded in a literature, the constituent elements of which are called documents. Both the source and the destination involved in the communication process have as one of their elements a file, or files, where representations of that knowledge are stored in an organized form. Examples of such files are human memory, library collections, computer tapes, and data banks. Communication takes place when information is transferred from the file of the transmitter to the file of the receptor, where it is rejected, stored for potential future use, or activated in the behavior of the receiving agent. The effectiveness of communication depends upon the extent to which the information communicated is relevant to the needs of the receiver, and the extent to which *noise*, unwanted information, is eliminated. *Noise* may be defined as any extraneous element that injects itself into the message—e.g., snow on a television screen, static in a radio signal, or ambiguity or irrelevant information in a message. Therefore, relevance is important to the librarian as an indication of the utility of what is being communicated.

ORGANIZING MATERIALS FOR THE SCHOLAR

Even in the world of the Ancient East, documents required organization, the only alternative being what Verner Clapp called "simian search," the random and haphazard ploughing through layer upon layer of the accumulated transcript. To solve the problem of adequate document organization, librarians evolved various systems of file organization. These were simple and, by present-day standards, crude, when documents were few in number and could be adequately stored in large jars or in pigeon-holes around a library room. But organization there was, and we may assume that the categories reflected the interests of the scholar-philosopher-scientist.

As the accumulated record grew in response to society's growth in knowledge, access to the intellectual content of documents became increasingly important. In the centuries before the development of modern scientific apparatus—the telescope, the microscope, and other devices for the exploration of physical and biological phenomena—the library was the "laboratory" of the scientist, who was then known as "natural philosopher." Scholarship in those early days was pursued by reading what one's predecessors had written, ruminating upon the contents, and eventually writing out for those who would follow one's own thoughts and speculations. Robert K. Merton, himself a distinguished social scientist, parodied the professors as he traced the origins of Newton's famous epigram, "If I have seen farther it is by standing on the shoulders of giants."[1]

Because of the scholar's dependence upon what had already been written as the source of his own intellectual activity, the organization of the record—i.e., bibliography—increased in importance as the record accumulated. Concurrently with the growth of recorded knowledge, file organization and bibliographic organization became increasingly complex for both librarian and scholar.

The ancients would not have known what systems theory is, but in their activities we can see its beginnings so far as its application to the organization of library materials is concerned. Systematic bibliography has long received the attention not only of librarians but also of the scholarly world generally. For example, in the second century A.D., Galen compiled a classified catalog of his works, and in 731 A.D., the Venerable Bede included a bibliography in his *Ecclesiastical History of the English People.* From the thirteenth to the fifteenth centuries there were, as Ernest A. Savage has found, a number of cooperative bibliographic enterprises undertaken by the monastic libraries.[2] In the sixteenth century Konrad Gesner, the Swiss physician and scholar who has popularly been called "the father of bibliography," compiled, in twenty volumes, a universal bibliography of world literature, the *Bibliotheca Universalis.* Unfortunately, his untimely death during the plague of 1565 prevented its completion.[3]

It was, however, the pioneering work of Paul Otlet and Henri La Fontaine, at the close of the nineteenth century, that led to the formation of the Brussels Institute of Bibliography, now FID, and its plans for a universal catalog, on cards, of all world literature. Using the Dewey Decimal Classification as a base, the Institute devised the Universal Decimal Classification, which is still popular in many parts of Europe.[4] Thus may be seen in the slow development of organized subject bibliography the first steps toward the dissemination of the fruits of scholarship and a solution to the problem of improving scholarly communication. Today such bibliographic monuments as the catalog of the library of the British Museum or that of the

Bibliothèque Nationale of France, or the *Gesamtkatalog der preussischen Bibliotheken* as well as our own *National Union Catalog* or the catalog of the Library of Congress, are a tribute to the success of the bibliographer in helping to ease the burden for scholars.

Bibliography itself has become a system, a network, composed of well-defined basic types and their subordinate variations: national and trade bibliographies; union catalogs of the holdings of more than one library, or the holdings of more than one library in specified fields; catalogs of individual libraries or special collections held by an individual library; and specialized bibliographies by subject, author, or any other restriction imposed by the compiler. One may regard the bibliographic system as a pyramid; national enumerative bibliography is the base, and the system becomes increasingly selective as the apex is approached. At the apex is the bibliographic essay, the most highly selective and most demanding in its scholarship of all types of bibliographic undertaking.[5] Thus it may be seen that bibliography is important to the present discussion because it was one of the earliest attempts to solve some of the problems of scholarly communication.

There were also other efforts by scholars to bring under control the accumulated knowledge of their age through communication. The rise of the scientific societies and their journals in the second half of the seventeenth century represented a substantial advance over personal correspondence and travel, which had previously been the main sources, other than books and bibliography, for the communication of ideas.[6] None of these techniques has made any other obsolete. Scholars still meet, exchange correspondence, seek grants for travel, and compile bibliographies.

Documentation emerged from librarianship at the turn of the twentieth century to meet the problem of retrieving from a rapidly rising tide of print the precise information, or data, needed by contemporary scholarship, particularly in the sciences. During its first decades documentation depended mainly on the elaboration of conventional library techniques in classification, indexing, and abstracting. By the 1930s, however, the librarians were beginning to question seriously the effectiveness of some of these conventional techniques that the documentalists had been elaborating. To accomplish their inquiries the librarians borrowed the methods and procedures of other disciplines, mainly from the social sciences, but particularly from statistics as applied to social phenomena. In this critical scrutiny of librarianship, the Graduate Library School of the University of Chicago played a leading role.

After the end of World War II, mechanization was introduced to facilitate the subject analysis of graphic records. Though many librarians were involved in the documentation movement, it developed largely apart from traditional librarianship and ran parallel to it. In short, documentation depended heavily upon "invention." Such pioneers as Ralph Shaw, Mortimer Taube, Calvin Mooers, and their contemporaries were "inventors," and serious effort was made by them and others to test the results of their work. Despite the early schism between librarians and documentalists, libraries slowly began to absorb, as Miss Overmyer has shown in the preceding chapter, the new techniques of the documentalists. S. C. Bradford, for example, who studied the dispersion of scientific contributions to a given field in the periodical literature, was a documentalist and the leading British enthusiast for the Universal Decimal Classification and other activities of FID. In the 1940s, Herman Fussler, a librarian, was one of the first, if not the first, to employ citation analysis in studying scientists' uses of the periodical literature and monographic literature of their respective fields. In his case he studied the habits of physicists and chemists. The special librarians in the United States and the information officers in Great Britain were experimenting with new types of classification and file organization.

By the early 1960s, a series of conditions surfaced which stimulated a paper flood that threatened to drown the scholar. This proliferation of print, this information overload, was serious in all fields of human activity, but particularly so in science, which had exploded into "big science."[7]

Of all the new experimentation, perhaps one of the most important experiments for the library is the attention being given to "systems." The growth of library networks, as well as new methods of file organization, is a comparatively recent phenomenon and one that may be expected to have important implications for future library development. Contractual arrangements between and among libraries are certainly far from new to the library world, but from management science, operations research, general systems theory, and other areas of exploration we should obtain a better understanding than we have yet had of the ways in which such cooperative efforts can be operated profitably for all contracting participants.

AN INCIPIENT INFORMATION SCIENCE

In the 1950s and early '60s, when the documentalists were vigorously pursuing their new methods for the design of information retrieval systems, work was going on elsewhere that was eventually absorbed into the explorations of the documentalists and librarians. No one can point to any single individual or book as the origin of what is today known as information science; this new area of activity was largely the result of strange new currents that were moving in the intellectual atmosphere of the day. Two influences, however, were particularly strong in the emergence of information science out of documentation. The first was the work of Shannon and Weaver on the information, or signal-carrying, capacity of a telephone wire, which they called "information theory."[8] The second was the work of Norbert Wiener in man-machine relationships, which he called "cybernetics."[9] Both of these studies fired the imaginations of the documentalists to explore a variety of work in other fields for possible utility in improving their work in information retrieval. All this activity was substantially encouraged by the ready availability of support from such governmental agencies as the National Science Foundation, the U.S. Air Force, the U.S. Office of Education, and the National Institutes of Health through the National Library of Medicine. Interest tended to focus on the improvement of scientific communication because it was the era of Sputnik and the race with the U.S.S.R. into outer space.

William Goffman, a mathematician, sees the origins of information science in the attempts to substitute the computer for human effort in controlling the proliferation of scientific writings that resulted from World War II and its aftermath. "This activity which came to be called at various times, without differentiation, documentation, information retrieval, information sciences, and finally information science, passed through a parade of clever schemes each of which was proclaimed by its inventor as the answer to the problem."[10] The failure of these attempts to solve the information problem, Goffman says, was blamed by some "on the computing machines themselves; they weren't big enough or fast enough. Others came up with get rich schemes: it's all a coding problem; it's only a problem in linguistics or mathematics or logic or indexing, etc." He sees information science "vying for academic respectability by capturing a name." It is Goffman's belief that if information science is to achieve the position of a legitimate discipline it must develop its principles independent of any physical system "involving the notion of information, while at the same time being applicable to all of them. That is we must begin seriously to question the foundations of the entire area of activity now called information science." Goffman thus sees as the central concern of information science the communication process, wherever it manifests itself in the biological, social, and physical worlds.

Phyllis A. Richmond who, unlike Goffman, is a librarian, depicts information science on an equally broad canvas. To her, this area of inquiry is defined as "that body of knowledge which concerns the collection, treatment, storage manipulation, and dissemination of information of all kinds in all subjects."[11] Her definition closely allies information science to library science. Both Goffman and Richmond were implicitly protesting the viewpoint expressed by those information scientists who would limit information science activities exclusively to communication in the sciences.

Harold Borko has seen in information science a true discipline:

> . . . that investigates the properties and behavior of information, the forces governing the flow of information, and the means for processing information for optimal accessibility and usability. It is concerned with that body of knowledge relating to the origination, collection, organization, storage, retrieval, interpretation, transmission, transformation, and utilization of information. This includes the investigation of information representations in both natural and artificial systems, the use of codes for efficient message transmission, and the study of information processing devices and techniques, such as computers and their programming systems.[12]

He holds that the science is interdisciplinary in that it derives from and relates to such fields as mathematics, logic, linguistics, psychology, computer technology, operations research, the graphic arts, library science, management, "and similar fields."

Information science, Rees and Saracevic told the 1967 conference of the Special Libraries Association, "cannot be equated with documentation, information retrieval, librarianship, or with anything else. Information science is not souped-up information retrieval or librarianship any more than physics is super-charged engineering."[13] In the view of these two writers, information science is an area of study and research which draws its substance, methods, and techniques from a variety of disciplines to achieve an understanding of "the properties, behavior, and flow of information. It includes systems analysis, environmental aspects of information and communication, information media, and language analysis, organization of information, man-systems relationships, and the like." Thus they arrive at a definition of information science as the "investigation of communication phenomena and the properties of communication systems."

It is obvious that this diversity of definitions lacks consensus and an understanding of the nature and behavior of information. To quote D. J. Foskett:

> Thus the organizational pattern for the future appears to be taking shape at the subject, national, and international levels. It remains to be seen whether the various vested interests can be made to develop in compatibility with each other, so that we may avoid wasteful duplication and the building up of enormous edifices of blocks of information that either no one wants or no one will use because of their faulty construction. The responsibility for this lies on the shoulders of librarians, information officers, information scientists—all, that is, who would lay claim to be specialists in the new discipline of "informatics."[14]

The Russians—stimulated by Lenin's insistence that libraries are an integral part of the educational system as it is related especially to the "enlightenment" of the masses and hence are necessary to the building of the Soviet state—have probably done more than anyone to direct attention to the sociological relationships of the information transfer process. In the U.S.S.R. the work devoted to the sociological relationships of information science is impressive. In a statement prepared by the Council for Mutual Economic Assistance of the U.S.S.R., for submission to the fifth session of the Central Committee to Study the Feasibility of a World Scientific Information System, convened by Unesco-ICSU, in September 1970, the authors wrote:

> Information Science is a discipline belonging to Social Science, which studies the structure and general characteristics of scientific information, and also general laws governing all scientific communication processes.[15]

The Russians were correct in relating information science to the study of society, but they erred in limiting it to scientific inquiry, unless by "science" they meant all forms of creative cerebral activity. "I emphasize the essentially social nature of what I will now call, for temporary convenience only, 'Information Sciences, Technologies, and Activities' ... I do this to curb a dangerous tendency to bring in every and any science or technique or phenomenon under the 'information' heading," Robert Fairthorne told the 34th FID Conference in Moscow in 1968. But he saw the only unity in this emerging discipline as coming "from overlapping techniques and technologies. It has not come from the application of common principles."[1][6]

In the 1970s information science is still a somewhat ill-defined area of inquiry that is in search of its identity. Fairthorne is quite right in condemning information science for being a collection of overlapping techniques and technologies without having been derived from a common body of principles.

"We have all the answers," Archibald MacLeish once told the staff of the Library of Congress, "it is the questions we do not know." Perhaps in its gropings information science will identify some of the problems and their solutions, which can improve the quality of library service. Meanwhile, this brief attempt to explain what information science is may be justified by the eagerness with which library schools have been adding courses in the area to their curricula.

NOTES

[1] Robert K. Merton, *On the Shoulders of Giants* (New York: Free Press, 1965).

[2] Ernest A. Savage, "Cooperative Bibliography in the Thirteenth and Fifteenth Centuries," in his *Special Librarianship in General Libraries* (London: Grafton, 1939), pp. 285-310.

[3] Theodore Besterman, *The Beginnings of Systematic Bibliography* (London: Humphrey Milford for Oxford University Press, 1935).

[4] S. C. Bradford, "Fifty Years of Documentation," in his *Documentation*, 2nd ed. (London: Crosby Lockwood, 1953), pp. 132-145.

[5] Henry B. Van Hoesen and Frank K. Walter, *Bibliography: Practical, Enumerative, and Historical* (New York: Scribner's, 1929). Examples of bibliographic essays are the *Annual Review of Information Science and Technology*, and Jesse H. Shera, "The Literature of American Library History," in his *Knowing Books and Men; Knowing Computers, Too* (Littleton, Colo.: Libraries Unlimited, 1973), pp. 124-161.

[6] Martha Ornstein, *The Role of Scientific Societies in the Seventeenth Century* (Chicago: University of Chicago Press, 1938).

[7] Derek J. de Solla Price, *Little Science, Big Science* (New York: Columbia University Press, 1963). Also, his *Science Since Babylon* (New Haven: Yale University Press, 1961), especially Chapter V, "Diseases of Science."

[8] Claude E. Shannon, "The Mathematical Theory of Communication," *Bell System Technical Journal* 27 (1948): 379-423; 623-656.

[9] Norbert Wiener, *Cybernetics* (New York: Wiley, 1948). Also his *The Human Use of Human Beings* (Boston: Houghton Mifflin, 1950).

[10] William Goffman, "Information Science, Discipline or Disappearance?," *ASLIB Proceedings* 22 (1970): 589-595.

[11] Unpublished definition.

[12] Harold Borko, "Information Science—What Is It?," *American Documentation* 10 (January 1968): 3-4.

[13] Alan Rees and Tefko Saracevic, "Education for Information Science and Its Relation to Librarianship," unpublished manuscript, p. 9. See also the same authors' "The Impact of Information Science on Libraries," *Library Journal* 93 (Nov. 1, 1968): 4097-4101.

[14] D. J. Foskett, "Progress in Documentation," *Journal of Documentation* 26 (Dec. 1970): 365.

[15] Moscow, September 1970, p. 7. See also: Jesse H. Shera, "The Sociological Foundations of Information Science," *Journal of the American Society for Information Science* 22 (March-April 1971): 76-78; and Glynn Harmon, "On the Evolution of Information Science," ibid. (July-August 1971): 235-241.

[16] Robert A. Fairthorne, "The Scope and Aims of the Information Sciences and Technologies" (manuscript of papers presented at the FID Conference, September 1968, *passim*).

SELECTED READINGS

The literature of information science is voluminous, repetitive, and often obscured by an idiosyncratic vocabulary and abstruse mathematical equations. A substantial proportion of the older material has been included in the hope that it will throw some light on the origins of the field. For current material, the best sources are the bibliographic essays in *Annual Review of Information Science and Technology*, issued under the auspices of the American Society for Information Science.

Bradford, S. C. "Fifty Years of Documentation." In *Documentation.* London: Crosby Lockwood, 1953. pp. 132-145.

Fairthorne, Robert A. *Toward Information Retrieval.* London: Butterworth, 1961.

Harmon, Glynn. "On the Evolution of Information Science," *Journal of the American Society for Information Science* 22 (July-August 1971): 235-241.

"Information Storage and Retrieval." In *International Encyclopedia of the Social Sciences.* New York: Macmillan and Free Press, 1963. Vol. 7.

Kochen, Manfred. *Principles of Information Retrieval.* Los Angeles: Melville, 1974.

Kochen, Manfred, ed. *The Growth of Knowledge.* New York: Wiley, 1967.

Machlup, Fritz. *The Production and Distribution of Knowledge in the United States.* Princeton, N.J.: Princeton University Press, 1962.

Meadow, Charles T. *Man-Machine Communication.* New York: Wiley, 1970.

Murra, Katherine O. "History of Some Attempts to Organize Bibliography Internationally." In Jesse H. Shera and Margaret E. Egan, eds., *Bibliographic Organization.* Chicago: University of Chicago Press, 1951. pp. 24-53.

Perry, James W., and Allen Kent. *Tools for Machine Literature Searching.* New York: Interscience, 1958.

Salton, Gerard. *Automatic Information Organization and Retrieval.* New York: McGraw-Hill, 1968.

Saracevic, Tefko, comp. *Introduction to Information Science.* New York: R. R. Bowker, 1970.

Shannon, Claude E., and Warren Weaver. *Mathematical Theory of Communication.* Urbana: University of Illinois Press, 1948.

Shera, Jesse H. "Documentation into Information Science," *American Libraries* 3 (July-August 1972): 785-790.

——————. "The Sociological Relationships of Information Science," *Journal of the American Society for Information Science* 22 (March-April 1971): 76-80.

Shera, Jesse H., Allen Kent, and James W. Perry. *Information Services in Documentation.* New York: Interscience, 1957. 2v.

Siegfried, A. *Germs and Ideas.* London: Oliver and Boyd, 1965.

Ziman, J. M. *Public Knowledge: An Essay on the Social Dimension of Science.* London: Cambridge University Press, 1968.

6

STRUCTURE, ORGANIZATION, AND RECORD

At the outset it would be well to begin this chapter by dismissing as fruitless the long-standing argument, often hotly debated, over whether librarianship is a profession. The noun, like the verb *to profess*, derives from the Latin *professio*, to believe, to be dedicated to, the public taking of vows in a religious order. Hence, a professor is one who teaches that which he believes. The classic use of the term, the learned professions, derives from the three faculties of the medieval university of theology, medicine, and law. *Webster's Second Edition* defines the term in part as "the occupation, if not purely commercial, mechanical, agricultural, or the like, to which one devotes himself; or calling in which one professes to have acquired some special knowledge used by way either of instructing, guiding, or advising others or of serving them in some art."

Serious thinking about professionalism and the characteristics of a profession seem to date from Abraham Flexner's classic study of social work as a profession, published in 1915. Briefly stated, and somewhat over-simplified, Flexner's criteria are: the involvement of intellectual operations with large areas of individual responsibility; the derivation of its materials from science and other forms of scholarship; direction toward practical and well-defined ends; the possession of educationally communicable techniques; self-organization, control, and discipline; and altruistic motivation.[1] But because of the prestige implicit in the term, the desire to make virtually every human occupation or activity a profession has so blurred these characteristics that the term has now lost much of its original meaning except, perhaps, as it has survived in the phrase "learned professions." "We all do believe that librarianship is a profession,"[2] wrote Pierce Butler in 1951, and librarians have seen no reason to change their opinion since his time. Frank Atkinson in his introduction to librarianship dismisses the whole argument by saying that the important consideration is not whether librarianship is a profession, but the kind of profession it is.[3] But it is not labels or respectability of the credentials that gives librarianship recognition as a profession. The proper focus of concern is on the place of the library in contemporary culture and how effectively it realizes its acknowledged aims.[4]

Just as futile as the argument over the credentials of librarianship as a profession is the long-standing controversy of whether librarianship is a science or an art. At the turn of the present century the English called the field "library economy," probably for much the same reason that Henry Fielding named his novel, *Tom Jones*, "a history," for want of any other term to apply to it. C. C. Williamson insisted that librarianship is not a science, but "a service," and so named the school at Columbia University, a precedent followed by Rutgers. Others have escaped the issue by using simply "librarianship," and the University of Buffalo uses "library studies." Finally, Oliver Garceau, in his volume on *The Public Library and the Political Process*, spoke, to the consternation of many librarians, of "the library faith." The urge of the librarian to be "scientific," like the drive toward professionalism, reflects the value system of our culture more than it reflects the characteristics of the librarian's practice.

Every discipline is, of course, both a science and an art, a theory and a practice, and the two must operate together—neither is superior or inferior to the other. A librarian who serves the informational needs of scientists must himself have a knowledge of science, but this does not imply that his practice of librarianship is "more scientific" than that of his colleague who serves the staff of an art museum. Both of them are librarians; in the pages that follow we will be considering the several types of librarianship, but one must not lose sight of the unity that is librarianship. Both librarians, though the materials upon which they work will differ widely, are engaged in bringing together the graphic record and the user. Kenneth Boulding once defined economics, for the present writer, as "what economists do"; perhaps this "definition," restated in library terms, is the best possible rejoinder to the combatants in this persistent controversy over professionalism and science.

STRUCTURE OF THE FIELD

Traditionally the field of librarianship has been divided into four areas, based largely on the clientele served: public libraries, school libraries (both elementary and secondary), academic libraries (including junior college, college, and university), and special libraries, a relatively new category encompassing a disparate variety that will be discussed later. Added to this broad categorization are a variety of libraries serving government at all levels, and privately endowed libraries that are open to the public for reference use.

Of all the types of libraries, the goals and objectives of the public library are probably the most difficult to define and implement. The public library is part of the public sector, and the public sector is always unbounded. The public library must stand alone and be self-sufficient; there is no parent institution to set its sights. It serves a wide and diverse clientele, from the pre-school child to the aging adult, from the most educationally disadvantaged to the most scholarly, from those for whom reading is little more than a means for allaying tedium to those who have a very specific purpose or problem. Moreover, it depends for continuing support on its ability to convince the electorate that it is important to the community, thus it must constantly think in terms of its public relations and image. Unlike the school and the academic library, it has no faculty expertise to guide its book selection or to advise on its services. It must strive to be all things to all men, knowing full well that it can never achieve such an impossible goal. Thus, it may be said to offer the greatest of library challenges and the widest opportunity for imaginative leadership. In many respects it offers a career for which our professional education is least well prepared to cope. But it stands, as Alvin Johnson said, as "the people's university," or perhaps more accurately, the library of the people's university. More than a century ago Horace Mann, that distinguished pioneer in universal public education, characterized it as "the crowning glory of our public schools."

For present purposes the school and the academic library may be considered together, for they have much in common. Both are integral parts of a larger organization that sets goals and determines lines of development. Both have a reservoir of talent in their respective faculties on which to draw for assistance. Both can approximate a measure of effectiveness in the degree to which they satisfy the needs of the students and the faculty. To a young librarian seeking a career they offer, especially the academic library, an intellectual environment. They do not have to fight with the departments of police, fire, street maintenance, and a host of other municipal agencies for their share of the public till. They do have to press for adequate financial support, but usually this is done in an environment basically hospitable to learning and where there is an awareness of the importance of a library to any educational institution. As our educators tend to put increasing emphasis on the student's individual work, the need for the library grows.

The history of the public library in the United States may be dated from Captain Robert Keayne's benefaction to the town of Boston in the middle of the seventeenth century, if not before. The history of the academic library goes back to the medieval university, but the special library is a comparative newcomer. John Cotton Dana, then librarian of the Newark, New Jersey, Public Library seems to have been the first to conceive of the special library as a unique form, and to recognize the opportunities for the public library to provide specialized service to business and industry. In 1909 he formed, with a small group of kindred spirits, the Special Libraries Association. Such libraries conventionally serve the needs of business and industry both in managerial and in scientific research. But gradually their scope has been broadened to include newspapers, museums, agencies of state and municipal government, independent research institutions, and a host of other enterprises that comprise modern society. Of the four types of libraries mentioned above they are the most sharply focused, since their services are provided mainly for a highly specialized and restricted clientele. They are dependent entirely on management for their support and hence are beholden to no one else. So long as they meet the needs of the staff of the parent company or organization they need have no other serious concerns. However, as a professional courtesy many will serve specific requests from the general public if the need seems worthy. One can argue with considerable conviction that in preparing for a career in a special library, professional preparation in the subject field or fields involved is more important than library training, though exposure to both represents the ideal. Pressures for productivity are probably heaviest in the special libraries since they are usually attached to business and commercial enterprises, but the financial rewards are greatest in these fields, too.

This four-part classification of the library world is fairly firmly fixed and well-defined in the minds of most librarians, but the categories are far from being discrete and there is a widespread blending of types. The public library serves students and faculties of schools and colleges, not infrequently setting up special accommodations for them. A few college libraries also serve as public libraries in their communities particularly when the community itself is not sufficiently large to provide an adequate tax base for library support. Miami University at Oxford, Ohio, received in the early years of the present century a grant from Andrew Carnegie with the understanding that it would be freely available to the citizenry of Oxford. In Oberlin, Ohio, the public library of the town is an integral part of the Oberlin College library. Special libraries draw heavily upon the resources of the public libraries in their communities, and on occasion will make their resources available to those not employed by their organizations.

Beyond these conventional groupings of libraries there is a substantial array of libraries that defy any specific categorization. First, there are those libraries that are independent establishments, founded by the generosity of wealthy donors, presided over by their own self-perpetuating boards of trustees, responsible to no one for their programs. Generally they are large reference libraries which serve anyone whose needs seem worthy. Their materials do not circulate but are for reference use only, though most of them will permit use outside their walls, through interlibrary loan, of all except their most valuable possessions. The more prominent of these are: the John Crerar Library and the Newberry Library in Chicago. The first is primarily a scientific collection, including medicine, the second emphasizes the humanities, including history, and has in addition an outstanding collection of the American Indian, as well as the Wing collection on the history of the book and printing. The J. P. Morgan Library in New York and the Henry E. Huntington Library in San Marino, California, are the outgrowth of the justly famous private collections of their donors, and both emphasize the humanities. The Linda Hall Library in Kansas City, like the Crerar Library in Chicago, is primarily a scientific collection, and the Folger Shakespeare Library in Washington, D.C., includes materials on fourteenth and fifteenth century England as well as those relating to "The Bard" and his contemporaries in Tudor drama. The Folger, founded by Henry Clay Folger who started the collection as a private enterprise, is curious because it occupies land given to it by the U.S. government and is presided over by the trustees of Amherst College. There are also quasi-public historical libraries such as the American Antiquarian Society in Worcester, Massachusetts, and the Western Reserve Historical Society library in Cleveland, Ohio. The William L. Clements Library is on the University of Michigan campus, and the John Carter Brown Library and the Ann Mary Brown Library are in Providence, Rhode Island. All of these tend to stress the humanities, history, and geography. One could go on and on with this listing, but perhaps enough has been said to suggest the breadth of the field. All of these are, of course, "special" libraries, but they are not so categorized as the term is generally understood. Often, too, they are staffed by subject specialists who have never seen the inside of a library school except, perhaps, to give an occasional lecture to courses in bibliography.

Also somewhat apart from the general library field are the law and legislative reference libraries. On university campuses the law library is generally attached to the law school, and its library reports to and is responsible to the dean of the law school rather than the university librarian. Law librarians have their own professional association and their own journal, as do the medical librarians; the latter, when part of the academic community, tend to be directly responsible to the dean and faculty of the medical school and are not infrequently associated with libraries for schools of nursing. Legal firms and hospitals often have their own libraries established to meet the needs of their own clienteles.

The federal government supports a vast network of libraries, at the center of which stands the Library of Congress, the National Library of Agriculture, and the National Library of Medicine, all of which are in the Washington, D.C., area. Many of the Departments have their own libraries, such as Interior, Labor, State, and Commerce, to name but a few. The independent agencies, such as the Federal Trade Commission, the National Aeronautics and Space Agencies, the Energy Research and Development Administration, and the Smithsonian Institution also maintain libraries. Opportunities for librarians to serve in foreign countries are available through the Armed Services and the U.S. Information Agency. Finally, one should mention archives—federal, state, and local—though these tend to recruit their professional staffs from the field of history rather than librarianship. Some library schools, of which the one at Case Western Reserve University is an example, offer courses in archival management. From this brief and necessarily superficial survey it is apparent that there are opportunities for librarians with virtually any type of subject interest or background, including the performing arts and the motion picture industry. No longer does the profession think of librarianship exclusively in terms of the town library on the village green, any more than it thinks of library materials exclusively in terms of books. The diversity of the profession will be made even more explicit in the discussion of professional associations that follows.

PROFESSIONAL ASSOCIATIONS

It has been said that if two Americans found themselves stranded on a desert island their first acts would be to form a National Association of Shipwrecked Persons, write a constitution and by-laws, elect officers, and call a convention. Certainly the voluntary association, for a seemingly limitless variety of purposes, has, since Colonial days, been an important aspect of American life. Librarians have shared in this enthusiasm for professional association. Three major associations, by virtue of the size of their membership, may be said to dominate the field, though there are many others representing specialized library interests that are both influential and important.

The oldest is the American Library Association, formed in 1876 at the Philadelphia Centennial Exhibition. An earlier attempt to form an association of librarians (in 1853) failed for a variety of reasons, most important of which was the absence of any permanent organizational machinery.[5] The American Library Association, with headquarters in Chicago, now numbers between 35,000 and 40,000 members, is governed by the Council, elected by the membership, and by the Executive Board, chosen by the Council from its own membership. The President, who is elected annually, outlines in general terms the program for the year in his inaugural address, and though the ultimate power in decision making rests with the Council, the Executive Board and the Executive Director, together with the Headquarters staff, are very powerful both in planning and in implementation. Only in crisis situations, such as the vote by the Council to move the Headquarters staff from Chicago to Washington, has the membership risen in revolt by petitioning for a vote of the entire membership. The power of the Executive Director and the Headquarters staff derives not from constitutional authority but from the fact that they are full-time, paid, high-level people who devote their full energies to the operation of the association, whereas the Council, the Executive Board, and the president are volunteers whose official duties must be assumed in addition to their regular jobs. Moreover, the growth of the membership imposes an additional handicap to democratic action. Only a distressingly small proportion of the "electorate," for example, regularly participate in the annual election. In short, even librarians, who are presumably dedicated to the principles of freedom and representative government, are finding it difficult to make democracy work effectively.

The ALA is, in reality, a federation of associations and divisions, each of which has an Executive Secretary on the Headquarters staff, and its own president and executive body. All of these are, of course, subordinate to the parent association, the ALA itself. Associations represent types of libraries, such as the Association of College and Research Libraries (ACRL), and the American Association of School Librarians (AASL), whereas divisions represent types of library activities, e.g., the Reference Services Division (RSD). Sections are sub-units of divisions, and Round Tables, which have no executive secretary at Headquarters, are unattached, such as the Library History Round Table (LHRT), the Junior Members Round Table (JMRT), which is open to all members under 35 years of age, and the Social Responsibility Round Table (SRRT).

The organization of the ALA and its Headquarters staff is shown in Figures 6 and 7 (pages 122 and 123) from the Association's *Organization Handbook* for 1975, and is, of course, always subject to reorganization or revision by action of Council and the membership at large. It should also be noted that each of the fifty states has its own library association, and though these associations are autonomous, each has its duly authorized official representative on the ALA Council.

Fig. 6. ALA Membership Organization*

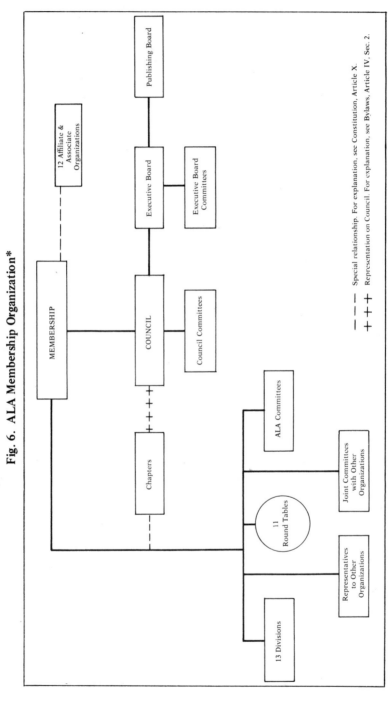

- - - Special relationship. For explanation, see Constitution, Article X.

+ + + Representation on Council. For explanation, see Bylaws, Article IV, Sec. 2.

Publishing Board

12 Affiliate &
Associate
Organizations

Executive Board

Executive Board
Committees

MEMBERSHIP

COUNCIL

Council Committees

Chapters

ALA Committees

11
Round Tables

Joint Committees
with Other
Organizations

Representatives
to Other
Organizations

13 Divisions

*From *ALA Handbook of Organization 1975-1976* (Chicago, American Library Association, 1975), p. 1.

Fig. 7. ALA Staff Organization*

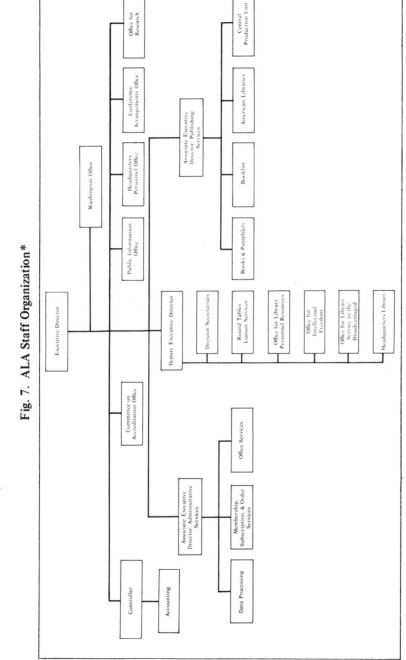

*From *ALA Handbook of Organization 1975/1976* (Chicago, American Library Organization, 1975), p. 66.

Membership in the ALA is open to anyone interested in librarianship, including library trustees, book dealers and publishers, and manufacturers of library equipment and supplies, as well as practicing librarians and those engaged in library education. Students in library school may attend conferences at a reduced conference fee during their period of enrollment. Membership is also open to librarians from other countries. Many Canadians, for example, despite the fact that they have their own Canadian Library Association and their provincial associations, are active in ALA, its boards and committees. Indeed, on two occasions Canadians have served as president of the Association. Toronto and Montreal have always been popular with Americans as convention sites. So far as librarians are concerned, the border scarcely exists, and only an occasional accent, a "zed" for a "zee," or "labour" for "labor" marks the difference. Librarians from Latin America have also been prominent in ALA programs.

Two conferences are held each year. The main conference, held in the summer, is moved from city to city to provide an opportunity for all members to attend at least an occasional conference. The mid-winter meeting, held in January, frequently but not invariably meets in Chicago. Both are program meetings as well as business meetings, and they last approximately one week each. The annual conference usually attracts some ten thousand librarians; the mid-winter session, which is mainly devoted to the transactions of associations, has a much smaller attendance. Both conferences provide exhibits of publishers and suppliers of library equipment, though the summer conference is by far the larger.

The Special Libraries Association dates its founding from the Bretton Woods conference of the ALA in 1908 and the work of John Cotton Dana, Director of the Newark, New Jersey, Public Library, to arouse the interest of librarians in the opportunities for specialized library service to the nation's burgeoning business and industrial community. At that conference Dana observed, "The library world has always been more or less academic, classic . . . The rapid development of special libraries managed by experts . . . is simply an outward manifestation that the man of affairs has come to realize that printed things form the most useful and important tools of his business, no matter what that business may be."[6] At the Mackinac conference of the ALA the following year, Dana made a vigorous attempt to secure the incorporation of his newly organized Special Libraries Association as an integral part of the older association. Subsequently he wrote in the *Library Journal*:

> My suggestions to the Executive Board in this line were as definitely ignored by the Board as have been many other suggestions from me. That there is a very active library organization, affiliated but not a definite part of the American Library Association is a fact which is not due to me but to shortcomings elsewhere . . .[7]

This new association, which by 1975 had some 8,500 members, took as its slogan, "Putting Knowledge to Work," which symbolized its dedication to the dissemination and communication of recorded knowledge to a wide variety of enterprises, heretofore more or less neglected by the general library movement. There are forty-four regional chapters representing special librarians in cities (Cleveland, Pittsburgh, San Francisco); states (Minnesota, Texas); and regions (Heart of America, Pacific Northwest, Hawaiian Pacific, European). There are also two municipal chapters in Canada (Toronto and Montreal). Chapters receive support from the national association, and each member automatically belongs to the chapter nearest to his home or place of business. There are 26 divisions representing broad subject fields (Science-Technology, which is the largest; Museums; Arts and Humanities; Pharmaceutical) and information handling techniques (Documentation). Each member is entitled to membership in one division without payment of additional dues. These divisions elect their own officers and many publish a bulletin or newsletter. The organizational structure is not unlike that of the ALA, though the headquarters staff, in New York, is much smaller. In addition to the general sessions of the annual conference, the divisions often present programs on specialized subjects of particular interest to their membership. Local chapters have their own meetings, which tend to be either monthly or quarterly. The association maintains a variety of services for consultation, employment assistance for both employer and prospective employees, and technical assistance of a variety of forms.[8] The organizational structure of the Association is shown in Figure 8 (on page 126).

It would not be unrealistic to trace the genealogy of the American Society for Information Science (ASIS) back to that historic meeting of Paul Otlet and Henri La Fontaine, in Brussels in 1892; from that meeting emerged the Brussels Institute of Bibliography, which eventually became the Fédération Internationale de Documentation (FID), and plans for organizing bibliography internationally. Coincidentally with the activities of Otlet, La Fontaine, and their associates, the Royal Society of London began to address itself seriously to the problem of organizing systematically the literature of science. These early workers called this new field, for want of a better term, "documentation," a name which a generation later spread to the United States, though its use here had a somewhat different emphasis.[9]

The immediate occasion for the growth of interest in documentation in the United States was experimentation with the use of microfilm and the possibilities it seemed to offer for extending the bibliographic resources of the scholar. This experimentation was brought to a focus through the efforts of Science Service, dating from 1926. Science Service, it should be noted, was established by E. W. Scripps, founder of the Scripps-Howard newspaper syndicate, to provide journalists with current developments in all branches of science. The Scripps organization also received some support from the Chemical Foundation to further its bibliographic work. The U.S. Department of Agriculture's Bibliographical Service was organized in 1935, through the efforts of three progressive and far-seeing documentalists: Clarabel Barnett, librarian of the Department of Agriculture, Rupert Draeger, and Atherton

**Fig. 8. Special Libraries Association:
Its Organization and Communications, 1975***

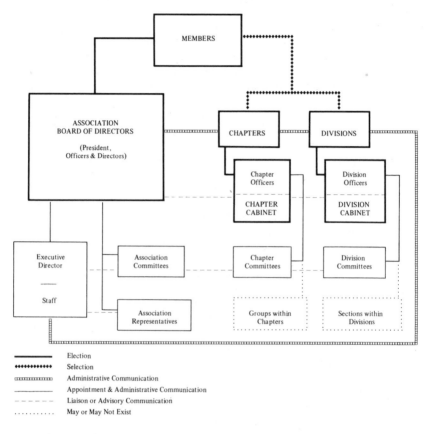

———————	Election
♦♦♦♦♦♦♦♦♦♦♦♦	Selection
▭▭▭▭▭▭▭▭▭▭	Administrative Communication
————————	Appointment & Administrative Communication
– – – – –	Liaison or Advisory Communication
. . . .	May or May Not Exist

*Courtesy of the Special Libraries Association and Rose L. Vormelker.

Seidel, the last two having been pioneers in the development of microfilming cameras. The object of this Service was to make the resources of the Department of Agriculture Library (today the National Library of Agriculture) as widely available as possible throughout the country. Emphasis on the dissemination of bibliographic information was intensified when, in 1940, Ralph R. Shaw was appointed as Miss Barnett's successor. Also, in the mid-1930s, the Carnegie Corporation established at the University of Chicago a microphotography laboratory to engage in research on the improvement and use of microphotographic techniques, and Herman H. Fussler was brought to the Chicago campus as the laboratory's first director.

Watson Davis, of Science Service, was responsible for merging the several interests, including those of the Microphotography Round Table of the ALA, and thus in 1937 the American Documentation Institute came into being. Membership in the new Institute was restricted to delegates from scientific and scholarly societies. Under the articles of incorporation a Board of Trustees was held responsible for the government of the Institute, and officers were elected by the Board from its own membership. The objectives of the new corporation were so broad as to make their full realization impossible, but a heavy emphasis was placed upon the development of microphotographic and other techniques of document reproduction; indeed, for at least the first ten years of its life such activity consumed most of the accomplishments of the organization. Throughout these early years there was a close affiliation between the ADI and the ALA's Committee on Photographic Reproduction of Library Materials; the *Journal of Documentary Reproduction*, which flourished from 1938 to 1943, was, in effect, resumed in 1950 as the ADI's *American Documentation*, both journals being under the editorship of Vernon D. Tate, director of the M.I.T. Library. In 1947, the Institute, which had been relatively inactive during the years of World War II, became the U.S. affiliate of the Fédération Internationale de Documentation, which by that time maintained headquarters at The Hague. The Institute, however, was careful to stipulate that such affiliation neither expressed nor implied official approval of the Universal Decimal System of library and documentary classification.[10]

By 1952 the Institute faced rebellion within its own ranks and the threat that a rival organization would be formed. Membership of the proposed organization would be open to anyone interested, and its program would not be heavily concentrated on the processes of documentary reproduction. As a result the Institute's charter and constitution were redrafted to acceed to these demands; eventually the photographic interests withdrew and formed the National Microfilm Association, the membership of which was largely composed of those concerned with the development, manufacture, and marketing of all types of equipment and materials for documentary photographic reproduction.

The membership of the ADI expanded rapidly, its programs began to encompass a wide variety of interests including classification, indexing, abstracting, and the use of computers for the analysis of bibliographic materials. There was, however, growing dissatisfaction with the name of the organization. It was believed that, in the United States at least, the term *documentation* was losing its earlier significance, and that calling the association an *Institute* did not reflect accurately its organic structure. There were, during the '50s and early '60s, repeated attempts to consolidate the Special Libraries Association and the ADI, to form an American equivalent of the British ASLIB (an acronym for Special Libraries and Information Bureaux) but these failed because both organizations feared the loss of autonomy. In 1968, the ADI changed its name to the American Society for Information Science, and *American Documentation* was changed to the *Journal of the American Society of Information Science*; both became definitely research oriented. ASIS also maintains affiliated local or regional chapters, many of which hold joint meetings with their respective chapters of SLA. The organizational chart of ASIS is shown in Figure 9. An annual conference is held in one of the major cities of the country, and in its program the special interest groups (SIGs) play a major role, as do the divisions of ALA. There are many librarians who belong to all three organizations (ALA, SLA, ASIS), doubtless because they fill quite different needs of the individual librarian.

In addition to these three major associations and their state and local affiliates, there is a substantial array of independent organizations devoted to a variety of specialized organized interests and concerns. Of these one might mention the Medical Library Association, the Law Library Association, the Music Library Association, the Association of American Library Schools, and the Catholic Library Association as examples. Also there are a number of "umbrella" agencies such as the Council of National Library Associations, the International Federation of Library Associations, and the Fédération Internationale de Documentation. Also of importance to the American librarian are the British organizations: ASLIB and the Library Association. At the margins of librarianship there are such organizations as the Bibliographical Society of America and the Society of American Archivists.

LIBRARY LITERATURE AND ITS BIBLIOGRAPHIC ORGANIZATION

Library Literature

Formal library literature may be said to have begun, at least in the modern world, with Gabriel Naudé's *Advis pour dresser une bibliothèque*, first published in 1627 and translated into English by the diarist John Evelyn, in 1661.[11] Naudé, who was the librarian of Cardinal Mazarin, set forth the basic principles for the acquisition, organization, and maintenance of the library collection. In the United States the first major work of this kind was Reuben A. Guild's *Librarian's Manual*, published in 1858.[12] Guild was the librarian of Brown University, and his treatise had been commissioned by the Librarians' Conference of 1853. However, in 1793, Thaddeus Mason Harris,

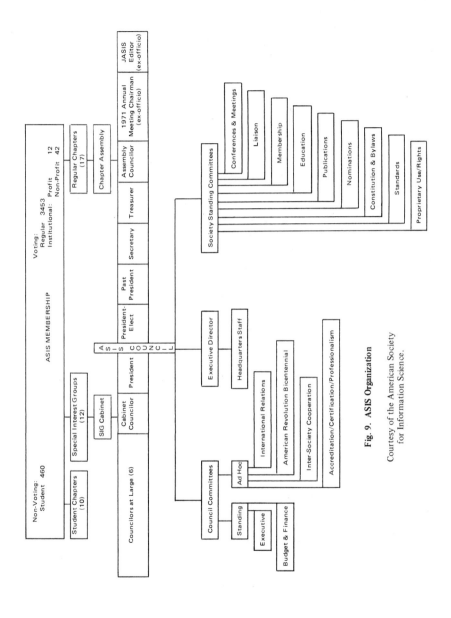

Fig. 9. ASIS Organization

Courtesy of the American Society
for Information Science.

then librarian of Harvard University, published from the press of Isaiah Thomas a small pamphlet listing the books he thought appropriate to form a social library.[13]

At a conference held at the University of Chicago in 1941, Ralph A. Beals classified all library literature into three major categories—Glad Tidings, Testimony, and Research. Despite its facetious tone, this partitioning was very appropriate at the time, and it is still meaningful today. Of Glad Tidings he wrote:

> Glad tidings, which comprise a somewhat large proportion of the periodical literature of librarianship, are of two kinds: speculative essays about what might, could, would, or should be true of public librarianship, and announcements, more or less unvarnished, of something about to be done or very recently undertaken. Glad tidings, like the apostle's faith, are the essence of things hoped for—the substance of things unseen. The point of view is anticipatory and optimistic. To the student of communication, the value of glad tidings as evidence of social influence is nil. . . . to the public librarian, as to the student of communication, glad tidings offer no valid evidence concerning the social value of public libraries.

> A second and still more numerous class of professional publications falls in a category that may be called testimony— testimony not in the legal sense, but in the sense commonly associated with religious sects: retrospective accounts of something done, of benefits conferred. Testimony is often, though not invariably, cast in the first person plural: we have thought; we have tried; we have accomplished this or that. Even when this formula is not employed, the implications are nearly always personal and, hence, likely to be idiosyncratic. The proof offered in support of testimony is experience, usually undifferentiated experience founded on the impressions and appraisals of complex phenomena by a person or persons whose predispositions tend to favor an *ex parte* conclusion. Now experience is the sole source of error as well as of truth; and in a substantial part of the published testimony about public librarianship one wonders whether the process of winnowing has been carried far enough to yield wholly trustworthy results; whether a particular project might not have succeeded even better under different (and usually untried) circumstances; how skilled an analyst and observer the reporter may be; whether the conditioning factors have been isolated and appraised with accuracy; whether group or central tendencies have been slighted for the picturesque, the unusual, or the fortuitous; whether the satisfaction that the librarian obviously finds in what he reports is shared by a

significant number of his readers. I should not wish to be understood as placing no value on testimony. On the contrary; for many stubborn questions the practicing librarian can find no answers elsewhere, nor is he likely to by any of the techniques thus far developed in our incipient "library science." But all testimony based on undifferentiated experience needs careful scrutiny, particularly by students of social communication.[14]

Of Beals' third category, research, there will be more said in the chapter that follows.

Of the limited amount of monographic literature in librarianship published before the early 1930s, a substantial portion could be called "instrumental"—tools for the librarian's use and guides on library operations. Typical of the period were the ALA catalog rules of 1906, Cutter's rules for a dictionary catalog, Mudge's *Guide to Reference Books*, the 1876 report on the state of libraries in the United States issued by the U.S. Bureau of Education, and the four-volume survey of libraries published by the ALA in 1926-27. At the close of the 1920s the ALA inaugurated its *Curriculum Study Series* under the editorship of W. W. Charters, a series of texts for the basic courses in the first-year library school program. Of these volumes, those most remembered today are Margaret Mann's *Introduction to the Cataloging and Classification of Books* and Lucille Fargo's *The Library in the School*, both of which were issued in 1930.

In the 1930s, and particularly after World War II, the librarian's shelf of professional reading expanded at a dramatic rate. University presses, like those of Chicago, Columbia, Illinois, and Michigan, produced an impressive number of books relating to librarianship: research studies, conference proceedings, and doctoral dissertations. With the 1950s commercial publishing became an important factor, and publishers such as Reinhold, Interscience (now Wiley/Interscience), and McGraw-Hill saw librarianship as a potentially fruitful market. Specialized library publishers emerged in addition to the H. W. Wilson Co. and R. R. Bowker. Thus began the Scarecrow Press founded by Ralph Shaw, the Shoe String Press of John Ottermiller, and, a decade later, Libraries Unlimited established by Bohdan S. Wynar.

The structure of the periodical literature of librarianship can best be presented in tabular form.

■ ■ ■

Library Journal. Issued twice monthly except monthly in July and August. 1876– .

The oldest of the professional library journals in the U.S. Founded by R. R. Bowker, and during its early years also served as the official journal of the A.L.A.

American Library Association

American Libraries. Monthly. 1970– .
> The official journal of the Association, including both official news and substantive articles.

ALA Bulletin. Monthly. 1907-1969.
> Replaced by *American Libraries.* Began as a news sheet about the activities of the Association but was expanded in the 1930s, under the editorship of Beatrice Sawyer Rossell, to a full-dress journal publishing papers presented at Association conferences and other substantive articles.

The Booklist and Reference and Subscription Books Bulletin. Twice monthly. 1905– .
> An annotated guide to current publications to assist librarians in developing their collections. Useful primarily to the small and medium-sized public library and to the school library.

College and Research Libraries. Bi-monthly. 1939– .
> The official journal of the ALA's Association of College and Research Libraries. Contains major articles of primary interest to the academic librarian.

Library Resources and Technical Services. Quarterly. 1957– .
> The official journal of the ALA Technical Services Division. Replaced the earlier *Journal of Cataloging and Classification,* 1944-1951. Of primary concern to librarians employed as catalogers, classifiers, and processors. It should be noted that "technical services" relates to the preparation of books and other materials for library use, and should not be thought of as library service to science and technology.

RQ. Quarterly. 1960– .
> Official journal of the Reference and Adult Services Division of the ALA.

School Media Quarterly. Quarterly. 1951– .
> Official journal of the ALA's American Association of School Librarians. Original title was *School Libraries.*

Top of the News. Quarterly. 1946– .
> The official journal of the Children's Services Division and the Young Adult Services Division of ALA.

Choice. Monthly. 1964– .
> Scholarly reviews of selected titles appropriate to college and university library collections. Lists current materials only. Published by the ALA under the auspices of the Association of College and Research Libraries.

Journal of Library Automation. Quarterly. 1968– .
Official journal of the Information Science and Automation Division of ALA. Articles tend to be technical, though not as technical or as heavily mathematical as those in the *Journal of the American Society for Information Science*, and are somewhat more closely related to specific library problems and applications.

Journal of Library History. Quarterly. 1966– .
Related to the work of the Library History Round Table of the ALA, but not under its sponsorship.

Journal of Education for Librarianship. Quarterly. 1966– .
Issued under the auspices of the Association of American Library Schools.

Special Libraries Association

Special Libraries. Monthly. 1910– .
The official journal of the Special Libraries Association.

American Society for Information Science

Journal of the American Society for Information Science. Bi-monthly. 1968– .
The official journal of the American Society for Information Science. Replaces *American Documentation* (quarterly, 1950-1967), which had been the official journal of the American Documentation Institute. *American Documentation*, in turn, had replaced the *Journal of Documentary Reproduction* (quarterly, 1938-1943), which had been sponsored by the Committee on Photographic Reproduction of Library Materials of the ALA.

Other Periodicals

Medical Library Bulletin. Quarterly. 1902– .
The official journal of the Medical Library Association.

Law Library Journal. Bi-monthly. 1908– .
The official journal of the Law Library Association.

Notes. Quarterly. 1934– .
The official journal of the Music Library Association.

Library Quarterly. Quarterly. 1931– .
Founded by the Graduate Library School of the University of Chicago, with a grant from the Carnegie Corporation of New York. Its major purpose is to provide a medium for the publication of serious library research. Tends to emphasize research by both students and faculty of Chicago, and particularly the publication of condensed versions of theses and

dissertations, but its pages are open to any writing that represents serious research. Its book review section is particularly strong, and one issue a year is devoted to the papers presented at the annual conferences sponsored by the Graduate Library School at Chicago. For more than a decade after its inauguration it was justly regarded as the most prestigious of American library journals, and though it now has more competition than in the past, its standards are still high.

Library Trends. Quarterly. 1952– .
Sponsored by the Graduate Library School of the University of Illinois. Each issue has a guest editor, and each is devoted to some specific aspect of librarianship—e.g., library administration, rare books, personnel, library automation.

Wilson Library Bulletin. Monthly except for July and August. 1914– .
Established by the H. W. Wilson Company, first as a house organ and public relations piece, but later expanded to the publication of material particularly useful to the school and small to medium-sized public library. However, under the direction of such editors as Stanley Kunitz, John Wakeman, Kathleen Molz, and William Eshelman, it has become one of the major library journals. Earlier titles were: *The Wilson Bulletin* (abandoned because of a conflict with an ornithological journal of the same name) and *Wilson Bulletin for Librarians.*

Bulletin of Bibliography. Irregular. 1897– .
Published by the F. W. Faxon Company of Boston, Mass. Usually appears twice or three times a year. Each issue is devoted to one or two bibliographies in a field of current interest. Particularly useful for its listings of new periodical titles that have appeared since the previous issue, and those titles which have been discontinued during the same period. Each issue also contains a biographical sketch, with portrait, of a leading librarian.

School Library Journal. Nine times a year during the school term. 1954– .
Issued by the R. R. Bowker Company, it was once bound with *Library Journal* but is now available only as a separate issue.

Journal of Academic Librarianship. Bi-monthly. 1975– .
Published by the Mountainside Publishing Company, Boulder, Colorado. Would seem to have a somewhat broader scope than *College and Research Libraries.*

In addition to this list, the state and regional library associations issue bulletins, usually quarterly, and a few of the large research libraries issue journals customarily devoted to the materials in their collections: the *New York Public Library*; the *Yale Library Gazette*, and the *Huntington Library Bulletin.* The weekly *Library of Congress Information Bulletin*, reproduced in photo-offset, is largely devoted to activities and happenings around the Library, but it also frequently contains useful information concerning the library world. It does have official sanction.

Foreign and International

Canadian Library Journal. Bi-monthly. 1972– .
The official journal of the Canadian Library Association. It should be mentioned that Canada, like the United States, also has regional and provincial journals, such as the *I.P.L.O. Quarterly*, published by the Institute of Professional Librarians of Ontario.

Library Association Record. Quarterly. 1899– .
The official journal of the (British) Library Association.

Journal of Documentation. Quarterly. 1945– .
Published by ASLIB (the British Association of Special Libraries and Information Bureaux). One of the most important journals in its field.

ASLIB Proceedings. Monthly. 1949– .
Ranks with the above as one of the major journals in special librarianship and documentation, including information science.

Journal of Librarianship. Quarterly. 1969– .
One of the newest journals from England.

Revue Internationale de la Documentation. Monthly. 1934-1965.
The official journal of the Fédération Internationale de Documentation, at The Hague. Articles were published in the language in which they were written, including English.

Unesco Bulletin for Libraries. Bi-monthly. 1949– .
Issued in Paris by the library division of Unesco, and published in a number of languages. Since Unesco has been very active in the encouragement of libraries around the world, this publication is particularly important.

Libri. Irregular. 1950– .
An international library review published in Copenhagen, Denmark. Articles, which are published in the language in which they were written, are scholarly.

The above selected lists might be regarded as the "hard core" of library literature for the American librarian; many other countries have their own periodical publications for librarians, such as the U.S.S.R., India, Australia, New Zealand, and many others. Also, for the United States, there are a number of journals of marginal interest to the librarian, such as *The Papers of the Bibliographical Society of America*, *The American Archivist*, *Datamation*, and *Information and Records Management*, to suggest only a few.

Bibliographic Organization

Librarians, like the legendary shoemakers whose children were supposed to have gone unshod, have been so preoccupied with classifying, cataloging, and indexing the writings of others that they have, at least until recent years, neglected the bibliographic organization of their own professional literature. The English were the first to index library literature. In 1927, the American Library Association published the American edition of Harry George Turner Cannons' *Bibliography of Library Economy* (issued in London by The Library Association) and thereby laid the cornerstone of American library literature. The compilation was, as its extended title-page said, "A classified index to the professional periodical literature in the English language relating to library economy ... 1876-1920." Titles were classified by subject only, and there was no author index.

In the 1930s, the Junior Members Round Table of the ALA, in searching for a professional undertaking that would give the newly formed organization a unity and at the same time make a worthwhile contribution to the library field, decided "to bring Cannons up-to-date." Accordingly, Lucille Morsch assembled a sizable group of Junior Members to abstract and index current library literature. Thus, in 1934, the ALA published *Library Literature, 1921-1932*, under Miss Morsch's editorship. The success of the publication prompted the H. W. Wilson Company to assume responsibility for the undertaking and to add it to their list of bibliographic services, and *Library Literature*, with its own permanent office and staff, became a reality. Over the years the coverage has been greatly expanded to include foreign, as well as American, publications, and those in foreign languages as well as in English. Issues appear quarterly and are cumulated annually, with major cumulations every two or three years. Arrangement is by author and subject, and brief abstracts are given under the author, or main, entry. *Library Literature* is the single most important source for the literature of librarianship.

At this point we return to the tabular listing:

The Year's Work in Librarianship. Annual. 1928-1950.
> Published by the (British) Library Association. A series of bibliographic essays in the several fields of librarianship by recognized English authorities. The point of view and the emphasis are, of course, on developments in the United Kingdom, but there is much material that relates to the United States. The essays are outstanding for their excellence and still have historical value.

Five Years' Work in Librarianship. Quinquennial. 1951/1955– .
> Successor to the *Year's Work*.

Library and Information Science Abstracts. Bi-monthly. 1950– .
> Issued by the (British) Library Association. Prior to 1969 the title was *Library Science Abstracts*.

Annual Review of Information Science. Annual. 1966– .
Sponsored by the American Society for Information Science. Contains bibliographic essays relating to the year's work in the several fields that comprise information science. Essays are prepared by specialists in the respective fields.

Advances in Librarianship. Annual. 1970– .
Presents each year a series of "state of the art" papers in various aspects of librarianship by specialists in those fields. The compilation, which is published by the Academic Press, is somewhat comparable to *The Year's Work in Librarianship.*

American Reference Books Annual. Libraries Unlimited, Inc. 1970– .
Includes a chapter on librarianship and library science, which provides the librarian with descriptive and critical reviews of the monographic literature of librarianship, with an emphasis on American publications. Reviews are written by specialists in the appropriate fields.

■ ■ ■

Bowker Annual of Library and Book Trade Information. 1955/1956– .
Not a bibliographic source, but important to the librarian as a tool for keeping abreast in the library field—in a sense, a kind of *World Almanac* of the library world.

Finally, though they do not come under the rubric of bibliographic organization, there are the directories, which should be mentioned because of their importance to the practicing librarian. The first of these for the United States was Charles Coffin Jewett's *Notices of Public Libraries in the United States* (Washington, D.C.: Printed for the House of Representatives, 1851). Eight years later William J. Rhees issued his *Manual of Public Library Institutions and Societies in the United States and British Provinces of North America* (Philadelphia: J. B. Lippincott, 1859). Today, the main source of such information is *The American Library Directory*, which provides not only the name of the library and its supporting institution, together with the name of the librarian or director, but the heads of departments, the total number of volumes held, and special collections in the library's holdings. Apart from the membership lists issued at irregular intervals by the several library associations, information concerning individual librarians is to be found in *A Biographical Directory of Librarians in the United States and Canada* (5th ed., ALA, 1970; formerly *Who's Who in Library Service*). The title, however, is misleading. It is not, strictly speaking, a "who's who," but a biographical listing of all librarians who took the trouble to return the biographical questionnaire. Because the volume is published irregularly the information is often seriously out-of-date.

From even the limited survey above it is apparent that librarianship offers ample opportunity for the young librarian to find an outlet for his thoughts and investigations; the library school, in addition to stimulating his intellectual capabilities, should provide him with the opportunity to express himself clearly and precisely. The world of librarianship needs good writers as well as good readers.

NOTES

[1] Abraham Flexner, "Social Work as a Profession," *School and Society* 1 (June 26, 1915): 902ff.

[2] Pierce Butler, "Librarianship as a Profession," *Library Quarterly* 21 (October 1951): 237-238.

[3] Frank Atkinson, *Librarianship: An Introduction to the Profession* (London: Linnet Books, 1974), Chapter II.

[4] Jesse H. Shera, *Foundations of Education for Librarianship* (New York: Wiley, 1972), pp. 66-74.

[5] George B. Utley, *The Librarians' Conference of 1853* (Chicago: American Library Association, 1951).

[6] Chalmers Hadley, *John Cotton Dana: A Sketch* (Chicago: American Library Association, 1943), pp. 88-89.

[7] Ibid.

[8] Special Libraries Association, *Special Libraries Association: A Resume* (New York: Special Libraries Association, 1974).

[9] S. C. Bradford, "Fifty Years of Documentation," in *Documentation* (London: Crosby Lockwood, 1953), pp. 132-143.

[10] Vernon D. Tate, "Introducing American Documentation," *American Documentation* 1 (January 1950): 3-6.

[11] Gabriel Naudé, *Advice on Establishing a Library*, with an Introduction by Archer Taylor (Berkeley: University of California Press, 1950).

[12] Reuben A. Guild, *The Librarian's Manual* (New York: Charles B. Norton, 1858).

[13] Thaddeus Mason Harris, *A Selected Catalogue* (Boston: I. Thomas, 1793).

[14] Ralph A. Beals, "Implications of Communications Research for the Public Library," in Douglas Waples, ed., *Print, Radio, and Film in a Democracy* (Chicago: University of Chicago Press, 1942), pp. 165-166.

SELECTED READINGS

There are no comprehensive readings that cover the material in this chapter. The librarian's best sources are the major journals listed above, which should be read thoughtfully but selectively. There are no books *about* the organization of the field and its literature. There have not been any comprehensive histories written about the major library associations and their work, and only the ALA publishes a major organization manual. In this area, particularly, the student, with the aid of his instructors, must find his own way.

7

EDUCATION AND RESEARCH

Before Melvil Dewey opened his library school at Columbia University in 1887 and inaugurated professional education for librarians, the neophyte mastered his craft in one of two ways: by accepting a subordinate position in a library and slowly climbing the ladder of success as experience was gained and skill evinced, or by enrolling in a training class program of one of the larger libraries. These programs varied greatly in length and in the kinds of courses and lectures offered, and they were combined with part-time work in the library. Always the training offered was shaped by the library providing the instruction. Dewey's school at Columbia, which was later moved to Albany when Dewey was appointed State Librarian of New York, was very similar to the training classes of other libraries and was open to any competent high school graduate. The faculty was drawn from the staffs of the parent institution and neighboring libraries. For a generation the Albany school was *the* school, and "anybody who was anybody" in the profession received his or her training there (and in those days it was mostly her). By the end of fifteen years, five other schools had been established: Armour Institute in Chicago (the school was subsequently moved to the University of Illinois); Drexel Institute in Philadelphia; Pratt Institute in Brooklyn, New York; Simmons College in Boston; and Western Reserve University (now Case Western Reserve) in Cleveland. Curricula were much like that at Albany: informal, diverse in the multiplicity of offerings, and open to high school graduates or, at most, those with one or two years of college. But with the coming of these schools the earlier training class programs in the individual libraries did not die; indeed, some persisted even into the 1930s.

By the end of the first decade of the present century a sufficient number of schools had been established to justify a professional association, and the Association of American Library Schools was formed, with membership limited to the schools per se, excluding the training programs in individual libraries. At the end of World War I, the ALA launched its "expanded program," employed its first full-time executive secretary, Carl H. Milam, established headquarters in Chicago, and, among other activities, began to take a serious interest in library education. Accordingly, Charles C. Williamson, a trained social scientist as well as a librarian, was employed by the Association to make a study of education for librarianship with recommendations for its improvement. The Williamson study, financed by the Carnegie Corporation, was published in 1923.[1] At the time of its appearance it was said to have "struck like a thunderbolt," so critical was it of librarianship's professional education. Williamson recommended:

1. That admission to the professional schools be restricted to students who had successfully completed the four-year baccalaureate undergraduate program, and in addition had passed certain diagnostic tests which indicated their personalities were in harmony with a library career.

2. That all schools be affiliated with universities, either as departments or professional schools.

3. That full advantage be taken of the parent university's scholarly resources to enrich and broaden the library school students' educational experience.

4. That the curricula be restructured to provide a first-year basic program in general library principles and practice, followed after an intervening period of well-planned and expertly supervised practical work by a second year of library specialization.

5. That texts and other teaching materials be developed.

6. That provision be made for the continuing education of librarians in service in the field.

7. That there be voluntary certification for professional librarians.

8. That there be established a system for the accreditation of library schools.

Williamson was particularly critical of the curriculum, which he regarded as being overloaded with techniques to the neglect of basic principles and theory. The Williamson report, landmark that it is, did not have the impact that it should have had; nevertheless, it did bring about certain desirable changes. It sounded the death-knell of the training class. The New York Public Library program and the school at Albany closed their doors, and Columbia University re-instituted library education in the new School of Library Service, opened in 1926 with Williamson as its director. The Carnegie Corporation, which had funded the Williamson study, provided Columbia with a substantial grant to set up the new school and provided an equally substantial sum to the University of Chicago to establish the Graduate Library School there.

In 1924 the American Library Association, through its newly created Board of Education for Librarianship (B.E.L.), began the accreditation of the library schools. Their accreditation standards recognized three types of programs, of which the most prevalent led to the degree of Bachelor of Library Science. By 1949 there were twenty-one schools offering this degree, to be taken after completing an academic year or its equivalent in summer sessions.

By this time five schools also offered the master's degree for a second year of full-time study, and the Graduate Library School of the University of Chicago had, since the late 1920s, offered the doctorate as well. Prior to 1949 schools were classified by three types: those offering the master's degree were known as Type I schools; those offering the fifth-year BLS were known as Type II; and Type III was composed of those schools offering an undergraduate major in librarianship. This last type was largely limited to the training of school librarians.

Williamson had argued that the professional library schools should be affiliated with their institutional hosts even as other graduate professional schools were, and thus integrated into the academic milieu. In most, if not all, instances, however, the amalgamation for which Williamson hoped did not materialize, and the schools remained largely apart from the main academic stream. Today, this situation has been substantially improved through the introduction of inter-disciplinary programs at the level of the doctorate, and through the growing popularity of dual master's degrees.

YEARS OF REVISION

The closing years of the 1940 decade are a watershed in the history of education for librarianship in the United States. Pressure for the elimination of the fifth-year Bachelor of Library Science and the substitution for it of a professional master's degree had been steadily growing, and the schools finally yielded. With this change came the abolition of the categorization of the schools by type. In many schools the change meant the addition of a required course in research methods and an acceptable master's essay to demonstrate research aptitude. In some cases it was little more than the renaming of the degree. Initially only an academic year of full-time study represented the residence requirement, but in recent years this has generally been extended to a full calendar year. By the late 1950s, all but a few schools had eliminated the master's essay along with the foreign language requirement, which had never been rigidly enforced.

The decades of the '50s and '60s also brought substantial changes in the curricula. Originally the program of study was rather limited and rigid. Basic required courses were cataloging and classification; book, or materials, selection; reference sources; the history of books and libraries; and library administration. Provision was made for electives in such fields of practice as public libraries, college and university libraries, service to children and young people, and, somewhat later, special librarianship. Second semester courses included advanced courses in many of these, and specializations such as hospital librarianship, community service (including adult education), and others. In recent years these basic, or core, courses have been substantially attenuated through the use of survey, or foundation, courses that concentrate on the fundamentals, leaving the student more time to elect courses in his specialty, but without sacrificing the essentials of librarianship per se. The aim of these courses, however they may be named, is two-fold: first, to provide the student with a holistic view of librarianship emphasizing the elements of commonality by which the field is unified, and second, to minimize as far as is practicable the technical aspects of librarianship, enabling the student to enrich his educational experience with courses in the graduate subject fields. The earlier courses in book selection have been broken up into the three areas of scholarship—the sciences, the social sciences, and the humanities—with instruction in the selection of materials in their subordinate disciplines and the structure of the literature in them, demonstrating points of similarity as well as of difference. The time devoted to the foundations course and the literature sequences varies from program to program, but students are generally required to take two of the three sequences in the materials selection sequence, the choice being determined by the student's special interests. At the University of California in Los Angeles, and in most of the library schools in Canada, two academic years are required for the master's degree, which enhances the opportunity for advanced study and makes possible the use of the intervening summer for employment and practical experience in an operating situation. Through such policies and the double master's degree awarded for study in both librarianship and an academic subject discipline, the profession is beginning to achieve Williamson's aspirations for the enrichment of library education by the resources of the university.

In 1948, at the Graduate Library School of the University of Chicago and at Western Reserve University, there were offered, for the first time, courses in documentation, bibliographic organization, and related aspects of non-conventional access to the subject content of graphic records. At Western Reserve, in 1955, the Center for Documentation and Communication Research was established to explore the potential of automated information retrieval through the use of computers. From these beginnings emerged today's information science, which has come to be recognized as an important program of study in most of the library schools. With these new programs have come courses in communication and systems theory, scientific management, and other aspects of science, particularly mathematics, that were undreamed of even by Williamson. The task that faces the library educator today is one of reconciling the conventional, which is by no means obsolete, with the new, for there can be little doubt that librarianship is experiencing important, not to say drastic, changes, and library education, like all education, must look to the future. In the early 1960s, there developed a marked interest in library education on the part of university administrations which previously had looked askance at such professional schools. Today there are some sixty library schools throughout the country, not counting undergraduate programs for the training of school librarians.

The original Board of Education for Librarianship became the ALA Committee on Accreditation, and the plan for decennial inspection visits to the schools was abandoned in favor of an annual report from each of the schools relating to financial support, faculty changes, curricula, and other matters relevant to educational excellence. At the close of the decade new standards of accreditation were developed and there began a thorough review of all the schools, each of which was required to produce a detailed self-study and submit to a three- to four-day examination by a visiting team. The Canadian schools, which in general have adopted the American pattern, except for the two-year program, are also accredited by the COA. In library schools, as in other parts of the university, students and, in some instances, alumni are being given an increasing voice in the affairs of the school through representation on major committees.

Two other organizations concerned with library education should be mentioned. The Association of American Library Schools, though not a part of the ALA, meets annually prior to the mid-winter meetings of that association. Its membership is limited to faculties of the accredited schools, though others may attend as auditors. The organization, which issues the quarterly *Journal of Education for Librarianship*, has no authority over the schools and is mainly a forum for the discussion of common problems and the reporting of innovations. The Library Education Division of the ALA is much the same kind of organization, though its membership is open to any ALA member interested in library education. It supports program meetings at the annual conference, and each year it awards the Beta Phi Mu citation for an outstanding contribution to librarianship. Beta Phi Mu is the national library honor society to which each year the outstanding graduates of the accredited schools are elected.

THE ACADEMIC SETTING

Williamson was right, the library school is a part of the university community, and hence it must reflect the basic philosophy of higher education. Therefore, it is important to review briefly the underlying principles on which graduate study is based and the general philosophy by which it is animated.

When he was President of Princeton University, Woodrow Wilson said that what should be imparted to the students was "not so much learning itself but the spirit of learning." The eminent jurist Judge Learned Hand amplified Wilson's "spirit of learning" by referring to "the consecration to the spirit of the pursuit of truth." Robert Maynard Hutchins, when President of the University of Chicago, argued that higher education is "the training of the intellect." On the northern side of the international border, J. A. Corry discussed the aims of university education at a convocation held to mark the one hundred and twenty-fifth anniversary of the holding of classes at Queen's University, Kingston:

> The aims are many: the passing on of our inherited exact knowledge, the pursuit of new knowledge at the frontiers, the sharpening of intellects and the disciplining of minds to respect both facts and logic, . . . All this to lead on to an understanding

and compassion for the restless searching of the human spirit for the superlative in some form or other in a world that does not easily yield such prizes. And still further on to the refining of knowledge and judgement and sensitivity into the beginnings of wisdom about "the troubles of our proud and angry dust."[2]

All of these men, at different times and places, were saying essentially the same thing: that education is far more than stuffing the student with facts or preparing him to master particular skills, whether the skills are cerebral or physical. It is expected that the university will provide an environment hospitable to the cultivation of knowledge, wisdom, and truth, a place where the "spirit of learning" can be nourished and nurtured by both faculty and students. Allied in this environment we should find both teaching and research, for student and faculty are, or ought to be, partners in the exploration of the unknown. This statement is not meant to imply, however, that the universities are, or have been, totally apart from the practical concerns of the "real world," set up as ivory towers for those who "never had to meet a payroll."

As in Europe, so in North America, the first universities were established as professional schools. They began in Bologna and Salerno as faculties of law and medicine, and at Paris and Oxford as schools of theology. The earliest American universities, among them Harvard and Yale, saw as their primary purpose to provide training for those young men destined for the ministry. Training for the law, teaching, and medicine, all of which had begun with apprentice training, were soon added to the curricula, while engineering developed somewhat later. Ezra Cornell, when establishing the university which bears his name, and its first president, Andrew D. White, believed that a university should provide for every educational requirement, and that any citizen should be able to find there a course of study appropriate to his need. Lotus D. Coffman, president of the University of Minnesota, expressed the same belief as the goal of the state university. It was, however, the passage of the Morrill Act of 1862, which provided federal aid to the struggling agricultural and mechanical colleges, that flung open wide the door to technical training, and when Charles W. Eliot became president of Harvard, the rigid classical curriculum was opened to the elective system. With these drastic breaks with the German tradition in American higher education, it is not surprising that such library pioneers as Melvil Dewey and William Howard Brett thought of the universities as proper places for the establishment of formal library training. Despite these innovations, however, there remained considerable sympathy for the classical tradition. Happily, among library educators there does seem to be a growing belief in the value of a general, or liberal, education as an essential preliminary to the professional training of the librarian. In this attitude, library education is following in the tradition now characteristic of the professional schools of law, medicine, and theology. Even the engineering schools, in such institutions as M.I.T., are beginning to recognize the importance of liberal education as a basis for admission to their respective graduate professional schools.

It is easy to criticize library education, as Williamson did, for being too technique oriented, too much concerned with the *how* rather than the *why*, and there is no doubt about the validity of his complaint; but it is well to remember that education for librarianship followed the pattern of professional education generally, and that it is dealing with the same problems in much the same way.

RESEARCH

Valid research, perhaps even more than teaching, represents the training of the intellect and exemplifies a dedication to the pursuit of truth. Hence a program of research is essential to graduate education. Moreover, it is the key to the future of the profession and is an important means by which the instructional program is enriched. One cannot say that the Graduate Library School of the University of Chicago invented research in librarianship, but that school, during the decade when Louis Round Wilson was its dean, was the first to address itself seriously to research and to give it a formal structure and the beginnings of a sound methodology. The establishment of the school, through a grant from the Carnegie Corporation in 1926, raised the serious question of what research in librarianship should be. When Wilson became its dean in 1932, he directed it toward the field of the social sciences and applied to its problems the methodology of social science research. In this effort he was fortunate in having the assistance of such scholars as Douglas Waples, Pierce Butler, and Carleton B. Joeckel. This reorientation of librarianship away from the humanities and toward the social sciences is all the more surprising because, in the cases of Waples, Butler, and even Wilson himself, the background had been essentially humanistic. Moreover, Wilson was successful in attracting to the school promising young students who enthusiastically shared his views, and who went out from the Gothic towers of Harper Library to spread the "gospel." Admittedly, there were times when enthusiasm permitted form and method to be mistaken for substance, and of much of it Ralph A. Beals said, in his address quoted in an earlier chapter:

> A third source of evidence comprises publications that may, with some propriety, be described as research. This class is not limited to statistical studies, nor do all statistical studies, as such, necessarily fall within it: several statistical studies of librarianship bear out Andrew Lang's contention that some men use statistics as a drunkard uses a lamppost—for support, not for illumination. Any study in which a problem is defined and analyzed into its constituent parts, in which valid data are collected and related to relevant factors, in which hypotheses are formed and, through testing, rejected, amended, or proved—any such study, I take it, offers acceptable credentials as research.[3]

When Beals was writing, library research was so new that those who would engage in it needed precise instruction in its methods and techniques, particularly those in the behavioral sciences, and especially statistics. Beals was simply warning that the method should not be mistaken for the substance and that correlation does not necessarily prove causality. Even today such a warning is not amiss.

There is nothing recondite about research; stated in its simplest terms it is no more than a search for valid and relevant evidence, or data, that will provide an answer to a meaningful question. Research, then, begins in a knowledge of our own ignorance and proceeds through an examination and evaluation of evidence until the inquiry is concluded. As pointed out in the Prologue to this book, Niels Bohr, the great Danish physicist, was wont to tell his students, "Every assertion that I make should be understood by you as a question." In its broadest sense, then, research is in the realm of criticism—criticism of the question being asked to determine its relevance; criticism of the hypotheses, which are no more than intelligent guesses, on which the inquiry is based; criticism of the evidence to determine its relevance and reliability; and finally criticism of the results. In a sense, the highest research approaches art, for it involves both analysis and synthesis—tearing the problem into its constituent parts, as an artist analyzes the object he is representing, and putting it all back together, as the artist creates a work of beauty and understanding.

Darwin's great work on the origin of species provides an excellent example. "While on board the H.M.S. *Beagle*," he wrote in the introduction to *The Origin*, " . . . I was struck with certain facts in the distribution of the organic beings inhabiting South America, and in the geological relations of the present to the past inhabitants of that continent." Darwin surmised that these facts might throw some light on " . . . that mystery of mysteries . . ." the origin of species. Therefore, upon his return home, he began his inquiry " . . . by patiently accumulating and reflecting on all sorts of facts which could possibly have any bearing on it." Thus he turned to that which was immediate—the plants and animals of the farm and barnyard—and comparing them with their kind "in a state of nature" he reflected that the lesser variability to be observed in the wild might be " . . . due to our domestic productions having been raised under conditions of life not so uniform as, and somewhat different from, those to which the parent species had been exposed under nature."[4]

Both Darwin and his contemporary, the naturalist Alfred Russell Wallace, arrived at the same hypothesis concerning "natural selection" through the reading of Thomas Robert Malthus' essay on the growth of human populations. If Malthus were correct, they reasoned, then the same phenomenon would hold true for all living creatures, and only those species which were most adaptable and able to survive would reproduce their kind. Thus, in this principle of "the survival of the fittest" or, more accurately, the survival of the most adaptable, the doctrine of evolution was born. Here we cannot, of course, trace out the thread of Darwin's argument or set forth the development of the thinking by which he reached his conclusions, though it would be most instructive to do so. But in it is to be seen the almost perfect representation of the research process. Darwin was probably not even aware that he had embarked on "research," though in his autobiography he speaks of his mind as "a kind of machine grinding general laws out of large collections of facts."[5] He was simply following the admonition of Francis Bacon in *The Advancement of Learning*, that the task of the philosopher is to "unlock the secrets of nature" through which can be known the world in which we live and have our being.

Such has been the course of research from Archimedes to Paracelsus to Galileo and Newton to Einstein and Fermi. Even fantasy can have its role in research. The nineteenth-century German chemist Friedrich August Kekulé von Stradonitz admitted to having hypothesized the benzine ring from a dream of snakes with their tails in their mouths, revolving like pin-wheels. Each innovator with his own conception of the world, his own world view, shatters, or helps to shatter, the paradigm of science, to use Thomas Kuhn's term, that has gone before, and through research contributes to the evolution of man's knowledge of his universe. Shorn of any mysticism, research has always been, as was said above, an answering of questions by the assimilation of verified or verifiable facts, which leads to the formulation of generalizations or universals that correct or substantiate existing knowledge.

One cannot talk about the philosophy of modern research without going back to Francis Bacon; every serious investigator of natural and social phenomena since the seventeenth century is deeply indebted, consciously or unconsciously, to Baron Verulam, Viscount St. Albans. But Bacon's insistence upon the strict use of the experimental method for discovering the facts of nature has now been so fully absorbed into modern scientific practice, has become so commonplace with the passage of time, that one is apt to forget that Bacon was protesting the haphazard accumulation of observations. He knew, of course, that experimentation had been practiced long before his time, but, as he wrote, "The manner of making experiments which men now use is blind and stupid, wandering and straying as they do in no subtle course and taking counsel only from things as they fall out, they fetch a wide circuit with many matters, but make little progress, they make their trials carelessly and, as it were, in play."[6] The true research worker does not embark on a fishing expedition. Chemists do not make random mixtures to see what will happen, nor do biologists thrust under their microscopes the first living organism that comes to hand. Experimentation and inquiry come after hypothesis, not before it. Indeed, one can agree with Pierce Butler that there is no such thing as scientific research until a theoretical hypothesis has been formulated.[7] To be sure, Darwin's curiosity was aroused by the varieties of species, but he did not begin his systematic study of its manifestations in domestic animals and plants until he had hypothesized the probable outcome of his inquiry.

But it was Bacon who established the pattern. "For hitherto," he wrote, "the proceeding has been to fly at once from the sense and particulars up to the most general propositions, . . . my plan is to proceed most regularly and gradually from one axiom to another so that the most general are not reached till the last . . ."[8] Again, he wrote in one of his most famous passages: "The men of experiment are like the ant, they only collect and use. The reasoners resemble spiders who make cobwebs out of their own substance. But the bee takes a middle course: it gathers its material from the flowers of the garden and of the field, but transforms and digests it by a power of its own."[9]

Clearly, to be an effective research investigator one must emulate the bee—one must be purposeful, industrious, and imaginatively selective in the assembling of evidence. Moreover, for an inquiry to qualify as true research its results must be generalizable. Darwin's work has implications, applications, and consequences far beyond the boundaries of biology, and Bacon well knew that axioms "rightly discovered will draw after them trains and troops of work."

The end of research, like that of formal education, is the perfectability of human knowledge through the pursuit of truth, a goal that can never be obtained but must always be assumed to be attainable. "The deeper we penetrate into the nature of the atom," Enrico Fermi once observed, "the more we become aware that Nature always keeps two jumps ahead of us." He was saying graphically that the search for knowledge is interminable, that it has no end, that there is always someplace else to go. His statement is not the counsel of despair but a challenge to initiative. Research does not have to have an immediate and practical end. Bacon spoke of "experimenta lucifera," experiments of light, as distinguished from "experimenta fructifera," experiments of fruit. Over the years, Americans have probably devoted too much attention to immediate results, to the neglect of pure science. And librarians, too, have failed to look behind their operations to the basic principles of the organization of knowledge, its dissemination, and communication, which are the foundation stones upon which their professional practice rests. "Truth and utility, therefore, are here the very same thing and works themselves are of greater value as pledges of truth than as contributing to the comforts of life."[10]

Research, then, is a systematic attempt to discover new facts, or sets of facts, or new relationships among facts, through the formulation of a preliminary explanation, or hypothesis, which is subjected to an appropriate investigation for validation or disproof. The only rule that governs research is the rule of objectivity. Research is the stern disciplinarian that it is, not because it is esoteric, but because it leaves no place for the subjective. Yet it is pursued by human beings, who are themselves inescapable complexes of both reason and emotion, and in research the latter must be suppressed if the former is to prevail. Reasoning or observation that is diluted with emotion becomes sophistry or dogma. Wishful thinking is a particular threat to research in librarianship, for librarianship is essentially a service profession and a service is always in jeopardy from emotion. The librarian means to do good, and by dint of self-sacrifice he does what he means to do; therefore, he assumes that what he does *is* good.

The decade that immediately followed the end of World War II brought with it an even greater prestige for scientific research than had previously existed, an excitement and sense of urgency that reached a climax with the advent of Sputnik. Librarianship shared in this eagerness to promote research, stimulated by largess from such federal agencies as the National Science Foundation and the U.S. Office of Education. Research, so far as library education was concerned, came to a focus in the doctoral programs. Of the three score accredited library schools, there are today some fifteen offering either the degree of Doctor of Philosophy, usually offered in conjunction with the university's graduate school, or the Doctor of Library Science. These programs vary, of course, from school to school according to the aspect, or aspects, in which the school specializes; but even in those instances where they are not directly under the graduate school, the requirements are aligned with it. Almost universally, interdisciplinary programs are encouraged, if not mandatory. These are especially important, for a librarian is not just a librarian; he is a librarian in some area, or areas, of human knowledge, and he cannot perform his responsibilities adequately if his educational background is not enriched with the requisite substantive knowledge. "To restore to intellectual life," writes Arthur E. Bestor in *The Restoration of Learning*, "the unity that the forces of modern life are threatening to destroy, constitutes one of the most significant tasks to which thoughtful men and women are addressing themselves today."[11] In an address before the Rockefeller Institute, Loren Eisley set forth the thesis that science and art are not divisible but are essentially one, and he thus challenged, at least by implication, the doctrine of C. P. Snow of "the two cultures" in the scientific revolution. Thus he declared: "Creativity in science demands a high level of imaginative insight and intuitive perception . . . In the very dawn of science, Bacon, the spokesman for the empirical approach to nature, shared with Shakespeare, the poet, a recognition of the creativeness which adds to and emerges from nature, as 'an artist which nature makes.' "[12] Preserving the unity of intellectual life is certainly one of the major tasks for which the librarian as generalist should be prepared, while the librarian as specialist, if he fails to see his specialization in relation to the whole of human knowledge, is bound to go astray in a wilderness of fragmentations.

Because the work of the librarian, particularly the public and academic librarian, involves a variety of disparate disciplines, and because much of library research requires skills and knowledge for which the librarian, even under the most generous of educational opportunities, cannot be prepared, team research would seem to be particularly productive. If the team brings to bear upon the problem to which it addresses itself a variety of scholars, each contributing his own special competencies, results should be much more productive than would be possible with one investigator working alone. In a few instances doctoral degrees have been awarded to two scholars working together on a joint investigation and producing a single dissertation. Such a procedure is not common, but at least a precedent for it has been set. The traditional interdisciplinary barriers are breaking down, and increasingly the academic world is realizing that knowledge is unitary and that work in one area depends upon and has implications for work in another. For generations science has assumed that it was *amoral*; that its only task was to discover the truths revealed in physical and biological phenomena. What the world might do with these discoveries was not the scientist's concern. But one blinding flash and a mushroom-shaped cloud over the sands of Alamagordo changed all that, and scientists learned that what they had done had implications and repercussions far beyond the boundaries of their discipline. The librarian as educator can, in both his professional services and his research, do much to bridge these age-old chasms that have carved up the terrain of man's knowledge. Hence, for the librarian, a sound general education, as much advanced study as possible in an appropriate subject field, and professional training are essential.

In the final analysis, the best way to learn to do research is to do it. Courses in research methods and such readings as are listed in the bibliography appended to this chapter will help, but they are no substitute for experience. Wherever possible one would be well advised to apprentice oneself to an experienced investigator, and failing that to strike out boldly on one's own and submit the result to a competent and uncompromising critic. The famous American sculptor Lorado Taft was wont to say that the best way to appreciate good sculpture was to take a knife and a bar of soap, or a lump of clay, and try it out on one's own. The result would at least develop a healthy respect, not to say admiration, for the artist who can do it, and one might also discover an unsuspected talent. Excellence in research requires a lifetime of dedication.

It is true, of course, that few who enroll in library school will ever be engaged in research, but this does not exempt them from the need for a basic understanding of what research involves and the rules and procedures by which sound research is shaped. Every librarian, at one time or another, will be called upon to evaluate the research of others, both in the field of librarianship itself and in other disciplines. The librarian, therefore, must be equipped to evaluate such material, to analyze it in terms of rational thinking, and to see if its conclusions can be accepted. In the building of the book collection and in the application of operational procedures, every librarian must be a critic.

Except for senior positions in academic libraries and the faculty of library schools, there is little demand for the doctorate in librarianship. In special libraries, as is quite proper, the emphasis is generally placed on advanced study and the Ph.D. in the subject field of the library's specialization. Therefore, there has been developing a serious concern for an advanced non-research degree that would be academically respectable but not demand original research for its qualification. This movement has made little progress because it goes counter to academic tradition. Nevertheless, for public librarians, whose education should emphasize government, public administration, and community analysis, the proposal has much to recommend it. Care must be taken, however, that it maintain high academic standards and not be used as a consolation prize for those who cannot qualify for the doctorate.

THE HOLISTIC VIEW

From what has been said above about education and research in librarianship, it becomes possible to identify, with a reasonable degree of precision, the goals and objectives of the typical library school within the framework of the academic community. Such a statement cannot, of course, apply to every school, but it may help to establish a pattern against which the individual school can be measured.

The end of higher education, following Hutchins' doctrine, is the training of the intellect, by which is meant that its first responsibility is the making of a good citizen, one who is equipped intellectually to assume a position of responsibility in his society. Beyond that goal, higher education must prepare the student for a career, or at least must lay the foundation for one, since many careers necessitate special training beyond the undergraduate program. In addition, the university should contribute, through active programs of research, to the extension of man's knowledge of himself and his environment. To achieve these goals the university should foster flexibility in its constituent programs and encourage interdepartmental cooperation and dialogue. Its structure should encourage student initiative and freedom of inquiry within a wide spectrum of learning situations and opportunities.

The goal of a school of library science is to educate competent professional librarians and, where resources permit, information scientists, within the framework of, and utilizing the resources offered by, the academic community with which it is associated.

Apart from the obvious fact that there are many stubborn problems in librarianship for the solution of which research is needed, the new student may well raise the question of why there should be a required course in its methods. Students will argue, and quite rightly, that in a service profession such as librarianship very few of them will ever be themselves engaged in productive research, and that if offered at all, such a course should at least be optional. One could respond with the age-old argument that such a course, like preparation in mathematics, trains the mind and helps to develop logical thinking on the part of the student. Such an argument has some validity, but the study of research has very practical ends, too. Every librarian, regardless of his career intentions, will encounter the "research," or what masquerades as research, of others, and the student must learn to be objective in his evaluations, to winnow the wheat from the chaff, to reject the spurious for what it is. Obviously, competent research workers are not made in a single course—"the lyfe so short, the craft so long to lerne"—but the student can gain some valuable insight into the research process and can learn some standards of evaluation even in a three-hour course in a single term, and it is an exposure that every student should have.

Perhaps enough has been said above to indicate that the education of the "compleat" librarian should be regarded as a system of well-integrated parts consisting of undergraduate general education and a subject major, professional study, and graduate training in a substantive field to at least a dual master's degree and preferably more in advanced work in the appropriate subject field. The library school's goal is to educate students who are prepared to function as practitioners hospitable to change and competent to deal with change in a field that is experiencing rapid and sometimes drastic innovation. Its graduates must be able to define and articulate user needs and to implement their procedures designed to meet those needs. Essential to the realization of this goal is an awareness that effective access to recorded knowledge involves intellectual and service activities as well as conditions favorable to the innovative developments relating to those activities.

The educational structure, then, is composed of six elements:

1. The underlying and fundamental principles of the profession
2. Specialized subjects and their relationships to each other and to professional practice
3. Implementation of the previous understandings in professional service, practice, and action
4. Knowledge of the clienteles to be served
5. An awareness of the social and informational environment within which the profession operates
6. The skills needed to evaluate results.

All students should be expected to develop the capacity to grasp and analyze ideas relevant to their concern as professional practitioners and to deal logically with the professional problems with which they are likely to be confronted. Such an admonition implies the formation of a mental attitude critically receptive to innovation and the adjustments that such changes may necessitate. Finally, the graduate should understand the need for continuing education as a source of enrichment not only for himself personally, but also for the institution he serves and for the profession generally. The educational system as an integrated whole is presented graphically in Figure 10.

A service profession has a three-part base: cognitive and normative *knowledge*, *skill*, and *experience*. Once acquired, these three form that conjunction which H. G. Cassidy speaks of as professional wisdom. Every service profession has accumulated knowledge and skill in terms of 1) *fundamentals* and 2) *specific subjects and their relations* which, if properly taught and studied, constitute *learning*. These fundamentals and specific subjects have been derived from and tested by *experience*, which results from 3) *professional action*. Professional action cannot be taught. It must be engaged in, practiced—that is why many schools offer field work.

Fig. 10. Education System*

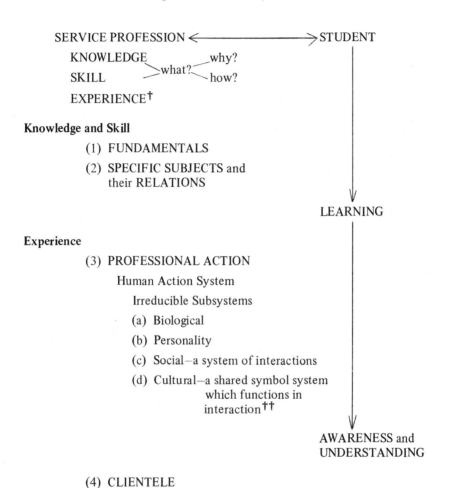

Knowledge and Skill

(1) FUNDAMENTALS

(2) SPECIFIC SUBJECTS and
their RELATIONS

Experience

(3) PROFESSIONAL ACTION

Human Action System

Irreducible Subsystems

(a) Biological

(b) Personality

(c) Social—a system of interactions

(d) Cultural—a shared symbol system
which functions in
interaction[††]

(4) CLIENTELE

(5) INSTITUTIONAL and SOCIAL ENVIRONMENT

---

*Courtesy of Conrad H. Rawski.

[†]H. G. Cassidy, "Liberation and Limitation," in F. Sweeney, *The Knowledge Explosion* (New York: Farrar, Straus, Giroux, 1966), p. 188.

[††]Charles Morris, *Signification and Significance* (Cambridge, Mass.: M.I.T. Press, 1964), Chapter 4, especially pp. 56-60.

CHOOSING THE "RIGHT" SCHOOL

To lecture anyone on the choice of a library school seems a bit presumptuous, not to say pontifical and even an elaboration of the obvious, for such a choice must be a highly personal matter. Yet we all know that such choices are all too frequently made according to fortuitous circumstance and without proper consideration of all the elements involved. Moreover, every dean or director of a library school has frequently been called upon to assist in such a decision, and a few guidelines may not be amiss.

In general, it can be said that all schools offer much the same basic curriculum and the ALA Committee on Accreditation does strive to make certain that standards are maintained. Yet there are substantial variations among the accredited schools, and there is no one "best" institution.

Someone has waggishly used the metaphor "to lie like a college catalog," and the catalogs of library schools are no exception. Every catalog lists courses that are not always offered, last-minute crises necessitate changes in scheduling, and not infrequently courses are listed even though they have not been offered for several years. But, withal, there is no substitute for a careful study of the major objectives of such material, remembering always that every school "puts its best foot forward." Visits to the most promising schools, whenever practicable, are highly to be recommended.

The first consideration is, probably, the nature of the program and the specializations that are offered to make certain that they fit the prospective student's needs, interests, and projected career. There is a wide variation among the schools respecting library specialization, and what may be excellent for one interested in children's work, for example, may be quite inadequate for a prospective information scientist. No school can include every specialization, so its offerings must reflect the interests and concerns of its dean and its instructional staff. From time to time, over the years, there have been surveys of library schools, as there have been of higher educational institutions generally. These are to be distrusted, for they reflect opinion, often idiosyncratic judgments, rather than fact. Excellence is not necessarily determined by democratic plebiscite. Reputations, for good or ill, tend to persist long after the original reason for them has disappeared. Prestigious institutions tend to rank high from a kind of "halo." The temptation to cite examples is strong, but at the moment it would be unfair and, after the passage of time, inaccurate. We are concerned here with no "stable commodity." Academicians are nomadic, and what is true today, even in the opinion of those best qualified to judge, may be quite erroneous tomorrow.

The standing of the faculty is, of course, a basic consideration—the areas of their specialization, their professional activities and research productivity. Possession of the doctorate is a guide, but not a guarantee of instructional excellence. We have all known excellent teachers who never achieved this "exalted" academic status, and conversely, those with the hallowed initials after their names who should have been . . . *ad lib.* The story has been told of George Lyman Kittredge, Harvard's most distinguished scholar in English literature, who, when asked why he never earned the Ph.D., replied, "Who would examine me?" Nevertheless, a school with a substantial number of faculty who hold the doctorate is to be given high marks.

One should also consider the standing of other departments of the university, particularly with the increasing emphasis on interdisciplinary programs. Such a consideration is important not only because of the possibilities for enrichment of the student's own program, but also because a university that has general strength throughout its program is unlikely to tolerate a mediocre library school.

The library collections are, of course, an important consideration. One should also give some attention to the school's physical plant and equipment; the latter is particularly noteworthy if one is interested in becoming a library media specialist. But do not be swayed by a pretty campus or spectacular architecture. Do not forget that Harvard lies in the dreary surroundings of industrial Cambridge, Yale struggles to rise above the shops of New Haven, and only the towers of Harkness Memorial and the Sterling Library succeed, and that Columbia, swallowed up by New York City, looks more like an agglomeration of office buildings than the groves of academe. Who would not enjoy the pastoral setting, as well as the intellectual stimulation, of a Princeton? Stately mansions for its corporate soul do not a great university make.

Finally, undergraduate, extension, and correspondence courses in librarianship should be avoided as the plague. The first presents librarianship at its lowest technical level and robs the student of time that should be spent on subject specialization. The second, due to the absence of adequate library resources and the inevitable fatigue that the evening hours bring to both students and teacher, cannot but detract from the learning process. Correspondence courses have a built-in inferiority.

Economic considerations should not be allowed to establish educational boundaries. Economic necessity must be recognized, but it is also important to remember that a penny "saved" in education may represent dollars lost in a career. A good student can rise above a mediocre education, but rarely; a good thing can come out of Nazareth, but it has happened only once. There are scholarships and fellowships available, and a work-study program, though it may lengthen the time spent in formal training, has its own rewards in the blending of education with experience. Surmounting economic barriers could well prove to be part of the challenge that education presents.

NOTES

[1] Charles C. Williamson, *The Williamson Reports of 1921 and 1923* (Metuchen, N.J.: Scarecrow Press, 1971), p. 49. The report of 1923 (the report of 1921 was suppressed because it was thought to be too critical) was published by the Carnegie Corporation of New York.

[2] J. A. Corry, *Farewell the Ivory Tower: Universities in Transition* (Montreal: McGill-Queen's University Press, 1970), p. 53.

[3] Ralph A. Beals, "Implications of Communications Research for the Public Library," in Douglas Waples, ed., *Print, Radio, and Film in a Democracy* (Chicago: University of Chicago Press, 1942), pp. 166-167.

[4] Charles Darwin, *The Origin of Species* (New York: Modern Library, n.d.), pp. 11, 13, 15.

[5] Charles Darwin, *Autobiography: Life and Letters* (London: Murrey, 1887), Vol. 1, p. 101.

[6] Francis Bacon, *The Advancement of Learning*, in Popular Edition, based upon the Complete Edition of Spedding, Ellis, and Heath, *The Works of Francis Bacon* (Boston: Houghton Mifflin, n.d.), p. 100.

[7] Pierce Butler, *An Introduction to Library Science* (Chicago: University of Chicago Press, 1933), p. 108.

[8] Bacon, *The Advancement of Learning*, p. 135.

[9] Ibid., p. 123.

[10] Ibid., p. 42.

[11] Arthur Bestor, *The Restoration of Learning* (New York: Knopf, 1956), p. 58.

[12] *Christian Science Monitor*, December 4, 1975, pp. 32-33.

SELECTED READINGS

Education for Librarianship

Danton, J. Periam. *Between M.L.S. and Ph.D.* Chicago: American Library Association, 1970.

Davis, Donald G. *The Association of American Library Schools, 1915-1968.* Metuchen, N.J.: Scarecrow Press, 1974.

Galvin, Thomas J. *The Case Method in Library Education and In-Service Training.* Metuchen, N.J.: Scarecrow Press, 1973.

Leigh, Robert D. "The Education of Librarians." In Alice I. Bryan, *The Public Librarian.* New York: Columbia University Press, 1952. pp. 208-369. (The Public Library Inquiry Series).

Leigh, Robert D., ed. *Major Problems in the Education of Librarians.* New York: Columbia University Press, 1954.

Shera, Jesse H. *The Foundations of Education for Librarianship.* New York: Wiley, 1973.

Shera, Jesse H., and Margaret Anderson. *Education for Librarianship in the U.S. and Canada.* Liverpool, England: Liverpool Polytechnic, Department of Library and Information Science, 1975. *Occasional Paper*, No. 5.

Trautman, Ray. *History of the School of Library Service, Columbia University.* New York: Columbia University Press, 1954.

Vann, Sarah K. *Training for Librarianship before 1923.* Chicago: American Library Association, 1961.

Vann, Sarah K. *The Williamson Reports: A Study.* Metuchen, N.J.: Scarecrow Press, 1971.

White, Carl M. *A Historical Introduction to Library Education: Problems and Progress to 1951.* Metuchen, N.J.: Scarecrow Press, 1976.

Williamson, Charles C. *The Williamson Reports of 1921 and 1923.* Metuchen, N.J.: Scarecrow Press, 1971.

Wilson, Louis Round. *Education and Libraries: Selected Papers of Louis Round Wilson.* Edited by Maurice F. Tauber and Jerrold Orne. Hamden, Conn.: Shoe String Press, 1966.

Research

Altick, Richard D. *The Art of Literary Research.* New York: Norton, 1963.

Bunge, M. *Scientific Research.* New York: Springer Verlag, 1967. 2 vols.

Festinger, L., ed. *Research Methods in the Behavioral Sciences.* New York: Holt, 1953.

Galtun, J. *Theory and Methods of Social Research.* New York: Columbia University Press, 1967.

Gillispie, Charles C. *The Edge of Objectivity.* Princeton, N.J.: Princeton University Press, 1960.

Goldhor, Herbert. *An Introduction to Scientific Research in Librarianship.* Urbana, Ill.: University of Illinois, 1972.

Goldhor, Herbert, ed. *Research Methods in Librarian Measurement and Evaluation.* Urbana, Ill.: University of Illinois, 1968.

Kaplan, Abraham. *The Conduct of Inquiry.* San Francisco: Chandler, 1964.

Northrop, F. S. C. *The Logic of the Sciences and Sciences and the Humanities.* New York: Macmillan, 1947.

Pullock, G. *The Organization of Inquiry.* Durham, N.C.: Duke University Press, 1966.

Scheffler, I. *The Anatomy of Inquiry.* New York: Knopf, 1963.

Shera, Jesse H. "Darwin, Bacon, and Research in Librarianship." In *Libraries and the Organization of Knowledge.* London: Crosby Lockwood, 1965. pp. 209-216.

Stevens, R. E. *Research Methods in Librarianship: Historical and Bibliographical Methods in Library Research.* Urbana, Ill.: University of Illinois, 1971.

Waples, Douglas. *Investigating Library Problems.* Chicago: University of Chicago Press, 1939.

Wynar, Bohdan. *Research Methods in Library Science: A Bibliographical Guide with Topical Outlines.* Littleton, Colo.: Libraries Unlimited, 1971.

8

LIBRARY AND INFORMATION SERVICES:
Components in Planning
for National Development

by Margaret Anderson
Assistant Professor
Faculty of Library Science
University of Toronto, Canada

INTRODUCTION

In the second chapter of this book Dr. Shera argues that the library, as a social instrument, takes its shape and purpose from the society and culture in which it is established. Taking the library to be a "social instrument" implies that it is, and has been, a part of the communication pattern of society, preserving, organizing, and disseminating the graphic records that society as a whole, or those in charge of it, have indicated to be the library's concern. Since 1945 such international organizations as Unesco and IFLA have sponsored many regional seminars on problems of librarianship and library development in various parts of the world. As the seminars proliferated and their published "Reports" and "Proceedings" appeared, certain characteristics of the role of library and information services in society were revealed to be more or less common to all nations, regardless of their level of technological development or their economic or political ideology.

Most governments, Josefa Sabor asserts, have long been convinced that "the future of our society depends primordially on our attitude to education";[1] but it has become a more recent conviction of governments that a part of the educational problem can be solved through proper organization and development of libraries. Every nation requires a dual base of both information and education for its economic and social development. The patterns of economic, social, and population development that have been observed throughout the 1960s and early 1970s indicate a need for increasing emphasis on planning of library and documentation services at both national and international levels. Among the developing nations we find many showing steady population increases and alarmingly high rates of illiteracy. In such countries as Bangladesh, Ethiopia, Mali, Togo, and Paraguay, the literacy figures for the entire population, albeit these are only estimates, vary between ten and twenty percent.[2] By contrast, Argentina boasts a ninety percent literacy rate for its adult population, and Chile cites over ninety percent of its entire population as literate, with the figure higher still for the urban areas. Brazil hopes to have its illiteracy eradicated by 1980, while in Algeria forty percent of the school-age children have not yet been given places in school. In Africa, both Nigeria and Egypt have been able to provide free, compulsory, and universal primary education, the former having begun to do so only in 1975. Several of the countries with high rates of illiteracy have embarked on large-scale campaigns to promote adult literacy, using various branches of the government, including the army, to handle such work. India and Morocco, among other states, make fairly extensive use of radio to promote adult literacy and adult education, and often arrange for the production of special, simplified-language newspapers as well, to allow those beginning to acquire the skills of reading and writing a chance to continue to make progress. Despite an intensive literacy campaign in India, the 1971 census figures indicated that only twenty-nine percent of the total population of the country was literate.

Such a situation means that an inordinately high number of the world's people are unable to avail themselves of information represented by the printed word; in areas where so many are totally illiterate we may postulate that, even among those who would be classed as "literate," many would have no more formal education than the completion of four to six years of elementary school. This achievement, if not followed by concerted efforts on their part toward continuing self-education through reading and discussion, will leave them in a state of functional literacy at best.

With so small a base of literacy, many developing nations have had very little, if any, experience with the traditions of library service. Along with their literacy campaigns, many of the governments of developing states have begun concerted campaigns to move these countries into the realm of technological and industrial development enjoyed by the more advanced nations. As they recognize the role that can be played by an institution which takes as its own aim the collection, organization, and distribution of information for all spheres of society, such library services as are already in existence (usually in the major urban centers and, of course, a part of the university complex, if one exists in the country) will need to be re-thought and expanded.

In the more developed parts of the world the challenging requirements in the growth of research, and in changing educational standards, indicate a need for more systematic delineation of library and documentation services there. All nations, rich and poor, are becoming increasingly subject to both economic and environmental pressures as they move toward realization of their national objectives, and all are growing more aware of the need to systematize the handling of information to avoid wasteful duplication of costly services. In the introductory section of the report prepared for the Organisation for Economic Co-operation and Development, 1971,[3] the subject of effective use of information services is discussed in this fashion:

The wise man does not act without attempting to know the consequences of his actions. Contemporary societies must be more prudent in their actions if technology is to be a boon rather than a curse for mankind. Information is the key to the wise management of our future. . . .

The organized processing and exchange of information has reached a peak of sophistication in certain fields of professional specialization. The logical structure and basic language of science is designed to facilitate the organization and creative use of technical information. Great progress in this direction has also been made in the social sciences. Contemporary technology for information handling now permits more efficient storage, retrieval, and exchange of information between specialists. But the challenge of modern societies is the effective use of such specialized information to guide the destiny of these societies.

Although the problems that confront librarianship, and that hence affect its incorporation into schemes for national development, differ in both nature and solution when we consider the developing and advanced regions of the world, they need to be examined in juxtaposition because the international transfer of materials and information is growing increasingly frequent. All types of information packages are being exchanged across international borders as governments, international organizations, and institutions require them: books, manuscripts, survey and experimental data in both the social sciences and technology (some of it processed data, some of it raw), scientific research information in the form of journals, technical reports, and partially processed statistics.

The international character of large-scale information transfer is of quite recent vintage, but two of the annual conferences held by the American Society for Information Science (ASIS) in the 1970s have focused on this topic.[4] In the introductory statement to the session pertaining to "International Systems under Development," at the 1972 conference, Carol A. Johnson pointed out that:

The development and operation of truly international documentation and information systems now are possible thanks to several recent developments. Among these are: (1) the growing acceptance of English as *the* international language; (2) the wide distribution and use of compatible computer and communication equipment; and (3) the increasing effectiveness of cooperation through international political bodies such as agencies of the United Nations.[5]

The links allowing transfer of information between nations are now primarily mechanized systems, and, in the field of scientific literature at least, it may soon be impossible for any nation to expect access to current bibliographic and information data bases except through access to automated information systems—the kind of specialized exchange referred to in the introductory statement of the Ad Hoc Group on Scientific and Technical Information already quoted.

Consideration of library and information services as part of the national development plan must be carried out at differing levels for the developing and the more advanced nations. In the latter, library and information services are already well established, some by governments, some controlled by the "private sector," and such national planning needs to work toward coalescing the already existing systems and services into a unified whole which will serve the national interest and make the adjustments that changing demands and conditions warrant. In the advanced countries we find public libraries linked, at the very least for interlibrary borrowing, into regional systems, and academic libraries moving toward the establishment of state or inter-state networks, linked by one or more of the following: telephone, telex, or computerized, cooperative, cataloging networks.

In the developing countries, the planning to include library and information services in the national scheme for development must often start with a consideration of how to establish the basic level of these services. Developing countries have one advantage over more advanced nations; by decreeing that library and information services are national resources, to be used to unify and develop the nation and to assist it in the field of international technology, they can avoid a proliferation of services in both the public and the private sectors. Library and information services can be placed entirely in the hands of government departments, much as educational systems are.

While there is not yet an abundance of literature on national planning of library services which can be consulted by librarians or others, some of the most useful works, at least for the developing nations, have appeared as the result of Unesco action. The International Institute for Educational Planning, a Unesco agency, has made it a policy to include, as part of its internship program, a seminar on the national planning of library and documentation services.[6]

When one assumes that library and information services must be considered in overall national planning, one must then work out a methodology that will facilitate this action. The concept of the library and information service functioning as a national resource, and therefore to be considered as a part of national development schemes, is a concept that requires definition, both within the literature of librarianship and as a concept to be offered to the laymen in charge of the governments. C. V. Penna has suggested using the definition of "planning" developed from the Ibero-American Seminar on Planning and Documentation Services, otherwise known as the Madrid Seminar, held in 1968.

> The planning of library and documentation services is regarded as one specific aspect of educational, scientific, and cultural planning within the social and economic planning of a country or

region, for only within this context can library and documentation planning acquire the foundations of support which it needs if
it is to be effective. Regarded in that way, planning of library
services requires a continuous systematized process of studying
educational problems at all levels, including adult education and
the problems of scientific research from the standpoint of library
needs; it also involves determining the aims of library services,
setting targets for attaining those aims and preparing realistic
decisions to ensure that the objectives will be reached through the
rational and reasonable use of available resources.[7]

In the terminology of the social sciences, planning on a national scale
occurs in one of two ways: macro-planning and micro-planning. Macro-
planning is the simultaneous consideration of all the combined educational,
social, and economic needs of the country and the available resources to
satisfy them, along with planning to help the nation achieve its full potential
on the international scene. In macro-planning the needs, problems, and
resources are parts of an interlocking whole. If political or economic
conditions make macro-planning impossible or inadvisable, it may be
necessary to proceed first with individual areas of the country, or units within
a system, working on the level of micro-planning. Ideally, for the national
system, macro-planning is better, but where resources are limited one may
begin with smaller units, hoping that ultimately the parts can be locked into a
unified, coherent whole. Whichever path a nation follows, all national
development schemes must be worked out in the light of the local situation
and the conditions that exist in that place and time.

Library and information services are international activities as well as
national, regional, and local ones, and if the activities involved in the
international transfer of information take on international characteristics,
then surely the discipline of librarianship must too. We need to recognize
international librarianship as a specific sub-field within the discipline, one
considering the various factors influencing the profession's development in
different regions of the world, partly comparing situations and perhaps
offering solutions based on the experience of others, and also providing a
method of collecting information on current library conditions and problems
which might serve as a basis for future international cooperation. Library
science, like some of its fellow social sciences which have taken more
emphatic shape since World War II, is now a discipline in search of an
underlying philosophy and methodology. By viewing some of the situations
facing those trying to work library service into the framework of planning for
national development, we may be able to suggest some general, basic,
methodological principles for the discipline.

THE NATURE OF THE PROBLEMS
FACING LIBRARY SERVICE IN DEVELOPING COUNTRIES

Between 1951 and 1956 Unesco organized three seminars dealing with problems of public library service in developing countries. Each focused on an entire continent, the three continents where the greater number of the developing countries exist.[8] Although the reports of all the Unesco seminars refer to "public libraries" in their titles, the discussions were not entirely confined to these libraries but dealt generally with the potential role of library services in helping to realize national needs and objectives for economic and social development.

It was stated above that one of the major problems faced by most developing states as they struggle to modernize is the high proportion of illiterates in their populations. Not only are there high percentages of adult illiterates, but in many instances, despite formidably mounted government schemes, universal primary education through ages twelve to fourteen has yet to be achieved. Money for schools, teachers, and materials has been hard to find; wars have disrupted entire populations (to say nothing of their economies); political systems are often unstable and subject to frequent change; populations are scattered over rugged terrain, and separating children from their families to attend regional boarding schools works undue hardship on the family's social and economic pattern.

High levels of illiteracy and the consequent lack of library traditions force the close linkage of the library and library services with educational planning in developing countries. The materials that libraries traditionally collect—books, pamphlets, films, and other such items—are both indispensable tools of education and tools for the dissemination of information necessary for advances in such areas as hygiene, farming methods, and vocational and technical training.

Such a linking of library services with the educational function raises two questions: what is the real nature of a library under such circumstances, and where ought the library to be located? If the library's stock of materials, in a newly literate society, is to be primarily devoted to providing the populace with the information that will allow them to improve their socioeconomic conditions, perhaps the role of the library's personnel, at least in the beginning, will be as much educational as oriented towards the Western concept of the librarian's service function. In many parts of the developing world the transfer of information—historical, technical, and social—has depended almost exclusively on the oral tradition, combined with a rudimentary form of numerical record-keeping. Even those who have achieved some considerable degree of literacy will need help in the actual handling of library materials and in the comprehension of their contents. In these circumstances the librarian's role will encompass both teaching and interpretation, functions considered in the Western world as being reserved for teachers, and these must be combined with the traditional library functions of acquiring, organizing, and disseminating the materials.

If one admits the educational function as part of the role of the library and the librarian, then some thought must be given to the location of the library, particularly when it is being introduced to the community. Many of the developing countries do possess at least a limited library tradition: in the Arab states those leaders who hark back to the glorious past of the Islamic Empire speak proudly, and with justification, of the library collections held in its mosques and religious schools; in the early nineteenth century public libraries were established in Buenos Aires (1810) and Lima (1820), and were later converted into national libraries for their respective countries;[9] those former colonial states, such as India, which had developed educational systems past the secondary school level, had libraries attached to universities. In all these cases, however, the implication was that the libraries were reserved for the scholarly minorities, and the nature of the collection was determined by whatever such groups might care to study. The library tradition that did exist then, indicated that libraries and library service were intended for the exclusive use of the privileged few. If the patterns of library building in Britain and North America are introduced in the developing countries, making the library a separate building in the towns and villages where it appears, not only will the costs of library operations rise, but the populace will likely be slower to accept the new, somewhat isolated service, and to avail themselves of it.[10] The adults and children living outside of the major urban centers in the developing countries associate reading and the use of such library materials as pictures, films, and pamphlets, with adult literacy classes or with the schools. Since most are still only in the learning stages of using these tools, it would seem logical to keep the tools and the training system together. From both the practical and financial standpoint, placing the library in a section of the school building would seem to make maximum utilization of its facilities more likely.

This creates a staffing problem, since economic considerations will probably dictate that only one person can be hired to staff the library. It must be decided whether the library should be staffed by someone whose training is better suited to the library's educational function, or someone who has been trained in the professional program for librarianship. For a considerable portion of the library's early period of existence, the librarian may be required to do some regular teaching, perhaps of the type that more advanced societies associate with continuing education courses.

The question to be addressed in these circumstances is whether or not one regards the library as an educational institution in the formal sense of the word. Historically, this had been the case in the Anglo-American world, particularly in Great Britain, where William Ewart and his supporters trying for the passage of The Public Libraries Act argued for the educational goals of libraries.[11] Through the use of libraries the working classes could achieve self-improvement, both in the trades and in moral virtues. They would read to upgrade their skills, and the uplifting literature available would keep them from such vices as drinking and gambling. Early efforts for public library legislation in the United States did not, perhaps, stress the educational facet of the library as strongly as the British had done, but the same spirit of adult self-education permeated the American continent in the nineteenth century. Lyceums and literary circles were followed by the Chautauqua movement, and it in turn was superseded by the adult education movement and the interest in the "Great Books." In both the United States and Canada early in the twentieth century, public libraries sought to develop their professional identity by establishing patterns of community service.

We find, then, historical precedent in the Anglo-American library traditions for the argument that the library is an educational institution,[1][2] but the precedents are not congruent matches for the situations in the newly literate developing countries. The nineteenth century saw substantial literate populations in both Europe and North America; while, at least in North American circles, there may have been some discussion about the interpretive educational function of the librarian (this was certainly true of the early years of the twentieth century), this function was rarely seen in terms of assistance to the newly literate. It was more likely to have been discussed in terms of the differing literacy requirements of the immigrants who needed to learn English. If, by locating their libraries in the schools, the developing countries emphasize the formal teaching function of the librarians, we might in turn postulate that the librarians' formal training should encompass training in both disciplines—education and library science.

Another major problem facing library service in developing countries—a problem that also arises from the high levels of illiteracy—is that of finding adequate supplies of material in the languages, and at the level of difficulty, that the local readers can use. In many parts of the developing world there has been widespread use of two major world languages for business, government affairs, and post-secondary education. These are the languages of two of the former colonial powers, English and French. Despite the fact that these languages are used at the upper levels of society for certain types of business, they are by no means the languages of the majority of the populace. In South Asia alone we can find twenty-three major literary languages with an almost incalculable number of potential readers for each. The cost of producing reading materials in the various native languages is very high, since it would take time to build up to a situation where there might be high-volume sales. Only in the Arabic-speaking states have there been long-established publishing systems publishing in the local languages and using the non-Roman script, but there has nowhere been any tradition of publishing materials in any language for the newly literate adult. A recent study of one developing region, anglophone middle Africa, reported that:

> the vast majority of titles published are in English, with the notable exceptions of: lower primary schoolbooks, much of the literacy learning and followup materials, handbooks for the marginal and traditional sectors, and some popular and classical literature. English has become, through the education system, the first reading and writing language of the book buyers in the modern sector. This results in rural populations' being denied access to this influential material and being further limited, if not

by illiteracy, then by the small volume of publishing in vernacular language, which is itself limited by poor rural distribution and small readerships.[13]

One might expect that Africans and other writers in the countries of the Third World would be concerned to write for, and to, their fellow countrymen, and hence in languages their compatriots would understand; however, the majority of writers from the African intellectual community publish outside Africa—in Britain, the United States, and France. In part, publishing abroad is a matter of prestige, in part it is a function of the minuscule African market for non-fiction and scholarly works. Writers publishing abroad find that their choice of topic and their writing styles tend to be influenced by the demands of the foreign market, which wants material on African affairs for its own educational and research purposes. Even African writers of fiction aimed at a local market find themselves, to a certain extent, dependent on such Western publishing houses as Heinemann Educational Books, publishers of the "African Writers Series," Macmillan and Company, and the Oxford University Press. Some local publishers handle African fiction and include some self-study items among their wares,[14] but most materials available for educational purposes, whether in English or in the vernacular languages, are handled by multinational firms with head offices in Britain.[15] Some foreign texts, especially in mathematics and elementary science, could be easily adapted and/or translated locally for use by the newly literate in the appropriate vernacular, but the multinational firms have tremendous economic advantages in publishing, since their capital allows them to wait out the period needed to recover printing costs through domestic sales.

If libraries are to perform fully their functions in the newly literate rural and village centers, and particularly their educational function, they must be able to offer their clientele indigenous materials; several black African states now do have state-owned publishing houses in operation. These list from 100 to 400 titles as being available at any one time.[16] The books, development oriented, are intended for both primary education and continuing adult education, and more than half of the titles are in the vernacular.

Perhaps because of the high capital investment required to open new printing firms, perhaps because the educated civil service consider the items offered by the multinational publishing houses for world distribution to be nearly all the reading materials they require, the development of indigenous publishing in many of the developing countries has not been considered when determining overall development plans. If left unchanged, this situation bodes ill for the rapid eradication of illiteracy since it lessens the chances of the newly literate receiving library materials geared to their reading levels and their specific needs.

Multinational publishers have not diversified substantially from their home-based function of publishing books for formal education, thereby reinforcing habits of identifying books with education and school, to the detriment of informal and non-formal education and leisure reading. They have, for example, not invested heavily in literacy followup material or books for the young, even though such items are most vital to widening the reading habit, increasing the size of the book market, and fostering widespread development. The multinationals have neglected literacy and young peoples' materials because illiteracy and linguistic fragmentation mean short print runs, and lack of profits, because the purchasing power of the potential readers is low or absent, and partly because concentration on formal educational and up-market publishing serves both the elites' and the multinational publishers' short-term interests.[17]

Library service in developing states is not confined to working on the problem of eradicating illiteracy or supplying continuing education materials. Most such countries have at least one national university, many have several, and library services are found there as well. Since a major concern of these universities is the training of qualified professionals to assist in the modernization of the country's economic and industrial potential so that it can function on the international scene, the libraries attached to them are concerned to develop research collections just as academic libraries in the more advanced nations are. The materials for research will have to be imported, mostly from publishers and data banks in the more advanced countries, and they will have to be paid for in "hard currency,"[18] a commodity usually in short supply in the developing states. Not only may the librarians experience considerable difficulty in securing a share of the country's limited supply of hard currency to spend on buying books and journals, but, having been granted the right to a certain share of it, they must then struggle with yards of sticky red tape trying to secure the permits that allow them to place the orders abroad and, later, those that allow them to clear the incoming books through customs.[19]

Developing states often cannot determine very far in advance how much hard currency will be available to them in any given year. This makes it difficult for them to assure any single component of the national develop-ment scheme a definite on-going allotment of foreign currency. This situation wreaks havoc with library ordering and bill-paying. From the latter standpoint serials are particularly affected, since dealers often demand payment for these orders in advance to provide protection for themselves against extended delays in payment. In one country, Sri Lanka, an entire year's subscription to serials was lost to the country's libraries in 1973 because the authorities would not release the hard currency to allow the libraries to pay the suppliers' *pro forma* invoices.[20] Saving both staff time and some of the budget by placing standing orders for subscription library materials is a luxury that many libraries in developing countries cannot avail themselves of.

An additional drain on the hard currency available to such libraries is caused by their having to pay handling costs for materials. The postal and shipping costs, usually figured into the total invoice, are charges that reflect the distance of the developing world libraries from the source of the materials. If they opt for the lower charges of surface mail, they must wait much longer than Western Europe or North America for their purchases; on the other hand, if they ask for airmail subscriptions to assuage the demands of their patrons—for example, in the case of scientific journals, which it is important to read before the contents are superseded—the cost of the individual journals may nearly double. Such added charges cut down the number of subscriptions these university libraries may receive, and the quality of their service is thereby diminished.

Problems of foreign payments, and bureaucratic impedimenta placed in the way of library orders (even to the point of requiring libraries to give the business to local booksellers rather than allowing them to order directly from the publishing source) make it very difficult for many libraries in Third World countries to provide the basic research facilities their countries need on any regular basis. Whether or not a coherent statement of the place of library service in the national plan actually exists, some university libraries also double as "national libraries," and all of them are subject to government controls. Thus, it would seem reasonable that one way for the libraries to improve their research capacities with minimal financial outlay would be to allow them to offer their own country's publications to institutions abroad in exchange for titles they cannot afford to buy at home. Since the local publishing firms that do exist in these countries are usually government controlled and often government sponsored, acquisition of materials by one "government department" from another such department should be a routine procedure. But the local publishing firms are rarely large, and their priorities for publication must often be given to government documents. While these items may be of interest to foreign research and government libraries as exchange items, another economic factor plays an inhibiting role here. Printing costs are high and are steadily rising as the cost of high quality paper escalates. The fact that such paper must usually be imported (and the hard currency problem arises again here) means that documents may be printed in limited quantities. Local academic libraries will therefore receive few, if any, national publications for exchange purposes. They could conceivably acquire them by purchasing the documents themselves, and they could then mail them to their exchange partners. Thus a substantial portion of the local library budget might be spent on buying multiple copies of indigenous publications and on paying the postal costs of mailing them abroad. Since funds allotted to the libraries are rarely increased in total amount, and certainly not in proportion to the rate at which book and journal prices are raised, the serials budget, no matter where it is spent, will eventually come to constitute the bulk of purchase allocations, cutting drastically into funds available for buying books and microforms. This again leads to a forced reduction in the level of service the research library in the developing state can offer.

The exchange method for acquiring foreign periodicals is further complicated by another factor: printing paper is not only costly, it is often scarce, and this scarcity delays the production of domestic publications. When paper is scarce, priority is given to essential government printing jobs, in sufficient quantity for local use only, and any additional printing must wait. Libraries in developing countries cannot guarantee their exchange partners a prompt and consistent flow of materials, whether these are government documents, university publications, or other items.

Even assuming an abundant supply of printing paper and a steady, guaranteed flow of publications within a developing nation, its research libraries may still encounter difficulties in offering exchange lists, since one can only offer those titles to which one has access and of which one has knowledge. In most of the Asian and African states, nationwide distribution schemes for publications have yet to be developed, and often the trade bibliographical lists of current publications are not distributed throughout the country, if they are even compiled at all.[21] Such bibliographical tools as are published in Europe and North America are primarily national and trade bibliographies for these regions, and they rarely cover more than a few Western language publications from the Third World. The *African Books in Print* project being developed at the University of Ife Press in Nigeria[22] is designed to provide a buying guide and index to in-print materials (excluding serials), compiled on the basis of information supplied by publishers. While Zell urges its importance as a buying tool for librarians in Africa and elsewhere, he also admits that the response from the 600 publishers, institutions, and organizations contacted was far from total, and that both governmental and francophonic publishers seemed remarkably reluctant to contribute lists of available titles. In Asia, the state of bibliographic coverage, with the appropriate tools, ranges from that of Afghanistan, where such tools are non-existent in any form, to multi-lingual nations like India and Pakistan, where there are some trade catalogs, actual national bibliographies prepared and published, and the *Accessions Lists* issued by the American Libraries Book Procurement Center of the Library of Congress. The national and trade bibliographies in these countries appear irregularly, and there is a considerable time-lag between the publication of the material and its listing in the bibliography; the *Accessions Lists*, the chief bibliographical tools of the PL-480 Program,[23] are quite selective in content. Even keeping informed of the publications coming from within their own countries creates a major problem for the research libraries in the developing countries.

Although the exchange system does allow libraries in the Third World a better chance of keeping up with current journal publications, it does little to alleviate the problems that arise when a library tries to establish a retrospective collection of research journals. A quick perusal of dealers' catalogs will indicate how costly such backruns can be on the open market. In the light of their currency shortages libraries in developing countries can acquire such research materials only by ordering them when they are listed for free distribution by foreign institutions and national and international agencies.[24] The recipients of such free acquisitions must still reimburse the sender's postal and shipping costs, and local post offices often create problems when they are faced with substantial demands for international reply postal coupons.[25]

Outright gifts of both subscriptions and runs of journals are valuable additions to library collections, but they are of greatest value if they are made after consultation with the recipients, and if they are made on a regular basis. If overseas libraries were to establish a regular pattern of donating their discarded bibliographical tools (such as interim cumulations of the *National Union Catalog* or the *British National Bibliography*), and perhaps form a cooperative organization to do so, some of the processing chores faced by the new research libraries would be facilitated. Regular consignments of such tools to the countries of the Third World would also promote common bibliographic standards, which would facilitate quicker understanding of specific international bibliographic requests.

Developing library services at either the macro- or micro-level in many parts of the Third World are faced with some very definite problems, due in part to local constraints and conditions—from petty bureaucracy to currency and paper shortages—and also due in part to the geographic separation from the publication centers of both library materials and bibliographical tools. Some of the problems facing librarianship in the Third World are similar to problems in more developed nations; since many Asian and African library students take professional training in Anglo-American schools, it seems reasonable to consider the similarities and differences in the problems facing the two sectors, in order to reach an understanding of how library and information services can be incorporated most expeditiously into national planning.

THE SITUATION IN THE DEVELOPED, INDUSTRIALIZED WORLD

By contrast to the Asian and African situation, the nations of Europe and North America have both high levels of literacy and long records of library tradition. Owners of large private libraries willed their books and manuscripts to form the nuclei of collections at the universities of Oxford and Paris,[26] and the major collections housed in the Bibliothèque Nationale and the British Museum date from the fifteenth and eighteenth centuries, respectively. Research collections, even though small, were part of the facilities available to the Fellows of the Royal Society from its inception in the seventeenth century, and scientific societies on the European continent had similar resources to rely on. The scientific societies also published papers and transactions, many of which they exchanged with each other, and scientists visiting abroad were often made honorary members of each other's societies. The tradition and skills of bibliography are also long established on these continents, going back to the manuscript era when Jerome and Cassiodorus, in their respective monastic retreats, concerned themselves with textual bibliography. There is general agreement that modern bibliography began under the aegis of Johann Tritheim, twenty-fifth abbot of Sponheim, who was elected to office in 1483.[27] The concept of universal bibliography appeared in the sixteenth century when Konrad Gesner, working in Switzerland, published his *Bibliotheca Universalis* (1545). The library tradition was well established in the United States before the American Revolution, and private collectors were also in the habit of bequeathing their libraries for the use of others. One Captain Keayne (d. 1655/56) bequeathed his collection to the town of Boston.[28] Thomas Bray's parish libraries and the individual town collections of the seventeenth and early eighteenth centuries, as well as the social libraries of the eighteenth century, offer ample testimony to the persistence of a library tradition from the colonial period to the present.

Since the seventeenth century the industrialized world has developed library and information services for nearly every level and interest of society: school libraries, public libraries, state and provincial libraries, legislative libraries, university and research libraries, special libraries of every type from legal to industrial, and, at the other end of the spectrum, major national collections such as are encompassed in the National Library of Medicine and the National Agricultural Library in the United States, the National Library and the National Science Library in Canada, the British National Library, and many others.

Despite the longer tradition of library service found in the technologically developed states, there was no concurrent growth of the idea that the libraries and the information contained in their collections should either be viewed as major resources or really seriously considered in national planning. There was a major exception to this state of affairs. Andrew Aines points out that:

> With the exception of Communist governments, countries did not pay too much attention to scientific and technical information. Scientists from the days of the royal societies onward have been deeply concerned about the flow of information, but, in truth, with few exceptions, centered their interest on scientific meetings and scientific publication. The "invisible collegium" was enshrined along with the primary journal, the cornucopia for individual recognition and progress. When publication began to grow, professional societies recognized and supported secondary publications to provide for better housekeeping. When the economics of publishing got out of hand, the government provided subsidies in the form of page charges and funds from R&D coffers to help professional society secondary services mechanize their services.[29]

Not until the 1950s and 1960s did Western governments follow the lead of the communist regimes and become involved with scientific and technical information programs, and not until the 1960s did the idea of national planning of information systems achieve true respectability in the West. Early in 1969 the Organisation for Economic Co-operation and Development set up the Ad Hoc Group on Scientific and Technical Information under the chairmanship of Pierre Piganiol. This Ad Hoc Group was expected to:

a)   explore the nature, magnitude and implications of the needs for scientific and technical information and data in science, the economy and society, and how these needs may be met through changes in the structures, technologies and policies and management concepts in relation to information;

b)   present their conclusions and recommendations for the developing role of scientific and technical information and data systems and the policy and programme resources required for them to fill this role effectively in Member countries.[30]

The Ad Hoc Group presented its report to the Secretary-General of OECD in September of 1970, a report that recommended the establishment of goals for a national policy on scientific and technical information. Piganiol pointed out in an accompanying letter to the Secretary-General that:

> The problem of scientific and technical information seems to be closely linked with economic growth from two different points of view. On the one hand, the diffusion of information throughout the scientific and technical community facilitates effective progress in research and development; on the other, information transfer offers industrial management the chance of taking optimal production decisions on a sound basis.
>
> ... Development should be coherent, and in consequence those responsible for macro-economic decisions require clear information not only on what is happening now, but on what is likely to happen later.[31]

In the year following the creation of the Ad Hoc Group, a special commission with similar responsibilities was created in the United States. The National Commission on Libraries and Information Science (NCLIS) was formed and given the responsibility of providing advice to the President and to Congress on the implementation of a national policy for library and information needs. It, too, was expected to provide a program of goals for a national policy that might lead to the establishment of a national library network. Some of its suggestions and recommendations will be described below.

The general tenor of activity on the North American library scene has been quite the reverse of a pattern that might establish a national library network, although several smaller types of network have been created. North American librarianship has spawned a diversity of special interests, and consequently there have been specialized efforts to solve problems of particular libraries, or particular types of library, often without much reference to more than the specialized needs of their immediate clientele. Certainly some of the philosophy developed in North American librarianship has concerned itself with the national scene, but it is chiefly among the academic research libraries that cooperative, national philosophy has been converted into action.

Although the public library has a long-established place on the North American scene, the economic recession of the 1970s and the consequent shortage of funds and donations has, to a certain extent, forced it to rethink and re-assert its role in the community, to ensure that it continues to receive the funds it needs for both staff and materials. In the developing world the public library is a new phenomenon except in the major urban centers; because it is moving into a newly literate society, it must give considerable thought as to whether it can function best if it labels itself as an educational institution. In North America the public library, styled as a form of "public utility," is, in trying to work out its role in the community, scrutinizing carefully the part it can play in the inner-city, low-income areas of the cities, in the areas housing large numbers of non-English-speaking immigrants, and in the rural sections of the country. At least in the first two instances the focal point around which it may have to develop services is illiteracy—not precisely the same form of illiteracy that faces the public library in the Third World, where there has long been reliance on the oral tradition and where books and writing are "foreign objects," but the illiteracy that shows in the abysmally low scores on standardized reading tests given in crowded ghetto schools. The immigrant, too, is illiterate in the language he needs to allow him a better job, to become a citizen, or to take advantage of the many social services his new country can offer. Both in Western Europe and in North America librarians continue to debate the issue of the educational function of the library and its personnel, not so much in terms of whether this role ought to exist, but in terms of how the public library can both provide educational facilities for those of its clientele, real or potential, who may need them, and also provide recreational and other aspects of public service as well. Along with making meeting rooms available for use by community groups, sponsoring film showings, programs for senior citizens and handicrafts groups, some public libraries style themselves as community information centers or house such facilities under their roof.

Librarians in the Anglo-American world perhaps debate the question of the library's educational function more strongly because they traditionally have held the view that an educational institution is involved with formal instruction; while they recognized that the library's materials could be used for self-instruction and continuing education, they were not altogether ready to admit the teaching function of the librarian. Viewing the library as an "informal educational institution" makes it very difficult to make specific statements about the educational function of the librarian. Perhaps even in the developed parts of the world we have not yet established sufficient evidence as to the exact nature of the communication patterns that constitute the learning process. There are, among the public librarians, some who would argue that, until the full nature of the learning process is understood, the public library should confine its efforts to acquiring, organizing, and disseminating all the materials that society requires, assuming only that these requirements meet a minimum level of social acceptability, and not take the initiative in informing or even guiding the community.[32]

In some few areas of the Western world public libraries face a problem similar to that found in the developing countries—the problem of obtaining indigenous publications from national writers. It is not so much that the libraries do not know what has been published, nor that the national writers write in a foreign language; it is more a problem of whether the writers are able to get published at all. Certainly in the United States, Great Britain, France, Germany, and the U.S.S.R. there are well-developed publishing industries, handling both national and foreign authors' works (although in the U.S.S.R. one does have to be "approved" to be published), and libraries in these countries have no trouble acquiring the output of national writing and thought. In Canada, however—a much smaller country in terms of population—there is some question of whether or not a national publishing industry is a viable economic operation, and whether it can, even though it attempts to publish Canadian writers, compete in the marketplace with the multinational concerns and their international array of authors. Without a national publishing industry, unknown authors often find it difficult to manage their first publication; the respective Canadian associations of publishers and authors have been concerned to impress upon both Canadian libraries and the Canadian government that Canadian publishing should be subsidized, if necessary, in order to ensure libraries and the public a steady supply of Canadian materials. The "battle" was carried, with some considerable success, into the realm of periodical publishing: the Canadian government was persuaded to remove the status of tax benefit when Canadian firms advertise in journals published and sold in Canada by foreign-controlled publishers. If the Canadian content level of these publications falls below the 80 percent level, the Canadian advertisers cannot claim their advertisements for tax deductions.

Although it has been suggested that the public library's underlying philosophy is being subjected to some serious rethinking to determine how its role in community service may be better charted, this is not to be taken as an indication that public libraries have been functioning in splendid isolation as they review their problems. Certainly there has been cooperative activity among them on various levels; we have seen the formation of large metropolitan library systems, multicounty systems, and programs for statewide cooperation. There have also been some efforts at interlocking with the offices of the United States government, although not for the purposes of working out a national plan. The government's library programs have been administered through the Office of Education's Library Programs Division, housing four major programs: Library Research and Demonstration; State and Public Library Services; Library Education and Postsecondary Resources; and the School Media Resources Branch. There is a newly created executive office, the Office of Libraries and Learning Resources (OLLR), charged with controlling the funds these programs administer. Its main purpose is to "effect better coordination and utilization of the Nation's libraries and instructional resources; enhance learning; and improve information services for children, college students, and adults."[33] Through the program dealing with state and public library services, grants are allotted to the individual states by formula with the hope that the management of public library programs at the state level can be improved, especially in such areas as library building, and reader services to special groups in the community.

The larger academic research libraries in the United States realized the need for some form of national action in the early 1940s; World War II was threatening the very existence of the great scholarly collections in European libraries, as well as removing from the lives of North American scholars the opportunity for travel to Europe for research purposes. If the clientele of these libraries was to be provided with the means of continuing research at an advanced level, it would be necessary to expand considerably the collections already in American universities, and it was seen that this might involve cut-throat competition among university libraries as they competed for some of the more rare and expensive materials scholarly research would need.

In 1932, some of the major research libraries formed an interlibrary organization, the Association of Research Libraries. This organization, which is still functioning actively, is now composed of ninety-nine members representing the most prestigious collections in North America. While its membership consists chiefly of academic libraries, a few federal and public research institutions also belong. The ARL faced the problem of expanding collections by adopting a plan that contained a "proposal for a division of responsibility among American libraries in the acquisition and recording of library materials."[34] The plan was named the Farmington Plan since it was devised during an October meeting at Farmington, Connecticut, 1942. The project was developed initially through the Executive Committee of the Librarian's Council of the Library of Congress, and it was given its name when the ARL took it over in 1944.

The Farmington Plan began with two distinct facets: "one, the use of subject responsibilities for the acquisition of publications from Western Europe, Australia, Mexico, and South Africa; two, country-wide responsibilities, especially for countries with a poorly organized book trade or with languages not commonly handled within the majority of American institutions. The Plan itself was intended to be world-wide in scope, but its early years focussed on Western Europe."[35] Because the Farmington Plan did continue to focus on acquiring materials from Europe, it became necessary to establish new cooperative systems to obtain materials from other areas, particularly to support the area studies programs which sprang up on university campuses across North America in the 1950s. The Middle East, the Far East, South Asia, Africa, and Latin America attracted the attention of those scholars doing research in both the social sciences and the humanistic disciplines, and there was considerable demand for both historical and current materials. Additional cooperation and planning became necessary. While the ARL played a major role in these areas, it needed, and received, assistance from both the United States Congress and the Library of Congress to secure quantities of material from the Third World. That assistance from the Congress was provided is a reflection of government realization in the 1950s and 1960s that substantial collections of foreign materials in the major research libraries were important to the national interest.

Congress passed the Agricultural Trade Development and Assistance Act in 1954, an Act which allowed surplus agricultural products to be sold abroad for payment in local (rather than "hard") currencies. Since the local currencies could not be used outside their respective countries, they remained there to be spent as and when necessary on projects, or for items, approved by that country. This Act of Congress was entitled Public Law 480, and in 1958 it was amended through the efforts of Congressman John Dingell to, among other things, authorize the Library of Congress to use the surplus funds available in several of these countries to acquire "books, periodicals, and other materials" for deposit "in libraries and research centers in the United States specializing in the area to which they relate."[36] The costs of binding, processing, cataloging, and even repairing and translating were also to be paid out of these payments for surplus food. While the amendment passed in 1958, it was not until fiscal year 1962 that Congress actually approved the declaration of the funds overseas as surplus and then proceeded to authorize the Library of Congress to begin overseeing an experimental program to bring books and journals from overseas to the research libraries of North America. The libraries that agreed to join in the experiment were to pay into a central fund the sum of $500.00 for each country from which they wished to receive books. In exchange for this payment they would each receive, as far as possible, all the current research publications from the country chosen. The first three countries selected for the experiment were the United Arab Republic, India, and Pakistan. Six additional countries were added later: Indonesia (1963), Israel (1964), Nepal and Sri Lanka (1966), Yugoslavia (1967), and Poland (1972). Some of these programs have now been terminated—notably Indonesia (1969), Yugoslavia (1972), and Sri Lanka (1973). As many as twenty-five research libraries were involved in the acquisitions programs bringing books from the United Arab Republic and from Israel. Local procurement centers were established in each country to handle purchasing, processing, shipping, etc.; while they were selecting the books and journals, the staff at each of these centers also prepared *Accessions Lists* for monthly distribution to the participating research libraries. These *PL-480 Accessions Lists* have become valuable bibliographical tools for current publications both in the nations where they are prepared, since their own national bibliographies are either non-existent or appear hopelessly late, and in libraries in the West. While they are certainly not complete lists of all current publishing, they do cover most of the monographs, serials, and documents that would be of use to research collections. The *Accessions Lists* present each item in a bibliographical format that conforms to the Library of Congress standards for preparing cataloging entries, so the materials can be processed quite rapidly when they are received

Cooperation among research libraries is not limited to the North American scene. The Europeans have made some international arrangements as well. In 1971 the Ligue des Bibliothèques Européennes de Recherche (LIBER) was established. An international, non-governmental organization, its aim is to establish "close collaboration between the general research libraries of Western Europe, particularly national and university libraries, and in particular to help in finding practical ways of improving the quality of service these libraries provide."[37] LIBER too, has set up subgroups to concentrate on different regions of the world, with the intention, it appears, of fostering cooperative programs for the acquisition and processing of materials for European libraries.

Increasing amounts of material, increasing user demands, and decreasing amounts of available funds are all factors that have combined to push Anglo-American libraries into closer cooperation in order to provide maximum service to their patrons. We can find, as was observed earlier, metropolitan library systems, and regional and statewide systems; but we also find, looking at library organization, increasing reference to the term "network," sometimes referring to libraries and sometimes referring to information. It is necessary, then, to examine the term as it relates to library service.

LIBRARY AND INFORMATION NETWORKS

The term "network" has existed as a part of the English language since 1560, according to the *Oxford English Dictionary*, but its meaning has varied with the centuries. Not until 1658 was it used to signify "structures," and then only as found in plants or animals; it was only in the nineteenth century (1839) that it was used to denote a complex collection or system of things such as canals or rivers. By the mid-1970s it has become the "in" word with reference to libraries,[38] and at least five different contexts have been noted for its use, each with a different bearing on how problems of information transfer and handling were dealt with.[39] Overhage has identified the five different modes of usage and provided an actual example of each:[40]

Context	Example
1) Science literature	Citation-linked papers
2) Organization structures	ERIC clearinghouses
3) Cooperative arrangements	Interlibrary loan
4) Communications systems	Press wire services
5) Computer-commission systems	NASA RECON system

Overhage is primarily concerned with information networks and the transfer of information by electric signals in his article, but he does not state that this is the sole characteristic of the organization. An explanation of the term "network" that may be more comprehensible to librarians is that given by Elizabeth Miller, who defines the term as

... a cooperative system established by libraries and information centers which are brought together by a common subject, geographic proximity, or other common grounds, to share informational resources, human resources, equipment, technologies, and all other elements essential for providing effective information service.[41]

Certain characteristics have been determined to be essential to network organization:[42]

i) a network's function is to marshal resources from its environment to accomplish results beyond the ability of any one of its members;

ii) a network has developed an organizational design and structure that allows it to establish an identifiable domain and exercise appropriate influence over the members;

iii) it has a base in communication technology.

By way of amplifying the first of these, one might add that the goals of the network are clearly spelled out for and are understandable to the users of the system, and that the managers of the network are in agreement as to what these goals are.

It should be pointed out to the novice in the field that because of the various contexts in which the term "network" has been used there is still confusion over the distinction between library networks and information networks. Miller and Tighe view library networks as being a subset of information networks handling a particular kind of information transmitted for or by librarians,[43] and they would seem to agree with Launor Carter that an information network requires time-shared computer systems and a good, high-speed, high-data-rate communications system.[44] The general, basic properties around which network activities are organized are these:[45]

i) they have information resources;

ii) readers or users are usually remote from the main sources of information;

iii) schemes are used for the intellectual organization of documents or data;

iv) resources are delivered to readers or users;

v) there is a formal organization of cooperating or contracting information agencies for presenting different data bases and/or groups of users;

vi) there are bidirectional communications, preferably using high-speed, long-distance electrical signal transmission with switching capabilities and computer hookups.

The ultimate aim of the network is to provide the individual user with the materials he wants in the form, at the place, and at the time he requires them.

> The United States should work toward a time when the availability of knowledge will not be severely limited by the ability of certain individuals to pay for it, by the fortunes of geographical location, or by associational membership. Knowledge should be treated as a universe, and availability of knowledge should be considered in relation to the total needs of all the individuals and institutions which make up the nation.[46]

Networks are not spontaneously generated original organizations that are suddenly created out of nothing and planted in the world of librarianship; rather, they are built, over a period of time, on the foundations of already existing institutions. Nearly all professional societies that are concerned with producing, disseminating, or using information now have committees on networks. The foundations on which a network can be built often encompass more than one type of library. In 1959 the Association of College and Research Libraries, in adopting its standards for college libraries, included a statement urging the need for cooperation with the other library facilities within the community, to benefit both students and faculty, and also to benefit the community outside the campus. In June 1967 interlibrary co-ordination proponents received a major boost when the boards of directors of four ALA divisions, the Associations of Public, State, School, and College and Research Libraries, approved a joint statement outlining the urgent need for cooperation among libraries in the face of accelerating reader demands, spiralling costs of materials, and rising quantities of published materials. Urging the principle that libraries acting together could more efficiently satisfy their users, the joint statement set down some principles for meaningful interlibrary cooperation:[47]

i)   that primary responsibility for each type of library to its special clientele must be defined before interlibrary cooperation can be established to augment service;

ii) that effective cooperation depends upon adequate resources, administrative capability, and efficient communications;

iii) that although the primary responsibility of each library must be respected, each library must realize its responsibilities to the network and assume its appropriate share of responsibility;

iv) that all libraries must maintain an attitude of flexibility and experimentation.

Network planning and development in the United States has moved mainly along geographic lines as research libraries scramble to expand their services to their users; thus, we find such arrangements as NELINET (New England Library Network), RLG (Research Libraries Group–Harvard, Yale,

Columbia, and New York Public Library), the Association of Southeastern Regional Libraries, and OCLC (Ohio College Library Center). A primary consideration of the membership of these networks is resource sharing.[48] The resources may be materials or equipment, or they may be people, money, or time. Sharing library materials in a coordinated fashion means that some purchasing and processing costs are saved, and sharing equipment, especially the time-sharing of computer-based processing activity, avoids considerable duplication of effort, as in the shared-cataloging, remote catalog access system developed by OCLC.

Two examples of somewhat different types of network are MEDLINE, the nationally available literature search and retrieval system of the National Library of Medicine, and the Museum Computer Network (MCN). Through their access to MEDLINE, designated centers in the United States and Canada can request information from the data base at the National Library of Medicine. The data base covers the publications listed in the *Index Medicus*, and searchers using MEDLINE can request full bibliographic data concerning citations, or can do a complete search of the data base for all the material pertaining to a specific subject. Because of its widespread network of access points, several users can search the system simultaneously.

The Museum Computer Network was formed in 1967.[49] It began as a pilot project with the goal of examining the feasibility of a computerized catalog of the holdings of 15 museums in the New York area, most, but not all, of which were in the art field, and the holdings of the National Gallery in Washington. While some of the original participants have had to drop out of active participation in the project due to financial problems, the Museum of Modern Art cataloged its entire collection within the MCN system, and the Metropolitan Museum of Art managed to record a substantial amount of its own holdings as well. Such a network is of great help to those interested in preparing comprehensive exhibits, since one can expect to locate through the data base all items that might be borrowed to comprise such an exhibit.

Library and information networks operate within the framework of allowing the members access to a centralized data base. It is at this point, according to Carter, that people become very fussy when discussing networks; what kind of data base is best?[50] One type of data base provides the basic bibliographic information concerning the materials held by the network, so that one can request catalog cards, bibliographic lists by topic or author, or even specific publications by a specific person in a given year.

> But that for some purposes is not adequate. You may want the kinds of information you have in secondary sources. You may want to have indexes, abstracts, citations, etc., and so some kinds of data bases have that kind of information in them. But that may not be adequate. Maybe what you will want is full text, and you may want to have it transmitted very rapidly.[51]

This raises the question of copyright. Has one violated copyright by putting the full text into the computer data base, or is copyright violated only if and when the text is displayed on a cathode ray screen in answer to a user's request?

In the fields of science and technology, information held in individual data bases in a given country may well be demanded by those doing research in another country. At the beginning of this chapter it was mentioned that the development and operation of international information systems is now possible. But, although international computer networking can be managed almost as easily as the connecting of telephone hookups between different nations, it seems likely that national policies of the individual governments will have some considerable effect on international networking. Nations are likely to be increasingly concerned with controlling the flow of information across their borders, whether it is entering or leaving the country. Charles C. Joyce asks the question:

> Is it in the interest of the U.S. to encourage the greatest possible world access to its resources of scientific, technical, and commercial information? Is the scientific norm of maximum dissemination of research findings applicable to all types of U.S. knowledge, especially in view of substantial and growing importance of knowledge and information-based activities in the U.S. "post-industrial" economy?[52]

Should data processing and data banks be treated as national resources, to be shared only when a given government has decided to permit such sharing? If so, this would place the less developed nations even further away from a state of industrial development, since, if they must develop their own technological data information banks instead of sharing those already developed, they must count on spending far more time and money.

National policy with respect to the treatment of data banks and their contents is not the only obstacle to international networking. In Europe, where a European information network plan has been developed (EURO-NET), one has to contend not only with a multiplicity of national policies but also with a multiplicity of languages.

> The multiplicity of languages used in Europe is not only an obstacle to communication between the planners of cooperative systems and networks; it is above all an obstacle to the use of single-language data bases by scientists unfamiliar with the corresponding languages. This problem is the more difficult to solve as promotion of the national language is a matter of prestige in many a European country.[53]

Even the international exchange of bibliographic data from one national bibliographic network to another faces interchange problems, despite the agreed-upon International Standard Bibliographic Description. The MARC format developed by the Library of Congress varies somewhat from the MARC format used in Britain, and even more from the French

MONOCLE, which is used for the national bibliography in France. Someone in a fourth country attempting to design a national system of bibliography that would be able to draw upon data from the other three would have to develop yet a fourth program incorporating the variant MARC forms in it. Standardization of bibliographic entry and quality control of data bases are both problems which must be faced by those constructing networks and advocating their wider use. Miller and Tighe summarize their discussion of networks in this fashion:

> Because networks are believed to be the most viable means known now for distributing and manipulating data from diverse sources to dispersed users quickly and accurately and at a tolerable economic cost, they will probably continue to expand and multiply, and to merge and consolidate. There does not appear to be any significant technological barrier to their continued growth, and much research, though uncoordinated, is providing solutions to particular technological problems. Curiously, the barriers to growth appear to be social, political, and economical behavior—some of the same factors claimed as stimuli to network growth. ... At this point, the problems of how a network should operate, how it should be governed and supported, whom it should serve, and what services should be provided are not generally resolved. The phenomenon is too new, the alternatives are not fully explored, and there is a great diversity of approach. ...
>
> ... We see that networking is expensive, in that it requires drastic reallocation of scarce financial and human resources by many people and institutions. This reallocation takes the form of renewed interest in standardization and quality control, and of the introduction of skills not formally considered part of either librarianship or computer science. The development of this phenomenon appears to be at a crucial stage. Goals, mutually acceptable to individual institutions as well as networks, to network managers as well as users, and to private citizens and society at large must be identified.[54]

THE UNITED STATES BEGINS CONSIDERATION OF NATIONAL PLANNING

It was stated above that, despite the fairly long tradition of librarianship in the Anglo-American world, the idea of viewing it in relation to national planning has only appeared here quite recently. As national governments became more aware of the advantages to be gained from information technology, various information modules were developed both by divisions of government and by facets of the private sector; modules which could conceivably have been fitted together as components of a national system. Aines and Day[55] offer some examples of these modules, including the National Library of Medicine's Medical Literature Analysis and Retrieval System (MEDLARS), NASA's RECON system, the Department of Agriculture's Agricultural Sciences Information Network, and such commercial systems as those of Systems Development Corporation, Tymnet, Informatics, and bank and legal information systems. They also make this observation:

> In the absence of concerted planning on a national scale, there is emerging a profusion of information systems and networks in the United States where growth and interconnection may suffer from a lack of standardization. The problem becomes even more serious on an international scale. A good deal of ingenuity and buffering hardware and software is necessary to overcome the resulting incompatibility. Standards-setting, as practiced by the American National Standards Institute and the International Standards Organization, always lags behind the growth of data banks and data delivery systems. The emergence of new information technology, which rapidly passes through succeeding generations of sophistication, imposes a difficult burden on standards makers.[56]

Since the early 1960s several studies have been conducted in the United States which have recommended the need for policy formulation and coordination concerning scientific and technical information matters. In 1962 the Office of Science and Technology was established in the Presidential Executive Office, under the direction of the Presidential Scientific Adviser. In the same year the Federal Council for Science and Technology sponsored the Crawford Report, which called for

> the establishment of a central authority to define objectives; to plan, develop, and guide the organization of government information activities; to develop criteria with which it would be possible to review and evaluate federal agency information programs; and to provide systems research, engineering and development.[57]

Outside government circles the major effort toward urging the development of a national policy for the handling of scientific and technical information was made by the Committee on Scientific and Technical Communication (SATCOM), sponsored by the joint efforts of the National Academy of Sciences and the National Academy of Engineering. The SATCOM report, published in 1969, advanced as its fundamental philosophy:

> Our recognition that a basic element of strength in our country's over-all scientific-and-technical-communication effort is the *participation of the members of the scientific and technical community* in its development and administration. As a result of

their broad participation, our extraordinarily diverse communication programs and services have maintained a flexible responsiveness to changing and newly emerging needs as well as fulfilling a variety of other functions not entirely relevant to communication but reflecting firmly established traditions and work habits of scientists, engineers, and practitioners or of the organizations with which they are associated.[58]

The report went on to argue for the delineation of the respective roles of both the federal government and private organizations in the community of scientific and technical information, and for a thorough study of the economics of information services and the impact of new techniques on scientific and technical communication programs and practices. As its first major recommendation it stated:

We recommend the establishment of a Joint Commission on Scientific and Technical Communication, responsible to the Councils of the National Academy of Sciences and the National Academy of Engineering. This Commission should be conversant with activities in scientific and technical information and should provide guidance useful to public and private organizations in the development of more-effective scientific and technical communication. The Commission should be a group with as broad a representation as feasible of the major scientific and technical communities and the principal kinds of organizations engaged in related information-handling activities. It should be supported by a professional secretariat. The Commission should be responsible for leading the private sector in the coordination of its interests and programs and in the development of broad and farsighted plans. It should also be responsible for working with appropriate government groups in formulating needed national policies and programs and for gaining broad acceptance of them.[59]

Despite the considerable effort which went into both the Crawford and the SATCOM Reports, as well as into several others not discussed here, their recommendations resulted in no major changes with respect to the handling of information as an element of national planning.

In 1970, by establishing the National Commission on Libraries and Information Science (NCLIS), Congress made it clear that

library and information services adequate to meet the needs of the people of the United States are essential to achieve national goals and to utilize most effectively the nation's educational resources.

Further, it asked the federal government to "cooperate with state and local governments and public and private agencies in assuring optimum provision of such services" and authorized the National Commission to promote research and development activities which will extend and improve the nation's library and information-handling capability as essential links in the national communication networks.[60]

In June 1973 NCLIS decided to begin preparation of a paper describing a national program for library and information services. Two drafts of this document were prepared, were widely circulated in the library and information world, and were revised in the light of the criticisms and suggestions received. Regional hearings were held across the country, and many concerned professional societies held seminars and workshops to study the draft proposals. While the plan was still being drafted into final shape, NCLIS, which has a budget for funding related projects and studies, helped set up a continuing education network for librarians (CLENE) and funded a study to consider the use of the Library of Congress as a national bibliographic center.

The third draft of the NCLIS document, entitled *Toward a National Program for Library and Information Services: Goals for Action*, was finished in the Spring of 1975 and presented to the annual conference of the ALA (July 1975) for endorsement. Although there was some argument in favor of postponing endorsement of the document until the 1976 conference, thus allowing more time for its perusal,[61] the ALA Council finally decided to vote to endorse the concept of a National Program as NCLIS had outlined it, a program oriented toward the American user population—both current and potential users.

Although NCLIS's chairman has suggested that a further revision of the Program will be made within two years, the goal toward which the Program is currently aimed is:

To eventually provide every individual in the United States with equal opportunity of access to that part of the total information resource which will satisfy the individual's educational, working, cultural and leisure-time needs and interests, regardless of the individual's location, social or physical condition or level of intellectual achievement.[62]

In order to move toward this goal the Commission has set up two major program objectives:

1) to strengthen, develop, or create where needed, human and material resources which are supportive of high quality library and information services; and 2) to join together the library and information facilities in the country, through a common pattern of organization, uniform standards, and shared communications, to form a nationwide network.[63]

Hopefully the Program will appear sufficiently viable to encourage full cooperation by state and local governments as well as by private agencies concerned with information transfer. While the Commission saw the use of federal funds as being necessary to help in the development of compatible state and multi-state networks, it did not envisage that there would be any problem of direct federal control over the operations of a national network, nor over the information content being exchanged on it. Some considerable care was exercised in spelling out what was meant by the concept of a nationwide network:

> It is important to point out that the concept of a "nationwide network" does not imply the absurd notion that only one copy of a particular book or publication will be sufficient for the entire country to use. People need material at the most immediate and most accessible level, and the Commission believes that a national plan must, therefore, be built upon strong local resources. An ideal nationwide network requires provision of local holdings of sufficient scope and quantity to satisfy the immediate needs of local users.

> In the same vein, the concept of a nationwide network does not imply the substitution of computer technology for human resources. As in the past, the bulk of user services would be delivered at the local level, but the network would provide the additional backup resources as well as the communication directions for reaching specialized materials and information in other libraries and information centers when these are needed locally.[64]

Beginning in 1976 NCLIS expects to be ready to recommend federal legislation to help with the implementation of the Program. This year, marking the centennial of the ALA, as well as the bicentennial of the nation, may see the United States begin the changes in jurisdictional arrangements, patterns of service, and funding practices that will earmark the beginning of concerted planning of library and information services on a national scale.

SUMMARY

The concept of developing national systems of library and information services has only recently received serious consideration in the Anglo-American world, and for this reason it has yet to be clearly defined or described in the literature specifically devoted to library and information science,[65] or in the broader range of social science literature which discusses developmental planning. One can find many components of national systems in both the United States and Canada, some of which have been in existence for a considerable period of time: components ranging from such practices as the ARL's agreement to divide acquisitions responsibility under the Farmington Plan, the various regional networks established by state, public, and academic libraries, to the nationwide availability of medical information from MEDLINE or the opportunity to buy scientific data base services from NTIS. A foundation for a national scientific and technical information system was established in Canada in 1924 when the National Research Council Library was designated as backup support for other scientific and technical libraries in Canada.[66] A revision of the National Research Council Act in 1966 established the position of the National Science Library in this service, making it an information transfer agency that works with all the major libraries in Canada through a system called CAN/SDI. The computerized bibliographic data bases available to the CAN/SDI service provide Canadian libraries, and hence their clientele, with access to over 15,000 journals in all fields of science and technology.

The main problem now confronting both Western Europe and North America results from the considerable proliferation of the components of national or international information systems with a concomitant lack of agreement on bibliographic or other standards which will allow the various bibliographic data systems to interface directly. But the problems of variant standards or the use of the various national languages for the information systems, annoying as they may be, are problems that can be solved. The most serious situation facing the nations of the industrialized world—a situation that has not yet been fully recognized by its officials—may be that outlined in the address given by Daniel Bell to the Keynote Session of the Annual Meeting of ASIS, Boston, 1975.[67] Bell argued that the framework within which one views events has a bearing on how policies are formulated, and our failure to perceive underlying structural changes in our environment, especially in the industrialized world, has detrimental consequences for policy formulation.

In the industrialized world, planning for development needs to be considered not only in the light of the stupendous increases in the available scientific and technological information, but also in the light of the rapid pace of change confronting our society. According to Rodgers' summary:

> What Bell and others have sought to give us is an awareness that the United States is in the midst of such a fundamental structural change. Bell calls ours a "post-industrial" society, and suggests that just as the industrial revolution brought about a metamorphosis in the previously dominant agricultural society, the post-industrial revolution will bring about basic changes in industrial society. . . .
>
> The result will be an information age where the creation of knowledge and information, rather than the creation of goods, will be the dominant economic activity. To Bell, information and knowledge are the "transforming resources" and the "key variables" of the information society—roles played by the created energy (electricity, oil), capital, and labor in an industrial society.[68]

In the developing world, with its lack of extensive library traditions, the major problems appear to be the lack of understanding of the library's role in society and its relationship to both individual and community development through its acquisition, organization, and interpretation of materials. Part of this failure to recognize the role of the library in developing countries comes from the fact that, except for those libraries and information services supporting industry and those supporting applied research at the academic level, the overall impact of libraries on the society itself is very indirect. It is relatively easy to establish quantitative measurements of needs in industrial, government, and commercial sectors of society, and to analyze the services provided to meet these needs; but general library service is far less susceptible to such quantification and analysis, a situation that inhibits its incorporation into national development plans.

In both the developing and the industrialized worlds the production and distribution of library and information materials possess a degree of interdependence with library services. Since 1966 there have been at least three Unesco-sponsored meetings[69] to examine the relationship of book production and national library services to the production of textbooks and materials for the general reader. Datus C. Smith points out that the interrelationship between publishing and library services is coming to be increasingly recognized in the developing areas:

> An additional aspect of the economic development factor in publishing is that, in order to serve the development purpose, book publishing must be responsive to the interests and needs of its own country, not to some distant nation. This fact is now very widely recognized not only by local educators and planners and by young publishers starting to surface in most Asian and African countries, but also by the enlightened new leadership in some of the same foreign firms which formerly scoffed at the idea of title lists' being chosen in the local country.[70]

While the changing techniques in communications technology, including the introduction of computers, miniaturization techniques, and satellite communications systems, are producing major changes in the handling of information in the industrialized world, where automated data systems and the use of electronic circuitry linking libraries into networks have become commonplace things, the developing states have yet to experience very much of this new technology. In some respects this places them in a very good situation, in that as they develop the managerial expertise needed to work on the development plans, they may then view the various technologies already in existence elsewhere and choose from among them what seems to be best for their own needs. Smith comments that it is likely, at least in the publishing area, that developing countries will make maximum utilization of technological innovations:

Developing countries also seem to evidence a greater flexibility toward the communications media as a whole than do Westerners. Rather than viewing electronic media as the natural enemy of print, educational leaders are alive to the possibility of electronic media as a promotional and supplemental system for books.[71]

In the developing world library planning and its implementation should be accompanied by a determined effort to promote public awareness of the need for library and documentation service. Perhaps successful pilot projects developed in one area of the country could be built upon or duplicated in other areas. Where the library tradition has been particularly conspicuous by its absence it might be best to follow the suggestions outlined by Penna:

> When presenting library development to the public, it should be shown not as an isolated phenomenon but as part of an extensive social plan. Again, it should be stressed that like education, library service (particularly public library service) is aimed at providing everyone with the opportunity for developing his potential and making the most effective contribution to social, economic and cultural development. Good library provision can do much to help bridge the social gaps between the highly educated minority and the less educated majority.[72]

In the Western world we need to remember that policy and planning must take into account the structural changes mentioned by Daniel Bell. Planning for national organization of information and its dissemination must occur if the projections for the increases in its quantity and in the number of agencies handling it are correct; but if the post-industrial society which Bell and others have postulated is the true picture of the future, then there are many questions that we need to be aware of, and to seek answers to, as we are considering national plans. Rodgers points out some of these:

> In an information society, where information and knowledge are the chief raw materials and the chief products, the distribution of information goods and services within society can be expected to be one of the major factors shaping society. Access to knowledge and information and to the channels through which it is conveyed will be important to a "piece of the action" in the information age, both on the domestic scene and internationally. Major questions are now being asked: Who shall have access? For what purpose? What will be the procedures for granting or denying access? What are the costs involved and how are they to be allocated?[73]

That national planning of library and information services must occur in all nations due to the mounting costs of handling needed information records appears to be indisputable. That specific operational plans for national organization of library and documentation services, also permitting international exchange of information, have not yet been formulated is also indisputable, but from the currently available literature much effort is being expended in devising them.

NOTES

[1] Josefa Emilia Sabor, "International Cooperation in the Training of Librarians," *Unesco Bulletin for Libraries* XIX, No. 6 (November-December, 1965): 285.

[2] The sources consulted for figures on literacy were *Europa Year Book, 1974* (London: Europa Publications, 1974), Vol. II.; *The Middle East and North Africa, 1974-75*, 21st ed. (London: Europa Publications, 1974). The figures for literacy/illiteracy among the various national populations are, for the most part, based on local government figures for the mid-1960s or for 1970-71.

[3] Ad Hoc Group on Scientific and Technical Information, *Information for a Changing Society: Some Policy Considerations* (Paris: Organisation for Economic Co-operation and Development, 1971), p. 17.

[4] American Society for Information Science, *Proceedings of the Annual Meeting* (New York, 1970, 1972), Vol. 7, "The Information Conscious Society"; Vol. 9, "A World of Information."

[5] Ibid., Vol. 9, p. 1.

[6] C. V. Penna, *The Planning of Library and Documentation Services*, 2nd ed. (Paris: Unesco, 1970), p. 15.

[7] Ibid., p. 16.

[8] The published *Proceedings* of these seminars were issued in the following books: Conference on the Development of Public Library Services in Latin America, São Paulo, Brazil, 1951, *Development of Public Libraries in Latin America: The São Paulo Conference* (Paris: Unesco, 1952); Seminar on the Development of Public Libraries in Africa, Ibadan, Nigeria, 1953, *Development of Public Libraries in Africa: The Ibadan Seminar* (Paris: Unesco, 1954); Seminar on the Development of Public Libraries in Asia, Delhi, 1955, *Public Libraries for Asia, the Delhi Seminar* (Paris: Unesco, 1956). A more recent seminar, devoted to problems of one particular region of the "Third World" is: International Congress of Orientalists, 28th, Canberra, Australia, 1971, *International Co-operation in Orientalist Librarianship: Papers Presented at the Library Seminars* (Canberra: National Library of Australia, 1972).

[9] Conference on the Development of Public Library Services in Latin America, São Paulo, Brazil, 1951, *Development of Public Libraries in Latin America*, pp. 21-22.

[10] Many developing countries are heavily dependent on both foreign advisers and foreign economic aid as they work out their national development plans. Often the foreign aid advisers advance the argument that certain practices in their own countries offer the most economical and practical solutions to problems in developing states, and very few foreign advisers have been particularly knowledgeable in matters pertaining to librarianship.

[11] Thomas Kelly, *History of Public Libraries in Great Britain, 1845-1965* (London: The Library Association, 1973), pp. 4-15.

[12] This same precedent exists in the Soviet tradition, if we view the writings of Lenin and his wife Krupskaia concerning the political educational function of libraries on the national scene.

[13] Keith Smith, "Who Controls Book Publishing in Anglophone Middle Africa?," *Annals, American Academy of Political and Social Science* 421 (September 1975): 141.

[14] Ibid., p. 143. These local publishing firms have flourished most prominently in parts of Ghana and Nigeria, usually around large commercial towns. Examples of the type of materials they provide can be found in: Emanuel Obiechina, *An African Literature: A Study of the Onitsha Market Pamphlets* (Cambridge: Cambridge University Press, 1973).

[15] Smith, "Who Controls Book Publishing . . . ?," p. 144.

[16] Ibid., p. 146.

[17] Ibid., p. 150.

[18] If, of course, the multinational publishing firms have subsidiaries in the developing state, they can import from the parent firm at lower costs and accept payment in local "soft currency," which, staying within the country, will cover the firm's local expenses.

[19] While one might take the position that long delays in customs are merely annoyances, one might remember that many developing countries are in the tropical zones, and in tropical, humid climates books sitting in customs sheds for any period of time are likely to be attacked by molds, mildews and incidental insects who like the taste of their binding.

[20] S. B. Bandara, "Provision of Periodicals in the Libraries of Sri Lanka," *International Library Review* 7, No. 1 (January 1975): 21.

[21] Datus C. Smith, Jr., "The Bright Promise of Publishing in Developing Countries," *Annals, American Academy of Political and Social Science* 421 (September 1975): 137-138.

[22] Hans M. Zell, "Publishing in Africa in the Seventies: Problems and Prospects," in D. A. Clarke, ed., *Acquisitions from the Third World: Papers of the Ligue des Bibliothèques Européennes de Recherche Seminar 17-19 September, 1973* (London: Mansell, 1975), p. 119.

[23] For a description and definition of this program, see p. 176.

[24] While many backruns of journals can be purchased in microform for less money than the cost of buying an actual run of bound journals, such purchases involve the expenditure of hard currency for microform readers as well.

[25] Bandara, "Provision of Periodicals," pp. 23-24. Postal authorities often suspect that a demand for large quantities of such coupons indicates that someone is trafficking in them for his own economic gains.

[26] The early libraries at Oxford owed their collections, and even their buildings, to the munificence of Thomas Cobham and Duke Humphrey, and the chief benefactors of the early working collections at Paris were Robert of Sorbonne and Stephen Langton, Archbishop of Canterbury.

[27] Theodore Besterman, *The Beginnings of Systematic Bibliography* (London: Oxford University Press, H. Milford, 1935), pp. 6ff.

[28] Jesse H. Shera, *Foundations of the Public Library* (Chicago: University of Chicago Press, 1949), pp. 19ff.

[29] Andrew A. Aines, "Internationalization of Scientific and Technical Information Programs: Opportunity and Challenge," in *Information for Action: From Knowledge to Wisdom*, edited by Manfred Kochen (New York: Academic Press, 1975), p. 140.

[30] Ad Hoc Group on Scientific and Technical Information, *Information for a Changing Society*, p. 5.

[31] Ibid., p. 12.

[32] For a brief but cogent discussion of the two points of view, see Cyril O. Houle, "Continuing Education in the Public Library: Two Theories," *Library School Review*, Kansas State Teachers' College (December 1969): 34-46.

[33] *American Libraries* 6, No. 11 (December 1975): 655.

[34] Philip J. McNiff, "The Farmington Plan and the Foreign Acquisitions Programmes of American Research Libraries," in Clarke, *Acquisitions from the Third World*, p. 145.

[35] Ibid., p. 146.

[36] William S. Dix, "The Public Law 480 Program and the National Program for Acquisitions and Cataloging of the Library of Congress," ibid., p. 160. Note that, although the ARL has Canadian members, they may not participate in a scheme funded by the Congress of the United States and so may not receive PL-480 materials on deposit.

[37] Clarke, *Acquisitions from the Third World*, p. vii.

[38] R. F. Miller and R. L. Tighe, "Library and Information Networks," in Carlos A. Cuadra and Ann W. Luke, eds., *Annual Review of Information Science and Technology*, Vol. 9 (Washington, D.C.: American Society for Information Science, 1974), p. 173.

[39] Carl F. J. Overhage, "Information Networks," in Carlos A. Cuadra and Ann W. Luke, eds., *Annual Review of Information Science and Technology*, Vol. 4 (Chicago: Encyclopaedia Britannica, 1969), p. 340.

[40] Ibid.

[41] Elizabeth K. Miller, "RUIN: A Network for Urban and Regional Studies Libraries," *Special Libraries* 64, No. 11 (November 1973): 498.

[42] Edwin E. Olson, Russell Shank, Harold A. Olsen, "Library and Information Networks," in Carlos A. Cuadra and Ann W. Luke, eds., *Annual Review of Information Science and Technology*, Vol. 7 (Washington, D.C.: American Society for Information Science, 1972), p. 279.

[43] Miller and Tighe, "Library and Information Networks," p. 175.

[44] Launor F. Carter, "What Are the Major National Issues in the Development of Library Networks?," *News Notes of California Libraries* 63, No. 4 (Fall 1968): 407.

[45] Olson, Shank, and Olsen, "Library and Information Networks," p. 280.

[46] "Working Group Summary on Network Needs and Development," Conference on Interlibrary Communications and Information Networks, Airlie House, 1970, *Proceedings* (Chicago: ALA, 1971), p. 15.

[47] Cited by Genevieve M. Casey, "Emerging State and Regional Library Networks," ibid., p. 45.

[48] Miller and Tighe, "Library and Information Networks," p. 182.

[49] Robert G. Chenhall, "Networks for Museums and Related Disciplines," in EDUCOM, *Networks and Disciplines: Proceedings of the EDUCOM Fall Conferences, Oct. 11, 12, 13, 1972, Ann Arbor, Michigan* (Princeton, N.J.: EDUCOM, The Interuniversity Communications Council, 1973), p. 43.

[50] Carter, "What Are the Major National Issues . . . ?," p. 407.

[51] Ibid.

[52] Charles C. Joyce, "National Policies and International Computer Networking," *Bulletin of the American Society for Information Science* 2, No. 4 (November 1975), 14.

[53] Loll N. Rolling, "International Networks: The European Situation," ibid., p. 19.

[54] Miller and Tighe, "Library and Information Networks," p. 204.

[55] Andrew A. Aines and Melvin S. Day, "National Planning of Information Services," in Carlos A. Cuadra and Ann W. Luke, eds., *Annual Review of Information Science and Technology*, Vol. 10 (Washington, D.C.: American Society for Information Science, 1975), p. 7.

[56] Ibid., p. 12.

[57] Ibid., p. 32.

[58] National Academy of Sciences–National Academy of Engineering, Committee on Scientific and Technical Communication, *Scientific and Technical Communication: A Pressing National Problem and Recommendations for Its Solution* (Washington, D.C.: National Academy of Sciences, 1969), p. 8.

[59] Ibid., p. 22.

[60] United States. National Commission on Libraries and Information Science, *Toward a National Program for Library and Information Services* (Washington, D.C.: National Commission for Libraries and Information Science, 1975; available from Superintendent of Documents, United States Government Printing Office), p. 1.

[61] See the Report on "Conference '75" in *American Libraries* 6, No. 8 (September 1975): 478.

[62] United States. National Commission on Libraries and Information Services, *Toward a National Program*, p. xi.

[63] Ibid.

[64] Ibid., p. xii.

⁶⁵ Quincy Rodgers, "Toward a National Information Policy," *Bulletin of the American Society for Information Science* 2, No. 6 (January 1976): 14.

⁶⁶ Jack E. Brown, *The Canadian National Scientific and Technical Information (STI) System: A Progress Report* (Philadelphia: National Federation of Abstracting and Indexing Services, 1972), Report No. 4, Miles Conrad Memorial Lecture, pp. 4-5. For a description of components of national library and information systems that exist in other industrialized countries, see Andrew A. Aines and Melvin S. Day, "National Planning of Information Services."

⁶⁷ Summarized in Quincy Rodgers, "Toward a National Information Policy."

⁶⁸ Ibid., p. 13.

⁶⁹ Penna, *The Planning of Library and Documentation Services*, p. 41. The three meetings were held in Tokyo (1966), Accra (1968), and Bogotá (1969), thus covering the three continents where the bulk of the Third World nations can be found.

⁷⁰ D. C. Smith, "The Bright Promise of Publishing in Developing Countries," p. 133.

⁷¹ Ibid., pp. 138-139.

⁷² Penna, *The Planning of Library and Documentation Services*, pp. 80-81.

⁷³ Rodgers, "Toward a National Information Policy," p. 15.

SUGGESTED READINGS

Books

Ad Hoc Group on Scientific Books and Technical Information. *Information for a Changing Society: Some Policy Considerations.* Paris: Organisation for Economic Co-operation and Development, 1971.

Anderla, J. Georges. *Information in 1985: A Forecasting Study of Information Needs and Resources.* Paris: Organisation for Economic Co-operation and Development, 1973.

Conference on Interlibrary Communications and Information Networks, Airlie House, 1970. *Proceedings.* Edited by Joseph Becker. Chicago: American Library Association, 1971.

National Academy of Sciences—National Academy of Engineering. Committee on Scientific and Technical Communication. *Scientific and Technical Communication: A Pressing National Problem and Recommendations for Its Solution.* Washington, D.C.: National Academy of Sciences, 1969.

Penna, C. V. *The Planning of Library and Documentation Services.* 2nd ed. revised and enlarged by P. H. Sewell and Herman Liebaers. Paris: Unesco, 1970.

United States. National Commission on Libraries and Information Science. *Toward a National Program for Library and Information Services.* Washington, D.C.: National Commission for Libraries and Information Science, 1975; available from Superintendent of Documents, United States Government Printing Office.

Periodicals

(The following periodicals frequently carry articles
useful in consideration of this topic.)

American Libraries

Bulletin of the American Society for Information Science

International Library Review

Libri

Unesco Bulletin for Libraries

See also the following two specific issues:

Annals of the American Academy of Political and Social Science 412 (March
1974), "The Information Revolution."

Annals of the American Academy of Political and Social Science 421
(September 1975), "Perspectives on Publishing."

EPILOGUE*

Et Haec Olim Meminisse Iuvabit

Whenever I stand before a commencement audience, robed in academic finery, I feel that I should say something very profound, very wise, and very learned—something worthy to echo down the corridors of time. But I am quickly brought back to reality, not to say sanity, by an inner voice that reminds me that no one ever actually listens to a commencement address—listens, that is, except to anticipate the end. Few things in life are more conventional, more stereotyped, and less fraught with meaning and substance than a commencement address. Half sermon, or preachment, half Fourth of July oration, and heavily overlaid with references to Alma Mater, the commencement address stands as the rhetorical embodiment of the classic example of the inverted climax, "For God, for country, and for Yale." No, no one listens to what is said on such an occasion as this: the students are eager to get their diplomas in their hands, their parents and friends are impatient to see their favorites endowed with their new academic titles, and the faculty and administration want nothing more than to see the whole business disposed of as quickly and painlessly as possible. What can the speaker say in such a predicament that will be a "challenge and a source of inspiration" to the graduates, yet not a soporific to those who have endured many such celebrations?

But we must remind ourselves, I think, that the conferring of an academic degree is the concluding sentence of a paragraph in the narrative of one's life, and as such it merits something more than the platitudes and sterile formalities with which, over the years, it has become encrusted. Commencement is the graduates' day, their "white plume," their *panache*. They have earned this symbol of achievement and they deserve its celebration. So the commencement speaker should make a serious effort to say something of substance, and there comes back to me a phrase from my well-worn Latin grammar: "*Et haec olim meminisse iuvabit.*" —And from time to time it will be useful to remember these things. Commencement, as the name suggests, marks the beginning of a new way of life, but it is also a time for remembering. "Bright college years with pleasure rife," may be said of graduate study, too. The pleasures may not have been particularly rife, but the brilliance should increase as you penetrate ever more deeply into the field of practice or inquiry that you have chosen for your career.

---

*Based on two commencement addresses, delivered, respectively, to the College of Library Science, University of Kentucky, May 11, 1974, and to the School of Library Science, Case Western Reserve University, May 30, 1975.

But permit me to put remembrance aside and talk with you about an aspect of librarianship that should have meaning for your future, and indeed the futures of all of us in the profession: namely, "What makes a good librarian?" I submit that the attributes of a good librarian are three: a comprehensive knowledge and understanding—mastery, if you will—of the materials of which he has custody; the ability to communicate that knowledge to others in ways that will be useful and meaningful to them; and a sense of humor.

Librarianship is one facet of the communication process by means of which a culture maintains itself; without communication there can be no culture. But communication becomes mere idle chatter if there is not something worth transmitting. The librarian, then, if he is to be a worthy communicator, must first of all be a master of a substantive field of knowledge; he must be a scholar in the broadest sense. It is not "love of books" that marks the good librarian, but love of learning, love of knowledge, and devotion to truth. When I was entering the profession there was a popular dogma to the effect that "the librarian who reads is lost." Small wonder that librarians were often stigmatized as knowing only "the backs of books" and nothing about what was inside them. As a kind of rejoinder to this cynicism, William Warner Bishop published, in 1926, a collection of his essays on librarianship under the title *The Backs of Books.* I hope that you, as you enter the profession, are bringing to it something more than a "smattering of ignorance." The longer I contemplate librarianship in general, and library education in particular, the more I become convinced that librarianship is ninety percent subject, or substantive, knowledge, and ten percent the skills of the craft—or, if one must be brutally frank, the tricks of the trade. I am unable to see how a librarian, with all the professional training in the world, can be successful if he does not know his materials, what they contain, and for what purposes they may best be used. It is for precisely this reason that I am enthusiastic about the double-master's program which has been inaugurated at Case Western Reserve University. It does not go far enough, but at least it is headed in the direction toward which Case Reserve has been working for many years.

I hope you have had the opportunity to exercise your intellectual powers on materials that promote a toughness of mind. I further hope that you have acquired an understanding of at least one good subject field, the structure of the literature of that field, its landmark works, and the human needs that it fulfills.

But all the knowledge in the world will be of small use to the librarian or his patron if it is locked up in an inability to communicate that knowledge to others. "Books are for use; every book its reader; every reader his book," wrote S. R. Ranganathan in his Five Laws of Library Science. There are, of course, certain bibliographic treasures which, for reasons of rarity or other measures of value, must be kept under lock and key and used only under the strictest rules of security. But for the vast bulk of the library's collection, the librarian is not a Fafner presiding over the golden hoard of the *Niebelungen.*

The good librarian, then, must be knowledgeable about both books and humanity. I do not mean to imply that you must be missionaries carrying the light of truth into the darkness of the hinterland, but it is important that your patrons do not leave the door of the library with a sense of frustration, or unfulfilled desires and needs. You must learn to take people on their own terms, to communicate with them on their own levels, to place yourself in their position, to understand their problems, to "walk a mile in their moccasins." Again let me emphasize that you must not play social worker or lady bountiful dispersing riches to the impoverished. There will be times, of course, when you will suffer frustration, irritation, and even despair—frustration over your own inadequate knowledge and the limited resources of your collections; irritation over the foibles and "irrationalities" of your patrons, and despair in your attempts to communicate with others in ways that are comprehensible to them. Librarians, particularly public librarians, are wont to speak of the "general reader," but there is no general reader; every library patron is "special" in his own eyes. He has his own needs, problems, desires, and ambitions, and he speaks his own language. The librarian must learn to have empathy with the patron if he is to fulfill his professional responsibilities.

Some of you may recall that in Christopher Morley's anthropomorphic dog story, *Where the Blue Begins*, his protagonist, Mr. Gissing, who is a bachelor, discovers one morning that three puppies have been left unceremoniously on his doorstep. To support this little brood that has been thrust upon him he eventually takes a position as a floorwalker in the community's leading department store. "He loved the throng and multitude of the city," Morley says of Mr. Gissing. "He loved people; but sometimes he suspected that he loved them as God does—at a judicious distance." And Morley goes on to say, "From his rather haphazard religious training, strange words came back to him. 'For God so loved the world . . .' So loved the world that—that what? That He sent somebody else."[1] The good librarian cannot afford a divine perspective, and cannot delegate his unpleasant tasks to "somebody else." The good librarian must learn above all else self-discipline, and there will be many times when he would do well to recall the words of the Chinese philosopher, Lao-Tze: "The good leader says little and does much, and when his work is finished, his task is complete, they will all say, 'We did it ourselves.' "

Thus I arrive at my third attribute of the good librarian, a sense of humor, which some of my friends have told me is the most important of all. I cannot agree, but certainly it is important. What is a sense of humor? I answer that it is a sense of perspective, a sense of relationship, the ability to perceive priorities. It is the ability to see life as Shakespeare saw it in *A Midsummer Night's Dream*—through a telescope in reverse. Perhaps Figaro, in Beaumarchais's *Le Barbier de Seville*, has given us the best insight into a sense of humor, when he says to Count Almaviva:

Loué par ceux-ci,
Blâmé par ceux-là, me
moquant des sots,
bravant les méchants,
je me presse de rire de
tout. . . de peur d'être
obligé d'en pleurer.[2]

In the years ahead you will be both praised and criticized, and you must ignore the fools and brave those who are evil, and many times you will press yourself to laugh for fear of being forced to weep. . . Therefore, though you must always take your work seriously, you must not take yourself seriously. It is all very well to have a crown of thorns, and I suppose that every sensitive person carries one in secret; but the times when it can be properly exposed to public view are very rare indeed, and even then it should be worn cocked over one ear. Solemnity should not be mistaken for cerebration. We say that the owl looks wise, when in reality he looks only grave.

A mastery of the records of human experience and knowledge, the ability to communicate that knowledge to others, and a sense of humor—these are the three great pillars upon which the library as a social structure rests. You may have noted that I have said little about the librarian as the purveyor of enlightenment to the masses, but you have probably already heard enough of that in the classroom. Here I deal with the librarian as intellectual, the librarian as scholar. The good librarian, like the good teacher, is concerned with the growth and development of the intellectual life of those who seek his assistance. Paul in his letter to the people of Rome (8:18) speaks of "the glory that shall be revealed *in* us." Mark you, he said "*in* us," not *to* us. It is the truth, the knowledge, the learning that we represent that marks us as good librarians as it marks the good teacher.

Thus, Archibald MacLeish has written, "No, it is not the library, I think, that has become ridiculous by standing there against the dark with its books in order on its shelves. On the contrary, the library, almost alone of the great monuments of civilization, stands taller now than it ever did before. . . The library remains a silent and enduring affirmation that the great books still speak, and not alone but somehow all together."[3] If the library is to stand as a beacon against the dark it will be because we as scholars have built the library's collections and preserved, organized, and serviced them. It is the mastery of the library resources that is the apotheosis of librarianship, the glory that is revealed in us as truly professional librarians.

I urge you to remember, as you strive for professional achievement, that you are not working for yourselves alone. In the eyes of the library world *you* are your school of library science, whatever that school may be. You are its product. By what you are and by what you have achieved will it be judged. Your successes will be its triumphs, and your disappointments its failures. You have a right to expect from your school continuing professional support in a variety of ways, but the strength and meaning of that support will depend on what you do for yourself.

This, my good friends, is the promised end. In a very few minutes you shall be awarded your degrees by one with the authority vested in him by the board of trustees of the university, and you will be admitted to the rights, privileges, and responsibilities appurtaining thereto. *Et haec olim . . .* "I greet you at the beginning of a great career," Emerson wrote to Whitman upon first looking into *Leaves of Grass*; thus do I greet you, and I leave you with Brutus and Cassius on the plain of Philippi: "And if we meet again why we shall smile, if not why then this parting was well made." *Ave atque vale.*

NOTES

[1] Christopher Morley, *Where the Blue Begins*, illus. by Arthur Rackham (New York: Doubleday-Page, 1922), p. 80.

[2] Act I, Scene 2.

[3] Archibald MacLeish, "The Premise of Meaning," *The American Scholar* 41 (Summer 1972): 362.

INDEX